Election 2016: Democracy in Disarray

A Campaign Bloated with Bombastry, Bigotry, and Blatant Lies

Election 2016: Democracy in Disarray

A Campaign Bloated with Bombastry, Bigotry, and Blatant Lies

SANDRA LEE STUART
AND
AARON JAFFE

Published by Barricade Books Inc.
Fort Lee, NJ 07024

www.barricadebooks.com

Manufactured in the United States of America
Library of Congress Cataloging-in-Publication Data

Stuart, Sandra Lee.
Election 2016: Democracy in Disarray: a campaign bloated
with bombastry, bigotry, and blatant lies / Sandra Lee Stuart
and Aaron Jaffe.
  pages cm
ISBN 978-1-5698-0810-8 (pbk.)
LCSH: Presidents–United States–Election–2016. | Clinton, Hillary
Rodham. | Trump, Donald, 1946- | Political culture–United States. |
United States–Politics and government–2009-
I. Title.
  JK526 2016.S88 2017
  324.973/0932–dc23

2016057275

Other books by Sandra Lee Stuart
The Last Chance Diet (New York Times bestseller)
Who Won What When
The Pink Palace: Behind Closed Doors at the Beverly Hills Hotel
The Dannon Book of Yogurt
The Silence, a Memoir of a Holocaust Survivor
Grand Cru (a novel)
Why Do I Have to Wear Glasses?, an illustrated book for children
The Pink Palace Revisited
The Restaurant Guy

By Aaron Jaffe
The Second Coming of Bob, a novel to be published in 2017

*To Allison, who was like a fleece Snuggie
(warm and supportive) during a difficult year.
And to Joe Rogan, in the hopes that he will
have Aaron on his show so more than
six people read this book.*

Table of Contents

Introduction xi

Chapter One: That's the FEC, not the SEC 1

Chapter Two: The Debating Delusionals 7

Chapter Three: Candidates with Legs 71

Chapter Four: Debate Jabs, Kicks and Knockouts 153

Chapter Five: Run-up to Philly and Cleveland 199

Chapter Six: A Tale of Two Conventions 213

Chapter Seven: On to the Issues—Sort of 247

Chapter Eight: He Didn't Just Say That 257

Chapter Nine: Clinton Missteps, Misspokes and
    the Pillorying of Hillary 263

Chapter Ten: The Trajectory of the Race 271

Chapter Eleven: Aftermath—Winners and Losers . . . 315

Introduction

WHEN DISTANT HISTORIANS look back at the 2016 run-up to the White House, they will use many words to describe it. There is a good chance "dumpster fire," "clown fiesta" and the smiling poop emoji will be among them.

The campaign, at times, seemed as if it was being waged inside an MTV reality show with some of the wannabes to rule the most powerful country acting as if the way to the Oval Office was to be more outrageous than their opponents.

Somehow, it's hard to imagine Honest Abe boasting about the size of his genitals during the Lincoln-Douglas debates.

This election saw a candidate labeled as "Lucifer in the Flesh" and the love child of Joe McCarthy and Dracula. A nominee threatening to lock up his opponent once elected as if he would be governing Nazi Germany. And more scandals than a season of "The Real Housewives of Atlanta."

This was all part of the craziness and unseemliness that had the rest of the world wondering if we had collectively lost our sanity.

It should be pointed out that Election 2016 hasn't been the only vicious, low-blow brawl for the presidency. The 1800 roast-battle between Thomas Jefferson and John Adams made Trump's efforts look like the schoolyard taunts of an angry 1st-grader with Tourette's. Jefferson backers took to calling opponent John Adams a "hideous hermaphroditical character, which has neither the force and firmness of a man, nor the gentleness and sensibility of a woman." Not to be outdone, Adams supporters said Jefferson was "a mean-spirited, low-lived fellow, the son of a half-breed Indian squaw, sired by a Virginia mulatto father."

Historically, wives have not been off limits, either. Andrew Jackson's wife, Rachel was branded a Jezebel, adulteress and bigamist after marrying Jackson while still married to her first husband. She died of a heart attack before Jackson took the oath of office, something Old Hickory blamed on the campaign vitriol.

In a pushback, Jackson people spread the rumor that while John Quincy Adams was ambassador to Russia, he tried to pimp out his maid to Czar Alexander I.

The first Republican presidential candidate, John Charles Frémont, was accused of being a cannibal. Abraham Lincoln was called a gorilla. Grover Cleveland opponents, who believed he had sired a bastard child, reveled in chanting "Ma, ma, where's my Pa? Gone to the White House, ha, ha, ha."

Trump's penchant for "a lot of people are saying" and throwing out false facts is not original, either. Whigs had "proof" that James K. Polk was a slave trader. Only problem was the proof came from a book's made-up excerpt. In retaliation, Polk's followers said Henry Clay was a whoremonger and broke all the 10 Commandments. The response when challenged to come up with evidence? It was "too disgusting to appear in public print."

When 17 Republicans and five Democrats announced

they were running, you had to know there were some interesting months ahead, especially since one of them was master of reality TV and spray-on tanning Donald Trump. Similar to a Michael Bay film or Lady Gaga's fashion designer, Trump seemed to be constantly trying to outdo his last bit of outrageousness.

People were hunkering down with cases of beer to watch the debates like they were UFC cage fights. Granted, a drunken stupor was probably the best state to process those early Republican free-for-alls.

And then there was Bernie Sanders, who got young voters more excited than a new Snapchat filter on #ThrowBackThursday. He didn't get the Democratic nomination, but millions of supporters #feltheBern. (There was another candidate who got impressive turnouts on college campuses—Sen. Eugene McCarthy in 1968, drawing students because of his stance against the Vietnam War. He was a nice, principled fellow, who, unfortunately, had less energy than a dead battery.)

Then it became Hillary versus Donald, both with more baggage than what passes daily through O'Hare Airport. She of the private email server, big fees speaking to Goldman Sachs and the attack in Benghazi, Libya. He with a list too numerous to count, even using all of his dainty little fingers. It is interesting to note that John Kerry was ridiculed in 2004 by the Republicans for being a "flip-flopper." Trump was constantly making statements, denying he made them (despite video evidence), changing positions, performing more flips than Olympic gymnast Simone Biles and making more flops than Nicolas Cage.

So, do read on for a comprehensive dissection of Election 2016. No self-important punditry. No blah-blah, harumph-harumph, heavy-handed analysis. It's an in-your-face smackdown of all candidates, including the Delusionals who couldn't get past the nastiness of Trump, the organization of Clinton and yes, Bernie. And finally, the improbable Trump Triumph.

Chapter One:
That's FEC, Not SEC

After Watergate, the great minds in Washington felt it best to set up a campaign-finance watchdog. Unfortunately McGruff the Crime Dog was busy staking out bleachers behind a middle-school gymnasium, and so the Federal Election Commission was born. The FEC is charged with enforcing disclosure of campaign-finance information, as well as limits and prohibitions on contributions, and to overseeing public funding of presidential elections.

The commission's work didn't get any easier with the Supreme Court Citizens United decision that deemed corporations equal to breathing humans when it came to throwing money at candidates. The distinction should have been simple. If you are trying to ascertain if you are dealing with a corporation or a human being, there is a surefire test you can conduct. Show the party in question the YouTube video titled, "The Sneezing Baby Panda." If there are no signs of human emotion, such as joy or mirth, and only concern with how to monetize it, you are either dealing with a corporation or Donald Trump.

Now the understaffed FEC had to contend with the possibility of foreign money making its way into presidential elections by the back door of contributing through American-controlled companies. When Obama brought that up during his 2010 State of the Union address, conservative Supreme Court Justice Samuel A. Alito was caught on camera mouthing "not true."

Move forward to 2016, and examples had been uncovered. A Canadian-owned subsidiary lavished $1 million on Mitt Romney. A company owned by two Chinese nationals, but incorporated in California, funneled $1.3 million to a Jeb Bush Super PAC. And there is the more circuitous route of trade associations—with non-American contributors and members—giving money to candidates who are felt will further their cause.

The FEC didn't even act on the Trump campaign's soliciting money from lawmakers in England and Australia, a blatant violation. The FEC has been called "toothless" for good reason. What do you expect from an agency that is headed by three Republicans and three Democrats? One Republican even tried to stop staff from Googling *anything* without permission. This undoubtedly led to some awkward exchanges. "Mr. Commissioner," we can imagine a poor staffer asking, "may I please Google, 'home remedy + hemorrhoids'?" Talk about a pain in the ass.

No wonder the 375 full-time FEC employees have been characterized as "demoralized."

But monitoring contributions is only one of the commission's functions. It receives all the many Form 2s, the official "statement of candidacy," from people filing to run. And what do you have to do to file? Not much. Fill in your name, address and party affiliation. Which may be why the FEC received thousands of Form 2s for the 2016 election. Among them Deez Nutts and his running mate

Limberbutt McCubbins, D-Ky., whose slogan was "Meow is the Time." Satan, a Republican. God, a Republican. Emperor Palpatine of the Concerned Citizens Party of Connecticut with an address in American Samoa. Disco Daddy, no party affiliation. Independent Nothing Wrong Hitlerdid. Bros Before Hoes. Have Sex With Me. The Muslim Dictator Trump. And what list would be complete without Anakin Skywalker and Mickey Mouse?

Up to this point, as you might guess, all is free. Download the form and you're in the running for the most powerful position in the world—despite what Vladimir Putin would have you believe. Form 1 is more serious. You have to name a committee, treasurer, where you're banking, stuff that 15-year-old Deez Nutts couldn't provide. Also, Deez probably didn't have $5,000 in campaign contributions needed to move on.

The FEC heavy lifting is from this point on with tons of forms and disclosures. How much money did you raise, from whom, what did you spend? And they are all public record, making journalists happier than a pharmaceutical lobbyist on valium.

Take Donald Trump's June 2016 filing. Trump declared loud and often during the primary season that he was self-financing his campaign. But it turned out the $47 million he "gave" to his committee were actually loans. That's like buying your parents dinner, but putting the bill on your dad's "emergencies only" credit card— "See how generous I am, Papa? Just DO NOT read your statement too closely next month." After Trump was criticized for the fudging, the FEC filing showed he had forgiven the loans. In the month of June, Trump managed to raise $27 million. Still, he only had $20 million in the bank, while

Hillary Clinton's campaign showed $44 million. Another fun fact? Trump, who didn't seem to believe in having much of a staff, spent $71 million through June. Despite forking over this small fortune, a large number of Trump staffers quit after reportedly not being paid. One former adviser told The Washington Post, "They use and abuse people. The policy office fell apart in August when the promised checks weren't delivered." Meanwhile, Clinton spent $230 million on staff.

If you want to slog through the different filings, you will be treated to other tidbits like Trump's agreement with the RNC. It looks as if Great and Mighty Dealmaker got the short end of that arrangement that set up two fundraising joint committees. Combined they raised $32 million. How much was sent Trump's way? A relatively small $2.2 million. That was from one committee. More may have been on its way from the other. *And* he only managed to get 14 private donors to chip in $450,000.

On the Hillary side of the ledger, between what she raised and what Super PACs anted up, the total came to $386 million, $301 million spent, leaving $85 mil.

Madame Secretary was not free of contribution controversy. It seems logical and right that a business getting government contracts should not be allowed to contribute to a political campaign. That's a worse conflict of interest than the American Diabetes Association being overseen by Krispy Kreme Doughnuts. Apparently, the memo never reached the staff of a pro-Hillary Super PAC. A Massachusetts construction company had been awarded almost $170 million in government contracts since fiscal year 2008. And yet, it sent money to Priorities USA Action. The

Center for Public Integrity uncovered this no-no, and the Super PAC returned $200,000.

The FEC also breaks down the top employers and professions of donors. Here's Hillary's list:

$24.7M . . . . Attorney
6.9M . . . . Homemaker
5.3M . . . . Consultant
4.4M . . . . .CEO
4.4M . . . . Physician
Donald's
$1.09M . . . . .Self-Employed
$0.09M . . . . Boch Automotive Group
$0.01M . . . Donald J Trump for President
$0.01M . . . . Acorn Advisors
$0.01M . . . . Twenty One Twelve

In case you're wondering about Twenty One Twelve, it's a digital-marketing firm specializing in high-end products and companies. And it's an English company. You have to suppose the employees doing the donating were American. Otherwise, the FEC goofed.

The biggest Hillary PAC donors were Haim and Cheryl Saban ($10.1 million). Saban has done lots of things to amass his $3 billion, including distributing that TV classic, "Mighty Morphin Power Rangers," teenage fighters of evil clad in Spandex.

Trump got the most money from Robert Mercer and his family ($3.8 million). Mercer is a hedge-fund guy and computer scientist. This is a fellow whose household staff sued him because he would shortchange their pay if they left partially filled shampoo bottles. And forget about overtime. Mercer had more trouble making up his mind during this campaign than Chris Christie at a Golden Corral Buffet—"None of these options are good, but what the hell. I'll take all of them." First, he threw money at Ted Cruz. Then for good measure, he sent some to Carly Fiorina. When no one else was standing, Trump was his boy.

The FEC will keep on slogging through its thankless job until the next round of elections. It would be nice if most of the campaign wrongdoings it uncovers were penalized before people hit the polling booths.

Chapter Two: Debating Delusionals

The question arises, what possessed these people to waste their time and money running for president? They didn't have a whit of a chance. But run they did.

If you have a cynical bent, you might think it was to meet deep-pocketed donors who could prove useful later. Or maybe they were just tired of watching reruns of "Duck Dynasty." Or they liked being fussed over by TV makeup types.

Whatever the case, meet the Delusionals of 2016, in order of disappearance.

Rerun Rick

"Rick Perry is what happens if Lex Luthor distilled down George W. Bush's essence in a laboratory and crossed it with gunpowder and semen from the finest thoroughbred in Lubbock and then strapped that concoction onto a nuclear missile and shot it into the f*cking sun."—Jon Stewart

Stewart's analysis is a little over the top. Yes, Rick Perry is a Texas boy through and through, but his trajectory will never take him as high as the sun. If anything, he's more of a cross between Jeff Spicoli in "Fast Times at Ridgemont High" and a former model from a John Deere catalog. His Texas roots stretch way back to the Texas Revolution. For unlearned Northerners, that was the set-to with Mexico that ran from October 1835 to April 1836, resulting in the Republic of Texas.

Little Ricky made his first appearance on March 4, 1950. Daddy Ray was a tenant farmer who raised cotton, wheat and cattle, which may be why Rick would later study animal science in college. Either that or no one told him communications was by far the easiest major. Ray, like almost everyone in Haskell County, was a staunch "yellow dog" Democrat. You know, "I'd vote for a yellow dog before I'd vote for a Republican."

When it came time for Rick to go to college, he chose the state's oldest public university—Texas A&M. Or maybe he didn't have the grades to get into The University. No, not Harvard, the University of Texas at Austin. He certainly did not have the grades to transfer. Ricky was a terrible student, probably spending too much time as a Yell Leader, which is the Texan way of saying "a glorified male cheerleader." You're out there on the football field doing the whoop and farmers fight, working the spectators into a frenzy. It was actually an elected position at school and made Rick a BMOC to be on the team. Maybe Perry thought this was a good presidential credential given George the Younger had been a cheerleader at Yale.

During one summer break, Ricky got a lesson in humility. He sold Bibles slammed door to slammed door. After graduating in 1972, Perry took to the sky as a commissioned officer in the United States Air Force, piloting C-130s. Captain Perry returned to civilian life in 1978, got hitched to his high-school sweetheart and went to work for Ray—sort of.

Papa Perry had a job managing some cotton and wheat fields. He turned the work over to his Number One (and only) son. When an owner checked on the fields, they had gone to weeds. Rick hadn't gotten around to tending them. Hey, young Perry, what's up? the owner asked. Rick had no time for chit-chat. He was on his way to hunt some birds. Talk to Ray if there was a problem, he said. "We chided him about that and told his father he was not to farm for us anymore," the owner said.

Perry's foray into politics began inauspiciously after a friend snagged him a job on the Texas Real Estate Research Advisory Committee. A few years later, in 1984, he went after a state rep's seat. In a district that would take four hours to go from one end to the other by car, Pilot Perry crisscrossed easily in his 1952 Super Cub monoplane. It was during this campaign that a friend, in writing stump speeches, came up with a joke that Perry reran frequently over the years. It went something like—Ricky graduated from his high school in the top 10, only thing was his class had 13 students. Along with hours logged playing "World of Warcraft," that's probably not something you should brag about in public. Even so, Rick did win. Also won a second term, both as a Democrat

In his second term, Perry showed up with a mouthful of orthodontic braces. "Everybody who noticed his braces suspected that [it was a career move], but no one confirmed it," says then-Sen. Steve Carriker, a West Texas Dem.

As it turned out, it wasn't the straightened chompers that gave Perry's political career a boost. It was another

instrument designed to grind the life out of things, Republican puppet master Karl Rove. Perry, because of his
anti-tax stance, looked like someone Rove could manipu-
late. Times were changin' in Texas where LBJ and Democrats had reigned supreme for so long. Congressman Phil
Gramm jumped the Democratic ship in 1983. The state
was seeing red over damned Northern liberals like Teddy
Kennedy and Jesse Jackson. In 1989, Perry, standing next
to Gramm, said he, too, was now a Republican and would
run against agriculture commissioner Jim Hightower. A
Republican, near enough to Perry on the stage, heard the
convert mutter, "What the hell did I just do?"

It was a good thing for Perry there was no backsies.

Hightower's take on the election was "I suppose Karl
Rove looked at him and thought, 'Here's a guy who'd look
good in chaps and who is an empty slate, and we can make
him an offer that he'll grab because he's a political opportunist.' "

The grab worked with Perry adding another W in his
column. As commissioner, he set out to show farmers he
was their bestest of friends by getting rid of Hightower
pesticide regulations. God dang, Perry would defend his
agricultural constituents from "food terrorists and stomach police." Curious, since most of us think of Taco Bell's
Cheesy Double Beef Burrito when we hear "food terrorists," not someone trying to prevent ingested carcinogens.

Perry's ascendancy continued when the state's lieutenant governor said he wasn't running for re-election. What
an opportunity for the political parvenu. Perry, however,
was not looking forward to debating on television. He
wangled a Friday night slot during football season. Think
about it. Friday Night Lights in El Paso. There's a bet-

ter chance that Texans would abandon all their guns for rhythmic gymnastic batons than watch that debate.

With Karl Rove, pulling strings like a maniacal Geppetto, Perry again won. Rove was also managing George W.'s run for the White House. Should he win, the strategist wanted a Republican lieutenant governor in place, at ready to ascend to the Texas State House. And so it was that Rick came to rule the land of the Lone Star. And rule he did for three more terms. The "rule" might be stretching it.

He didn't play well with his fellow Republicans, pushing his own agenda rather than the party's. His own agenda was often that of campaign donors. Take the bill that would have curbed texting while driving. Who could be against that besides Words with Friends addicts and auto-body shops? Rick Perry could. Telecommunications companies didn't like it. They make mucho dinero from texting charges. Was it a coincidence that AT&T had put $500,000 into Perry campaign coffers? "This is a big deal to AT&T. We live in our cars here," explained a state rep.

It couldn't be said Perry was a do-nothing governor. On the contrary, he did a lot—a lot of vetoing. During the 2001 legislative session, Perry overworked his veto stamp by shooting down 82 acts.

What was left for the guv but the White House? He threw his cowboy hat into the ring in 2012. He was doing pretty well at the beginning and was even the frontrunner for a brief moment. Then came his poor debate performances. In one, he had a mind deep-freeze after declaring he would eliminate three government agencies if elected. Unfortunately for him, he could only remember Commerce and Education. Energy he could not.

Trying to make up ground, on Dec. 6, prophetically just before Pearl Harbor Day, the Perry people released a YouTube video. In it, he falsely declared "there's something wrong in this country when gays can serve openly in the military, but our kids can't openly celebrate Christmas or pray in school." (The kids was the false part.) It was not well received and earned an impressive 850,000 dislikes. By comparison, the video of former "Seinfeld" actor Michael Richards' onstage meltdown only received 4,000 dislikes. You know you screwed up when people like your campaign advertisement 200 times less than a video of a man repeatedly yelling the n-word.

Such was Perry's first political loss. But he wasn't to be counted out. This guy had spunk. You need that if you are going to say to some tech bloggers "When [Texas] came into the nation in 1845, we were a republic. We were a stand-alone nation. And one of the deals was, we can leave any time we want. . . . So we're kind of thinking about that again." This statement exemplifies Perry's cluelessness. He was someone with ambitions to become president of the UNITED States, talking glibly about un-uniting them. He might as well have applied for a job as a forest ranger and joked about being a pyromaniac during the interview.

So it was that on June 4, 2015, Perry was back in the running. The braces had worked. Why not change his appearance again, this time donning dark-rimmed glasses? Perhaps he was hoping in a Clark Kent turn, it would hide his secret identity as a mild-mannered imbecile fighting a never-ending battle for nothing in particular. Voters saw through it with X-ray-like vision. Rerun ran out of gas quickly and withdrew Sept. 11, 2015, of all dates.

Dropout Walker

If people, other than his family, think back on Scott Walker, they will remember his union-busting record as governor of Wisconsin.

Scott was born Nov. 2, 1967, in Colorado Springs, Colo. Three years later, the Walker family of four drifted to Iowa where father Llew followed his calling as a Baptist minister. When Scott was 10, the Walkers again moved, this time to Delavan, Wis. Later, there would be many a Cheesehead who wished Llew's preaching had led him to, oh, Alaska, or better still, Palau. Anywhere far away from Wisconsin.

At Marquette University, Walker was known for always wearing a suit and tie in an era of hoodies and jeans. His run for school president was marred with dirty tricks on his side. Want a for instance? The school paper endorsed Walker's rival, adding "either candidate would serve the student body well." Suddenly, not a copy of the Marquette Tribune could be found on campus. A new edition came out with the headline "Revision—Walker unfit." He lost by 20 points.

Dropping out 34 credits short of graduation, he went to work for a short while for the American Red Cross before answering his true calling at 25. This guy was a political animal. He kept a picture of him and Ronald Reagan on his dorm desk, for chrissakes. He managed to snag a seat in the state assembly in 1992, and then he was on his way to the governor's mansion, with the moving vans arriving in 2011.

The voters of the Badger State may not have known what was in store for them. He talked a good game about creating 250,000 jobs in his first four years. (OK, so he only got to 145,000, but that was yet to come.) He did give a big hint about what he would do in office when he mentioned stopping local governments from being "strangled" by public employees. Who knew how he planned to do that? That turned out to be an all-out assault on collective bargaining.

Those bad state unions were to blame for the $3.6 billion budget deficit. Who cared if research showed that "[States] with larger unionized workforces do not have larger budget deficits"? No cause, no effect, lots of political malarkey (to borrow one of Joe Biden's favorite words).

Walker prevailed. Not hard considering Republicans held the majority in both houses of the legislature. But his anti-union, anti-public employee actions angered many voters, led to protests in the State Capitol and a recall effort. Walker was believed to have received an $8-million boost from the Koch brothers to beat back the recall vote, with lots more coming from other out-of-state conservatives. When the counting was over, Scotty was still brushing his teeth in the Executive Residence.

It was little wonder the Kochs were enamored with Walker, who looked vaguely like a distant relative of Howdy Doody. (And who might be pulling his strings?) Besides his union busting, there was his environmental record. Did the state really need such stringent iron-mining and wetlands legislation? What's a little more phosphorus in waterways especially if the pollution is coming from Koch Georgia Pacific paper plants? Who needs wind power when the Koch billions are tied to fossil fuels? Time to cut the budget of the University of Wisconsin's renewable-energy research center. Get rid of scientists at the Department of Natural Resources (DNR), which oversees the protection and management of air and water quality, forests and wildlife. When a kid asked him about climate change, Walker, a former Boy Scout, said he had learned to leave his campsite cleaner going out than when he came in. A bit disingenuous considering he was part of a suit opposing the EPA's Clean Power Act that called for reducing state power-plant emissions by 34 percent in 15 years.

As long as state unions had been emasculated, why not go after ones in the private sector? Again, with all his conservative pals in the legislature, Walker signed a right-to-work bill that said private-sector workers didn't have to pay union dues even if they benefited from union negotiating. Otherwise known as a free ride for the non-union workers.

Should it come as a surprise there were blots on Walker's resume? One was his Wisconsin Economic Development Corporation, set up to dole out loans to businesses, which worked its way up to $1.14 billion. Problem was auditors discovered 60 percent went to companies associated with Walker campaign donors. There was also the mucky question of whether his campaign illegally coordinated with outside conservative groups on his recall fight. Scotty, that is spelled C-O-R-R-U-P-T-I-O-N. Walker also had his own email controversy. While a county executive, his office was investigated for using a private email system for campaign work—on public time. That made it so much more precious when the Wisconsin Wonder decried Hillary's using one, too.

All of this only served to burnish his conservative credentials. To the point that word went out in 2015 that Walker had been anointed by les frères Koch as their favorite presidential candidate. No little deal since it was believed the boys were going to commit $1 billion to putting kindred spirits into the White House, Congress and state-level positions. Walker was considered a frontrunner at one point. Then came two ho-hum debate performances, and he was demoted to a political oopsy. He announced his candidacy on July 13, 2015 and was out on Sept. 21, eliciting a "holy cow" from Ted Cruz. As a parting shot, Walker urged the remaining Republicans in the running to unite against Donald Trump.

It should be added that one of Walker's lasting legacies will be his being punked into thinking he was talking to David Koch. The punker, Ian Murphy, suggested to the governor he "physically intimidate his Democratic opposition with a baseball bat, whip up a good counter-protest by dressing hobos in suits . . . plant troublemakers to discredit the pro-union demonstrators." Walker's response? "[W]e thought about that. . . . My only fear would be if there's a ruckus caused is that would scare the public into thinking maybe the governor has to settle to avoid all these problems."

Thus, Scott Walker became the 2016 version of 2012 Rick Perry—from front running to no running.

Jim Rambo

When it comes to flag waving, military swagger, and posing as the tough guy, that's always been a Republican thing. But the members of the Grand Old Party pale in comparison to Democrat Jim Webb. When it comes to toughness Webb, who looks like a perpetually angry Philip Seymour Hoffman, is the real thing.

Webb was born in Saint Joseph, Mo., on Feb. 9, 1946, into a military family. He is of Scots-Irish descent and has a relative that fought in every major American war (the Scots-Irish are best known for praying, potatoes and picking more fights than a drunken Conor McGregor at a UFC press conference). His father flew B-17s and B-29s during World War II, and growing up, the family jumped from base to base, living in Missouri, Illinois, Texas, Alabama, Nebraska, California and Virginia.

In 1963, Webb received a Naval Reserve scholarship to attend the University of Southern California. After graduating, he was appointed to the United States Naval Academy in Annapolis, Md. Webb was an exemplary cadet. He graduated in 1968, receiving the Superintendent's Letter for Outstanding Leadership.

After the Naval Academy, Webb was commissioned as a second lieutenant in the U.S. Marine Corps. At the time, the U.S. armed forces were busy trying to explode communism deep in the jungles of Southeast Asia. So, like many young men at the time, Webb headed to Vietnam. To say Webb's time there was eventful is like saying Bernie Sanders' hair is a tad unkempt. Accounts of Webb's heroism read vaguely like action sequences from the Sylvester Stallone movie "First Blood." For comparison, let's replace "Jim Webb" with "John Rambo" in this account of why Webb was awarded the Navy Cross for heroism.

> *"First Lieutenant Rambo was advancing to the first bunker when three enemy soldiers armed with hand grenades jumped out. Reacting instantly, he grabbed the closest man and, brandishing his .45 caliber pistol at the others, apprehended all three of the soldiers. Accompanied by one of his men, he then approached the second bunker and called for the enemy to surrender. When the hostile soldiers*

failed to answer him and threw a grenade that detonated dangerously close to him, First Lieutenant Rambo detonated a claymore mine in the bunker aperture, accounting for two enemy casualties and disclosing the entrance to a tunnel. Despite the smoke and debris from the explosion and the possibility of enemy soldiers hiding in the tunnel, he then conducted a thorough search that yielded several items of equipment and numerous documents containing valuable intelligence data. Continuing the assault, he approached a third bunker and was preparing to fire into it when the enemy threw another grenade. Observing the grenade land dangerously close to his companion, First Lieutenant Rambo simultaneously fired his weapon at the enemy, pushed the Marine away from the grenade, and shielded him from the explosion with his own body. Although sustaining painful fragmentation wounds from the explosion, he managed to throw a grenade into the aperture and completely destroy the remaining bunker."

Unlike Rambo, Webb could read at significantly higher than a third-grade level and attended Georgetown Law Center after his service was over. He graduated with a Juris Doctor degree in 1975.

From 1977 to 1981, Webb worked on the staff of the House Committee on Veterans Affairs. He also briefly taught at the Naval Academy before being booted. Not afraid to express a wildly unpopular opinion, Webb had written an op-ed piece titled "Woman Can't Fight," urging the armed forces against using females in combat. He did add, "It is good to see women doctors and lawyers and executives. I can visualize a woman President." In fairness to Webb, it was still eight years before Ronda Rousey would even be conceived, so how could he have known? And on the upside, we can be fairly certain that Webb isn't guilty of any atrocities like being racist, a devil worshiper or a fan of Hootie & the Blowfish because he surely would have told us all about it in an op-ed piece.

Webb served as the nation's first assistant secretary of defense for reserve affairs from 1984 to 1987. Then in 1987, he was appointed secretary of the navy by Ronald Reagan. This made Webb the first Naval Academy graduate to serve as the civilian head of the Navy. Unfortunately, his tenure was short lived. In 1988, the Republicans were cutting costs and wanted to reduce the size of the Navy. Webb refused and resigned from the post. While it's shocking that someone of Scots-Irish decent would be hotheaded, there are numerous accounts of Webb acting like a jackass during this period (or as the Mexicans call it, "Pendejo Trump"). President Reagan wrote, "I don't think the Navy was sorry to see him go."

After his resignation, Webb said he was "done with government." He spent the next 15 years writing books, articles and becoming more mature than an 8-year-old at Chuck E. Cheese's. Seven months before the beginning of the 2003 Iraq War, Webb wrote an essay for The Washington Post titled "Heading for Trouble: Do we really want to occupy Iraq for the next 30 years?" In it, he accurately laid out the pitfalls the U.S. would later encounter in Iraq. He questioned whether an overthrow of Saddam would "actually increase our ability to win the war against international terrorism." It's like he had a crystal ball. That or he was able to think through consequences instead of treating the U.S. military like a game of "Warcraft."

In late 2005, a Draft Jim Webb campaign began on the

internet, urging him to run for senator. In many aspects Webb is politically conservative. However, he has said he does not feel the Republican Party looks out for the interests of working-class people. So on Feb. 7, 2006, he obliged, announcing that he would seek the Democratic nomination for the 2006 Senate race against incumbent Virginia Sen. George Allen (a notorious "Pendejo Trump").

"Webb ran an unconventional campaign, going more with his intuition than with the advice of Democratic Party professionals, who at times despaired over him. He chose his own pacing and for a stretch in the summer evinced little interest in campaigning at all," Elizabeth Drew of The New York Review of Books wrote. When you consider that this was the same Democratic leadership responsible for the John Kerry campaign, perhaps that was a good thing. On Nov. 9, 2006, after the AP and Reuters projected that Webb had won the seat, Allen conceded the election.

Webb's time as a senator was only slightly less action packed than his tour in Vietnams, so let's hit a few of the early highlights:

Nov. 28, 2006—Webb disses President Bush at a White House reception for newly elected Congress members by skipping out on a photo op. Webb later said in an interview, "I'm not particularly interested in having a picture of me and George W. Bush on my wall."

Jan. 4, 2007—On his first day in the Senate, Webb introduces the Post-9/11 Veterans Educational Assistance Act, which he wrote. It would expand benefits for military families. It becomes law on June 30, 2008.

Jan. 23, 2007—Webb is set to deliver the Democratic response to the president's State of the Union
address, focusing on the economy and Iraq. He
goes rock star, tears up the draft written for him
and writes his own, delivering an emotional and
well-received speech.

March 26, 2007—Webb's senatorial aide, Phillip
Thompson, is arrested for carrying Webb's load-
ed pistol into the Russell Senate Office Building. Webb is very anti-gun control.

Despite the early fireworks, of which there were many,
Webb was surprisingly effective as a freshman senator. He
was able to spur on reform for veteran's rights and the
prison system, in particular. And as it turns out, Webb's
notoriously hot head may have cooled in his later years.
As Republican Chuck Hagel put it, "I think Jim Webb
is one of the smartest guys I've ever known. He has an
ability to think through issues. Not many here do. He
questions, he probes, he thinks through the consequences—we almost never do. We take an action—like going
to war—without thinking. He listens. He's not a blow-
hard. He'll hang back, and he'll listen. He's actually kind
of shy, kind of quiet."

Notwithstanding his success, one ride on the senatorial merry-go-round was enough for Webb. He opted
against running for re-election in 2012, and his presidential aspirations were even shorter lived. He made a formal
announcement of his candidacy on July 2, 2015. Then on
Oct. 20, 2015, after a lackluster debate and limited support, Webb dropped out of the Democratic presidential
race.

The Great Right RINO

Lincoln Chafee is an enigma. He is a riddle, wrapped up in puzzle, twisted around two political parties, nailed to the bottom of a horse's hoof. If that sounds confusing, so are many aspects of Lincoln Chafee's life.

Lincoln Davenport Chafee was born in Providence, R.I., on March 26, 1966. His father, John, was kind of a big deal. John Chafee was an officer in the United States Marine Corps, the 66th governor of Rhode Island, the secretary of the Navy and a United States senator.

Lincoln attended several different public schools in Rhode Island and later, Phillips Academy (aka a boarding school for the fabulously rich and most likely preppy). He enrolled at Brown University in 1971 where he was captain of the wrestling team and received a Bachelor of Arts in classics. That means he studied the languages and cultures of ancient Greece and Rome. Think of everyone you've ever known in your entire life. Do any of them have a B.A. in classics? No, because there is no conceivable reason you would ever need a B.A. in classics, but Lincoln Chafee has one. Then, after graduating, he chose a path that no graduate from Phillips and Brown had taken before. He said to himself, "I'm going to learn how to put shoes on horses."

It was on to the Montana State University Farrier School to learn the intricacies of attaching metal to the bottom of a 1,000-pound animal. Lincoln learned well. For the next seven years, he worked at racetracks as a farrier. This moved him one step closer to his goal of becoming a character from a John Steinbeck novel.

In 1985, Chafee entered the family business of politics by becoming the delegate to the Rhode Island Constitutional Convention. This part makes sense, at least. It's an obvious career path. Step 1, become a horse-shoer person. Step 2, get into local Rhode Island politics. Step 3, become U.S. senator. Step 4, president of the United States of America.

In 1992, Chafee continued his odyssey and was elected Warwick's first Republican mayor in 32 years. His clan must have been proud. His father was a Republican and his grandfather before him. So naturally, Chafee went on to be incredibly liberal, even while serving as a member of the Republican Party.

Chafee worked amicably with Democrats, who controlled seven of nine seats on the Warwick City Council. This should have been a red flag to fellow Republicans. As all career politicians know, it is written in the secret Republican handbook that you are supposed to butt heads with Democrats like a horny bighorn sheep. He also made conservation, environmental protection and wise growth priorities. In the ultimate hippie-liberal move, Chafee purchased 130 acres of open space and planted hundreds of street trees.

In 1999, Chafee's father decided he would not run for re-election to the U.S. Senate. So, in a political "I got dibs," Lincoln announced he would run for the seat. It would have been a graceful passing of the torch, but John Chafee died unexpectedly in October 1999. Gov. Lincoln (yes, another one) Almond appointed Lincoln to serve out the term. A year later, Chafee successfully ran for the seat, winning the election 57 percent to 41 percent.

During Chafee's time as a senator, the dominant conservatives began calling him a "Republican In Name Only," or RINO. Most notable among these was Human

Events magazine, which named Chafee "the No. 1 RINO in the country." So let's take a moment to examine exactly how liberal Chafee was.

For starters, he did not vote for President George W. Bush in the 2004 election. He told media that he wrote in former-President George H. W. Bush. There is no bigger burn than saying someone is less fit for a job than his 80-year-old father, especially if that job is as a Calvin Klein underwear model.

Chafee also opposed eliminating the federal estate tax. He voted against the 2001 and 2003 congressional budget bills that cut individuals' federal income taxes. He wanted to increase federal funding for healthcare. He was one of the few Republicans to vote against drilling in the Arctic National Wildlife Refuge. He supported affirmative action and gun control. He was the only Republican to vote against the Authorization for Use of Military Force Against Iraq. And in the unthinkable, he was pro-choice and supported federal funding for embryonic stem-cell research. As we all know, stem cells are to arch-conservatives as garlic is to a vampire. "C'mon vampires! Garlic has amazing health benefits, you'd like it if you tried it."

Despite being maybe the most liberal Republican ever, Chafee still wasn't liberal enough for Rhode Island. (Rhode Island is like a seven on the liberal scale. Ten being a bra-burning bonfire at Burning Man and one being Dick Cheney wearing a three-piece suit made entirely out of Confederate flags). When it came time for re-election, Chafee's Democratic rival attacked him on the few points where he had sided with the GOP. As a result, Chafee lost the general election 54 percent to 46.

In a move long overdue, Chafee officially left the Republican Party in September 2007. He was now an independent. He said that he did so because the Republican Party was drifting away from its core values, which is a polite way of saying, "They're all bat-shit crazy now."

In January 2010, Chafee declared his candidacy for governor of Rhode Island. President Obama did not endorse any of the candidates. Many viewed this as a silent nod for the independent Chafee over the Democrat running. Even more assumed Obama simply forgot Rhode Island is a state, which happens to most of us on a fairly regular basis. On Nov. 2, 2010, Chafee won the gubernatorial race edging out six other candidates with 36 percent of the vote.

Chafee began his governorship during one of the worst recessions in U.S. history. Unemployment peaked at 11.4 percent in the first months of his tenure. During Chafee's four years in office, the rate dropped to 5.9 percent, in part due to his sound budgets. The unemployment rate was now second best in the country. During this time, after campaigning for Obama's re-election, Chafee finally switched to the Democratic Party.

Great right? Now liberal Rode Island would embrace him with open arms. Think again. Like most things in Chafee's political career, what happened made very little sense. When it was time to run again, polls showed him trailing badly. Chafee announced in September 2013 that he was out of the race.

Perhaps this should have been a sign that he should move on from politics. There were a number of other professions he would have excelled in. He could have gone back to being a farrier, been an artisanal lollipop maker, started a commune for reformed lumberjacks or become a keeper of the rare Tormentil nomad bees. He didn't take the hint, though. On June 3, 2015, Chafee formally declared his candidacy for president of the United States. No one, probably not even Chafee, is entirely sure why. The race did not go well. There wasn't much to distinguish him, except his peculiar stumping point that America switch to the metric system. Then Chafee got slammed in his first debate for voting for a bill that allowed banks to grow larger, despite going after Hillary for her coziness with Wall Street.

"Glass-Steagall was my very first vote," Chafee explained. "I had just arrived. My dad had died in office. I was appointed to the office. It was my very first vote—"

"Are you saying you didn't know what you were voting for?" Anderson Cooper, the moderator, asked.

"I just arrived at Senate. I think we get some takeovers," Chafee said.

Perhaps the highlight of his candidacy was when talk-show host Conan O'Brien showed his support, sort of.

"Let's be honest," O'Brien said, "I'm not trying to get him elected. In fact, I'm personally not going to vote for him. But I think we should at least get him on the board so he's not humiliated. It seems like the nice thing to do."

O'Brien was even kind enough to write Chafee a theme song that included the lyrics, "He's only got 12 Facebook friends; he looks like Chris Matthews on a juice cleanse."

On Oct. 23, Chafee announced the end of his campaign.

So what does the future hold for Lincoln Chafee? Who can say, but it will most likely be perplexing, and we can hope it involves horses.

Exorcist Not-So Extraordinaire

Ohh, Bobby, Bobby, Bobby, what were you thinking? Sure, you filed with the FEC showing $1.4 million in your campaign chest. Still, wasn't there anyone you trusted sane enough to say running for president of the United States was a huge mistake when you couldn't run Louisiana?

There was a time Jindal was being called the Republican Party's great beige hope. He had a dream bio for a party looked upon as a bunch of middle-aged and old white guys. Along came Jindal. His backstory was wonderful. In 1970, Jindal's Indian mother was offered a scholarship to study nuclear physics at Louisiana State University's graduate school. Though excited at the prospect, Raj Jindal saw one tiny problem. She was pregnant.

Not to worry, said LSU. We'll give you some time off after the baby arrives. So Raj and her husband, Amar, packed their belongings and headed to the exotic-sounding Baton Rouge. Well maybe not so exotic sounding when you know it translates into English as "red stick." Here's where all that immigration rigmarole, even back then, gets somewhat convoluted. You might think that the couple would have applied for green cards based on Raj at LSU. But no, the cards came through thanks to Amar being deemed a highly skilled professional, having been an assistant professor of engineering at Chandigarh's Punjab University. This even though he didn't have a job in the U.S. If he had piggy-backed on Raj's card, he wouldn't have been allowed to work.

Papa Jindal proved himself a resourceful man. In that pre-internet era, he took to the old-fashioned phone book. As Bobby wrote in his 2010 "Leadership and Crisis" (not unexpectedly labeled "self-serving" by some reviewers, but hey, Bobby was a pol), "So he sat down at the kitchen table in early 1971 and opened up the yellow pages. Starting with the A's, he made cold calls to local business in his heavily accented English, eventually landing a job offer at a railroad," a subsidiary of the Kansas City Southern Railway.

With all the nutty birthers running around with nothing else to do, the question of Bobby being a natural-born citizen eligible to be president raised its dopey head later, though nothing came of it.

Now we have Baby Piyush making his appearance in Louisiana on June 10, 1971. By the time he was 5, he rejected that Piyush business and asked to be called Bobby from henceforth. Bobby after the youngest "Brady Bunch" boy. His parents should have been grateful their son wasn't enamored with Fonzie on "Happy Days."

Piyush/Bobby was being raised Hindu. As he grew older, he felt the religion was not absolute enough. It didn't provide him with definitive answers and guidance. So, in middle school, when a good buddy introduced him to the world of evangelicals, Bobby felt the fit. While other boys his age were in the closet reading Playboy, Jindal was reading the Bible.

Bobby finally came out of the closet and confessed his conversion sin to his parents soon before heading off to college. Luckily for the lad, they did not withhold payment for his tuition to Brown, which back then was about $15,000 a year.

Now you have Bobby wandering the liberal campus feeling like a crayfish out of water until he discovered the Christian Fellowship and Campus Crusade for Christ, groups super-dedicated to spreading the teachings of Jesus. This Bobby liked. Now, he was hooked on old-time Catholicism, of the type no longer practiced by the Vatican. But Bobby wasn't content with his newest conversion. He was out to bring others into the fold. Fellow Brownies recalled him as on a proselytizing mission.

Bobby was of the mind that Catholicism, at least the way he would practice it, should battle evil on an intellectual and physical level. Which brought him to his collegiate exorcism. Yes, you read that right. Bobby Jindal conducted an exorcism. A female friend was diagnosed with skin cancer, she was having "visions," and most telling of all, people said they smelled sulfur in her room—all sure signs that Satan had possessed her. Jindal chronicled this in the New Oxford Review, a Roman Catholic magazine. It is unclear if the devil stopped possessing her after the ritualistic rigmarole, though in a later essay, Jindal talked about a girl with a different name than the first who was saved from Satan.

After graduating from Brown, where he had been in pre-med, Jindal passed on attending Yale and Harvard medical schools to be a Rhodes Scholar, something of a good first step in American politics. You have N.J. Senator Bill Bradley, who dabbled in basketball earlier in his career; a later New Jersey senator, Cory Booker; Les Aspin, Wisconsin congressman and secretary of defense; another Wisconsinite, Sen. Russ Feingold; Indiana Sen. Dick Lugar; and the list goes on with the Rhodes' crowning glory being President Bill Clinton.

At Oxford, where Jindal studied health policy, he continued his conservative ways, preaching against abortion. And he was full of himself. According to a 2014 Mother

Jones piece, "He was sufficiently impressed with himself, one classmate recalls, that fellow students shamed him into dropping coins in a jar every time he mentioned he was a Rhodes Scholar. But for all his passion, Jindal projected more wonkiness than political magnetism."

He took that wonkiness with him back to Louisiana where with help from a political connection, he was appointed secretary of the Department of Health and Hospitals, a prestigious position for a 24-year-old considering the department gobbled up 40 percent the state's budget. Beefing up his resume more, at 28, he was named head of the Louisiana University System, the youngest person to hold that position. Then it was on to a federal job in 2001 under George W. Bush as assistant secretary of health and human services. Talk about a trajectory to greatness.

In 2003, Jindal hit a setback. He lost the gubernatorial race to Democrat Kathleen Babineaux Blanco. Undaunted, he almost immediately sought a U.S. Congressional seat and won two terms—the second by 88 percent. But it was the governor's mansion he coveted. In 2007, he beat two prominent Democrats for it with 54 percent of the votes.

With the win under his belt, Jindal set out to prove he was a man of his word, a man of the future. He was taking over a state that has been called "half under water, half under indictment," where the notoriously corrupt Huey Long ran roughshod and a former governor crowed the only way he wouldn't be re-elected was if he was "caught in bed with a dead girl or a live boy."

Bobby had declared he would change all this. There would be transparency in politicians' finances. He would back strong ethics laws. Bring competency to government.

He would make his Bubbas for Bobby proud. One influential conservative talk-radio powerhouse even called him the next Ronald Reagan.

You have to hand it to the boy-governor. He started out strong, calling two special sessions of the legislature. (Louisiana reps are not particularly hard working, meeting regularly only every other year. When they do convene, they are sequestered in the four-sided Pentagon Barracks—the fifth side was so shoddily built, allegedly because of graft, it had to be torn down—where they have a lot of barbecues.) Jindal got an ethics law passed and got rid of some taxes that, it was argued, discouraged businesses from investing in the state.

Oh, Bobby was on a roll that rolled him to winning a second term in 2011 by 66 percent. Yet, there were some nasty storm clouds on the horizon. Jindal may have been too confident in his vaunted wonkiness to realize his policies were leading him toward disaster. Hurricane Katrina had kept Louisiana's budget in good standing as billions in federal money poured into the state. Bobby took that opportunity to push through tax cuts—tax cuts for the wealthy and subsidies for businesses ($210 million more was given out than taxes the new companies generated).

But all good can come to an end. That was the case in Louisiana. The federal money tap was being turned off. Oil prices plummeted, taking a good chunk of state tax revenue with them.

As the situation worsened, Jindal, who had inherited a surplus, resorted to a tactic he had once assailed. Creative bookkeeping coupled with slashing and burning programs so taxes wouldn't be raised. Jindal genuflected before the temple of Grover Norquist, the anti-tax crazy.

So let's see. Fire 30,000 state employees. Who needs so many child-services workers, even if that meant a cutback on the number of abuse cases investigated? State universities, what's a bankruptcy here or there? Let patients with disabilities fend for themselves. What are reserve funds for except to be dipped into and depleted? But gosh, send state money to religious and charter schools, one of which said the Loch Ness monster disproves the theory of evolution. The list doesn't end.

When newly elected governor John Bel Edwards, a Democrat, took office in January 2016, he found his predecessor had left him an unwanted present—a budget gap of $2 billion in fiscal year 2016-2017. Louisiana would need $3 billion to maintain services. You can imagine the uproar when Louisiana State University announced it might have to suspend *football*. Talk about the pigskin hitting the fan.

All of this made Jindal a pretty unpopular fellow. Really unpopular. A University of New Orleans poll in November 2015 put his approval rating at a sad 20 percent. That included the 55 percent of Republicans polled who gave him a thumbs down. Even George W.'s lowest performance rating was 25 percent. A Republican sheriff called Jindal an idiot, adding, "Bobby Jindal was a better cult leader than Jim Jones. We drank the elixir for eight years. We remained in a conscious state. We walked to the edge of the cliff, and we jumped off, and he watched us and guess what? Unlike Jim Jones, he did not swallow the poison. What a shame."

In addition to this colossal governing failure, his constituents had become increasingly annoyed. OK, royally pissed that their governor was spending more time out of state talking at rubber-chicken dinners in his obvious run for the White House than in Baton Rouge. The Associated Press did the math and found in 2014, Jindal was not in state one out of five days. It was all about ambition. A lobbyist said, "If you cut that boy open from stem to stern, won't nothing bleed out but ambition."

That ambition and an incredible lack of a reality check led Jindal to declare his bid for 1600 Pennsylvania Avenue in June 2015. This despite him polling behind "None of the Above" by 2 percent. That must have hurt.

Reality finally set in on Nov. 17 when Jindal suspended his campaign. Let's give him credit. He did get off a great swipe at Trump during one of the debates—though Bobby never made it to the main stage.

"You may have recently seen that after Trump said the Bible is his favorite book, he couldn't name a single Bible verse or passage that meant something to him," Jindal said. "And we all know why, because it's all just a show, and he hasn't ever read the Bible. But you know why he hasn't read the Bible? Because he's not in it."

Three Amigo Hawk

At first blush, you might wonder why Lindsey Graham is clumped with the Delusionals. When he threw his name into the ring, this guy had been in Congress since the Ice Age, well, more accurately, 1993. His backstory was both tear jerking and commendatory.

This fine fellow of the South wailed his first on July 9, 1955. Father F.J. ran the Sanitary Café in Central, S.C., where Little Lindsey was born. It was a multipurpose establishment—restaurant, bar, pool hall and liquor store for those who needed something for the road. It was illegally segregated. Blacks could buy alcohol in the liquor store, but had to go elsewhere to drink it. "It's just the way it is," F.J. told his son.

When his parents died one after another when Graham was in his early 20s and in the Reserve Officers' Training Corps, he was allowed to attend the University of South Carolina so he could take care of his young sister, whom he adopted. Graham quipped at the end of the second presidential debate, the one held in the Reagan Presidential Library, that he "wasn't the best law student. By the end of this debate, it'd be the most time I'd spent in any library."

Despite his self-confessed lack of academic fortitude, Graham got his B.A. in psychology in 1977 and a law degree four years later. Then it was back to the military. From 1984 to 1988, the future senator was sometimes prosecuting attorney, sometimes for the defense in Germany in the Air Force JAG. (TV fans might remember the "JAG" series spawned the incredibly popular "NCIS.") Back in the States, he left active duty, but not the military, joining the South Carolina Air National Guard, then the U.S. Air Force Reserve. Hey, these are great patriotic credentials. He even got called back to active duty in the first Gulf War. OK, so he never left South Carolina, being charged with instructing pilots on the rules of war.

That did not end his military service. Come 2007, Graham was a reservist on active duty in Iraq, though not for long. Again, he was briefing on the rules of law and how to treat detainees. Two years later, he packed his duffel for Afghanistan, taking advantage of the congressional summer recess to deploy.

Come on. Is this good Clint Eastwood stuff or what? Graham's political career was not to be sneezed at, either. In the South Carolina House of Representatives from '93 to '95, U.S. congressman, '95 to 2003. Then the big break. Strom Thurmond, the U.S. senator older than God herself (well, only if God was younger than 100), finally saw fit to announce his retirement. This bigot, who it turned out had fathered a mixed-race daughter, served in the Senate for more than 45 years.

Nobody ran against Graham in the Republican primary, and he was soon off to Washington.

In the Senate, it would be no way an exaggeration to say the South Carolinian was a hawk. At one time, he, Joe Lieberman from Connecticut and John McCain (do we really have to ID him?) were labeled the Three Amigos. Shortly after he declared his candidacy in June 2015, Graham hammered his militaristic bent. Send 20,000 American troops to Iraq and Syria—Graham would kick out its barbaric president, Bashar Assad. And he would ramp up the number of U.S. troops in Afghanistan if he saw the need.

And forget about the Iran deal if he didn't like it.

Graham made it clear he didn't mind being called a warmonger. He took these positions "not because I like war, not because I want war, but because I want to defend our nation."

He didn't make any points in the Bush camp when he conceded that although he had backed the Iraq invasion, he now saw it as a mistake.

And where he hasn't made points for years was with the Tea Party, which would have liked nothing better than running him out of office for his willingness to work with

Dems on issues like immigration reforms. Oh gosh, he was being called "Flimsy Lindsey" and "Grahamnesty," as if he cared. But the incumbent senator got the loudest laugh in the 2014 senatorial election. He had six primary opponents. One thought the federal government was filled with members of the Muslim Brotherhood. He managed a whopping 5.34 percent of the vote to Graham's 56.42.

Graham doesn't seem to have many compunctions about changing his mind. For instance, he had recognized climate change. Then he said it was oversold. Then in one of the debates, he said, "You don't have to believe that climate change is real. [But] I have been to the Antarctic, I have been to Alaska. I'm not a scientist, and I've got the grades to prove it. But I've talked to the climatologists of the world, and 90 percent of them are telling me that the greenhouse-gas effect is real. That we're heating up the planet. I just want a solution that would be good for the economy that doesn't destroy it."

That little quip about not being a scientist is pure Lindsey. Like his policies or not, there is no question he is a funny man.

On Marco Rubio: "I learned that Marco has a good memory because he kept saying the same thing over and over again."

On his failed presidential bid: "I got out because I ran out of money. If you want to get money out of politics, you should have joined my campaign."

He wondered how Hillary Clinton, who he called the "most dishonest person in America," might end up as the next president "How could that be?" He answered, "My party has gone batshit crazy."

"If you killed Ted Cruz on the floor of the Senate, and the trial was in the Senate, nobody could convict you."

"That's the first thing I'm going to do as president: We're gonna drink more." (He was referencing Reagan's habit of knocking back a few with Democratic Speaker of the House Tip O'Neill, though Tipsy always looked as if he knocked back more than a few.)

And his personal best was when he called Ted Cruz "the love child of Joe McCarthy and Dracula."

A forever bachelor, he had to deny rumors he was gay: "I know it's going to upset a lot of gay men."

On mandatory budget cuts: "Sequestration is Latin for doing really dumb things."

On a Trump victory: "ISIL would be dancing in the streets. They just don't believe in dancing."

Graham's campaign sputtered from the get-go, although some called for him being moved to the prime-time debates, probably hoping for more one-liners if he shared the stage with Trump. Trump, oh yeah. Not high on Graham's Most Admired list. "He's a race-baiting, xenophobic, religious bigot. He doesn't represent my party. He doesn't represent the values that the men and women who wear the uniform are fighting for."

And so it was that the Graham for President—A Conservative Leader Who Gets Things Done campaign was suspended on Dec. 21, 2015. "While we have run a campaign that has made a real difference, I have concluded this is not my time."

Of course, Graham always had a big disadvantage. He's only 5 feet 7 inches. Hey, Americans like taller guys in the Oval Office.

George Who?

Given the American penchant for tall presidents, at 6'5", George Pataki should have been a frontrunner. On the other hand, he was George Pataki. Do a search for his one-liners, and Google wonders if you're kidding.

Born in Peekskill, N.Y. on June 24, 1945, his was a melting-pot family. Hungarian, Italian, Irish. Father Louis was a postman, volunteer fireman and farmer, which explains why George needed a scholarship to go to Yale. One of his classmates was another George, George W., who didn't need a scholarship.

From Yale, it was on to Columbia Law School. Pataki took his J.D. back to Peekskill where he practiced at Plunkett and Jaffe, which would have been no big whoop except he met Michael C. Finnegan, the brains behind Pataki's political successes. First, it was mayor of Peekskill. Then the New York State Assembly and Senate. In 1994, he had the temerity to go up against the three-term governor, Mario Cuomo, and win. And what put George P. over the top in his estimation? An endorsement by shock-jock Howard Stern.

Come 2015 and Pataki had a major problem. Nobody knew his name. He could have been a regular in the Cheers bar, and still nobody would have known his name. Granted, he was governor from 1995 to 2007. Still, on announcing his candidacy in 2015, a political analyst wondered why Pataki was bothering. "I don't know how people obtain these delusions. I don't take those drugs."

This is a sad commentary for a guy who once headed one of the most populous states in the union.

Pataki had made noises about running in 2008. He

decided not to, supposedly because Rudy Giuliani was going after the nomination. Conventional wisdom was Rudy had a good shot. He started out strong, leading in polls, but eventually fell to John McCain. Some observers attributed Giuliani's abrasive personality as part of the reason he lost. He did little to soften that image in his RNC 2016 convention speech, in which he spent 15 minutes mostly screaming. Humorist Andy Borowitz had fun with that, citing a "poll" in The New Yorker that found "an unprovoked attack by Giuliani now rivals immigration, terrorism, and the economy as a top concern of likely voters." Borowitz "quoted" a father as saying, "When I put my kids to bed last night, I told them, 'Don't worry, the bad man on TV can't hurt you.' I wish I could believe that. I really do."

But back to Lonesome George. Another problem was the timing. His somewhat moderate record was out of step with many of the rabid Republican primary voters. He acknowledged climate change, as governor signed legislation protecting the rights of gays and lesbians and horror of all horrors, had once tried to get the party to take an anti-abortion stance out of its platform.

Maybe Pataki thought his "fiscal conservatism" and tax cutting would earn him points. He liked to point out that "19 different taxes were cut 90 times" during his three terms in Albany. Of course, he did raise fees to offset the lost revenues. Fees, taxes, tom-ay-toes, toh-mah-toes. And the other way to close a budget gap that widened considerably because of spending, which rose 46 percent in six years, was to cut back on subsidies, to say, education. Near the beginning of Pataki's tenure, the state chipped in 63 percent of state college budgets, with tuitions accounting for 37 percent. That got switched around by 2005 when it was 49 percent state and 51 percent tuition. And transportation took a hammering, too.

His record on crime might have been attractive to red-meat voters. He did reinstate the death penalty. So what if the New York Supreme Court ruled it unconstitutional 10 years later? During his time in office, some 100 crime laws were strengthened and prison sentences lengthened. Of course, that isn't terribly popular in 2016 as even the ultra-conservative Koch boys are calling for prison-justice reform. "Three strikes and you're out" proved a disastrous policy.

So why, why did Pataki enter the fray? Not to be crass, but it might have something to do with a certain Vegas and Macau casino owner. No, not Steve Wynn. Try Sheldon Adelson. Adelson, a pro-Israel hawk, poured $53 million or maybe it was $150 million into the 2012 election. The disparity coming from purported contributions to political nonprofits, aka Dark Money, that don't have to be disclosed. Adelson didn't have a very good track record. Nine out of the 10 candidates he backed outright lost. But hey, his $15 million kept Newt Gingrich going.

Maybe that's what Pataki was hoping for—enough money to keep him around long enough for people to stop asking "George Who?" He had creds in the "Adelson Primary," that's what the conservative candidates bowing before the billionaire in Las Vegas had come to be called. Pataki was the spokesguy and co-chair for the Coalition to Stop Internet Gambling, which Adelson started and backs, figuring suckers losing their money online would eat into suckers losing their money at his gaming tables.

For a while, Marco Rubio was winning the Adelson

sweepstakes. He had a definite leg up on Pataki as he co-sponsored a Senate bill that would prohibit online gambling. In any case, Georgy dropped out Dec. 29, 2015. He never got off the kiddy stage in the debates, not with single-digit polling numbers as low as one. And his calling for boots on ground in Iraq to fight the self-named Islamic State didn't give him traction.

Who knows, the traction he might get is lobbying for Sheldon Adelson.

Mr. Rogers' Homophobic Neighborhood

Imagine you walk into your living room, plop down on your sofa and flip on the TV. A familiar PBS show flicks on the screen. It's Mr. Rogers.

"Hello, children," he says. Something seems different about him, but you can't place it. Maybe a plumpness of the face . . . or a spark of insanity behind the eyes?

He crosses the room, and you see the familiar toys lining the shelves. One group seems to be arranged suspiciously like a Nativity scene.

"Now, let's tie our shoes, children. Don't worry if you can't do it on the first try," he chuckles. "Inside every human being, there are treasures to unlock." That's the homespun wisdom you grew up on. "Also," he continues, "you need to pledge yourself to Jesus Christ. And never commit the heinous acts of homosexuality or abortion because those are sins against God, and you will never be able to tie your shoes with a tarnished soul."

What the hell!?!?! You squint. That's not Mr. Rogers. That's Mike Huckabee, a man who can give you the warm, fuzzy feels with words of wisdom one minute, then say something that is precariously close to hate speech the next. How does such a man come to exist? The answer is in a little southern town.

Mike Huckabee let out his first wail on Aug. 24, 1955, in Hope, Ark. Yes, that Hope, home of the Hope Watermelon Festival and birthplace of international man of mystery, Bill Clinton. Sadly, while it's fun to imagine a John Hughes teen-movie where Clinton dumps a high-school cafeteria tray on Huckabee's head, there was no interaction between the two in their early life. Clinton is 11 years older than Huckabee, and they had very different upbringings.

Bill's biological father, William Blythe, a traveling salesman and husband to four separate women, was killed in an automobile accident three months before Bill's birth. Tragic, but it does make a strong case for nature versus nurture. For the first six years of his life, Bill was raised by his mother and grandmother. In 1950, Bill's mother married Roger Clinton, a car dealer and abusive alcoholic. If Roger could have just added "peeping Tom" to his CV, he would have completed the slimeball trifecta. So, Bill grew up without a father figure. Conversely, Huckabee's father played a dominant role in his life.

Huckabee's father, Dorsey, worked as a fireman and mechanic, and was a strict disciplinarian. He was a salt of the earth, hard-nosed man's man. The type of guy that might insist his kids' placemats at the diner are at a perfect 90-degree angle and won't hesitate to take a warm hand to their face if they dare color outside the lines.

"My father was the ultimate patriot," Huckabee said. "You know, he'd lay on the stripes, and I'd see stars." Some people might suggest that Huckabee is glibly hinting at child abuse. Those are the type of people that Dorsey would kick square in the balls. Sissies. With an alpha-father in the house, a young Mike was often timid and awkward. Luckily, he found two major outlets—the church and music.

The fact that Huckabee turned to the church and music were almost a given. As he put it, "You know, in my hometown of Hope, Ark., the three sacred heroes were Jesus, Elvis and FDR, not necessarily in that order." You can picture a young Huckabee fretting between whom was a better role model, Jesus or Elvis. And more importantly, which one of them had better hair. We can deduce that Huckabee went with Elvis, at least as far as coifs are concerned, and his love for music continues today.

Huckabee still occasionally plays bass guitar for the Arkansas-based rock band, Capitol Offense (whose other members consist of Huckabee's gubernatorial executive staff). Let's save some time and anguish before you inevitably stop reading this book and rush to iTunes to purchase every Capitol Offense song you can find. Tragically, their work is not available on the popular music platform. Be strong. You will have to settle for bootleg videos on You-Tube and perhaps a pilgrimage to Arkansas to see them live.

Speaking of holy quests, the church played an even bigger role in Huckabee's development. It was after joining the Garrett Memorial Baptist Church in the mid-1960s that shy, young Michael made a life-changing discovery. He loved the sound of his own voice. Like really loved it, the way a meth addict loves meth or Justin Bieber loves staring at his reflection. He preached his first sermon as a teenager. He also landed his first job at 14, reading the news and weather at a local radio station.

After these experiences, Huckabee started coming out of his I'm-scared-of-my-father shell. His growing confidence saw him elected governor of the Arkansas Boys State. What is the Arkansas Boys State, you ask? Apparently, it's the male, teenage, political equivalent of the Miss America Pageant. Huckabee also continued to preach sermons in his high-school auditorium to classmates. This is probably the greatest sign of Huckabee's growing self-confidence. At that age, most guys are hesitant to tell a pretty girl they like her hair, let alone instruct their classmates on how to have a personal relationship with God. Mike was undaunted, though, and it was around this time, he met a young lady that struck his fancy.

Mike had his first date with Janet McCain (no relation to John) in 1973. She was tall and a straight baller as a standout on the girls' basketball team. It was love at first sermon. They were married a year later at Janet's house. As the story goes, Janet descended her staircase in a white dress her mother had made, and Mike, unable to afford a ring, slipped a soda-can tab around her finger, which, regardless of how you feel about Huckabee, is goddamned adorable.

Janet and Mike have been described as personality opposites. While he is much more focused and frenetic, she is fun loving and relaxed. Later, when Mike became governor, she was referred to as the "first tomboy of Arkansas." This nickname was undoubtedly earned because of her penchant for hunting bears and rattlesnakes, or perhaps was awarded after she took advantage of the National Guard's hospitality to fire off a rocket launcher. Regardless, they were a match made in Hope.

When asked to comment on this serendipitous and

blissful union, Mike's best friend since the second grade, Lester Sitzes III, answered, "Those two folks were virgins when they got married, I can tell you that." And we care because?

This marks yet another difference between governors Huckabee and Clinton. Let's refrain from being uncouth and speculating at what age Bill Clinton lost his virginity, but we can only hope it was in the double digits.

The Huckabee lovebirds attended Ouachita Baptist University, where Mike majored in religion and minored in speech. By all accounts, they had a grand time at Ouachita.

"When I was in college, we used to take a popcorn popper, because that was the only thing they would let us use in the dorm, and we would fry squirrels in a popcorn popper in the dorm room." If that doesn't sound like good (if not clean) Arkansanian fun, what does?

Following his 1975 graduation, Mike did not feel he had had done enough Bible thumping in a formal educational setting. So he enrolled at Southwestern Baptist Theological Seminary in Fort Worth, Texas, before dropping out to work for televangelist James Robison. This is the same James Robison of LIFE TODAY, a television program that allowed him to rake in piles of cash, Scrooge McDuck style.

Huckabee returned to Arkansas in 1979 to serve as a congregational pastor and was reunited with his true passion of hearing himself talk. This led to him becoming the head of the 490,000-member Baptist State Convention 10 years later. It was from there, like many wannabe messiahs before him, that Huckabee built a following. He used this power base to run for the Senate against the three-term incumbent Dale Bumpers in 1992. This is where we see the Huckabee-crazy for the first time.

During the campaign, Huckabee advocated separating people with HIV/AIDS from the general population, telling the Associated Press that "we need to take steps that would isolate the carriers of this plague." Now, Huckabee did not say this, but you have to wonder if he would have been onboard with isolating them in Utah so they could mingle with the Mormon population. By Huckabee standards, this would be a "two birds with one stone" scenario. It came out later that Michael is not a fan of the Church of Latter-Day Saints. Despite this strong platform of HIV-banishment, Huckabee suffered a resounding defeat.

Many people would have been deterred by what appeared to be complete disdain by his fellow Arkansanians, but not Mike. This is the guy who stood in an auditorium and told his high-school classmates they weren't loving Jesus the right way.

Fortunately for him, opportunity knocked. On the heels of Bill Clinton's election to president, a special election for Arkansas lieutenant governor was held in 1993. Mike slid right in there like Bill Clinton . . . well, you get the idea.

In yet another, even stranger Clinton coattails cross-over, Huckabee became governor in 1996 when Gov. Jim Guy Tucker was convicted on federal charges of fraud and conspiracy relating to the Whitewater scandal. If you recall, Whitewater was the investigation into the possibly illegal and surely shady real-estate investments of Bill and Hillary Clinton and their associates, Jim and Susan McDougal. Jim Tucker, Clinton's successor as governor, received four years' probation for his involvement. Susan

McDougal (who President Clinton later pardoned) served 18 months in prison for refusing to answer questions. And Bill? Of course, nothing stuck. Meanwhile, the true beneficiary of Whitewater was Mike Huckabee. He was elected to full terms as Arkansas governor in 1998 and 2002, then announced in 2007 that he would run for the Republican nomination for president. With his history as governor and pastoral credentials, Huckabee was the religious right's favorite guy with the opposition being scary Mormon Mitt Romney and shark-eyed John McCain. This was Huckabee's first exposure on a national stage. It was a chance to hear himself talk in front of millions of people. It was a dream come true.

Who would have thunk it? Huckabee won the Iowa Republican caucuses, receiving 34 percent and 17 delegates, compared to second-place Mitt Romney's 25. This cemented Huckabee as a real contender. What went wrong, you ask? What could stop Mike's ascent to the White House? In short, with the mounting exposure and pressure, Mike's full-crazy came out.

So, what does full-Huckabee-crazy sound like? Consider that these words actually came out of his mouth, intentionally, in a public setting. "Well, I don't think that's a radical view to say we're going to affirm marriage. I think the radical view is to say that we're going to change the definition of marriage so that it can mean two men, two women, a man and three women, a man and a child, a man and animal."

Yes, Huckabee equated gay marriage with bestiality. Perhaps he could have understood the difference if someone explained to him it to him in these terms, "Michael, it is OK for your wife to shoot a deer with her double-barrel shotgun, whereas it is not OK for her to shoot a gay person." Of course, it's possible that Mike disagrees with that statement in principle.

Trailing behind John McCain and Mitt Romney in delegate count and popular vote, Huckabee exited the race in March of 2008. McCain went on to become the Republican nominee and look old and pasty next to Barack Obama.

Even though Huckabee's brand of crazy was a little too strong for the Republican Party at large, it was Goldilocks-right for Fox News. They signed him shortly after the election, and Huckabee began hosting his own talk show on the Fox News Channel in September 2008. In 2012, he also began hosting "The Mike Huckabee Show," a radio offering produced by ABC. While it wasn't presidential, Huckabee could still hear himself talk to hundreds of thousands of people.

Mike declined to throw his hat in the ring during the 2012 election, although there was much speculation that he might become Mitt Romney's running mate. That would surely have been a disastrous political pairing. Huckabee once said Mormons believe that "Jesus and the devil are brothers" when asked about Romney. However, it would have made an amazing sitcom. They could have called it "Mike and Mitt."

"Don't touch me with your possessed magic underwear," Mike would say shaking a hand vigorously at Mitt. "That voodoo will burn my skin." Oh Mike, the audience would laugh!

With the persistence of Rocky charging face first into an Apollo Creed punch (in Rocky I, not Rocky II where he actually wins), Mike entered the 2016 election for president. However, after dropping gems like "So the Muslims will go to the mosque, and they will have their day of prayer, and they come out of there like uncorked animals—throwing rocks and burning cars," the Republican voters turned Huckabee away like a geek asking the homecoming queen for a prom date.

So, who is Mike Huckabee? A musician. A preacher. A politician. Someone who tried to follow in the footsteps of Jesus, Elvis and FDR, with no regard to how crazy he sounded along the way. But hey, that's Mike. A guy who will say what he believes, as warmly and personably as Mr. Rogers ever could. True, the people have resoundingly said they don't like this. True, Huckabee received a crushing defeat in the 2016 primaries. But do you think Huckabee cares about those stupid facts and figures? Nope. As Mike so eloquently put it, "I didn't major in math. I majored in miracles."

Irish Guitar Guy

It's easy to picture photogenic Democrat Martin O'Malley with his equally photogenic, accomplished wife and four cute kids gracing the White House Christmas card. O'Malley sure could, as well, but first he would have to suffer the slings and travel of a presidential campaign.

It all started on Jan. 18, 1963, when baby Martin was born in D.C. to Barbara and Thomas O'Malley. After serving as a bombardier in the Army Air Force (he saw the Hiroshima mushroom cloud while flying a mission), Thomas used the G.I Bill to afford law school and eventually was appointed an Assistant United States Attorney. Barbara was to become an aide to forever Maryland pol Barbara Mikulski, for whom she worked—and was still aiding in 2016—for 30 years.

As is often the case, a lawyer begat a lawyer. (Are toddlers taught torts on their mommy or daddy's knee?) Martin dutifully got his J.D. from the University of Maryland School of Law in 1988. But before that, while a lackluster student at the Catholic University of America, he took a step that started his political juices boiling or maybe simmering. He volunteered to work for Gary Hart, a 1984 presidential candidate. Marty was placed first in the Iowa office, then got moved to Columbus. When fellow workers hadn't heard from the 20-year-old for several days, they feared the worst and grabbed a plane for Ohio.

"We found him playing guitar, and he had a couple of good-looking girls with him signing up volunteers," Phil Noble, a Hart research director, said. "He told us when he got 500, he was going to knock off for the night."

Oh, the guitar. A very important part of the O'Malley saga. While at Gonzaga High School in D.C., he and his football coach formed a band, the Shannon Tide. It was 1979, so you would be forgiven for thinking they played covers of "Da Ya Think I'm Sexy?" and "Old Time Rock and Roll." Forgiven, but incorrect. The Tide, which morphed into O'Malley's March, had more of a Celtic folk rock propensity and played "This Land Is Your Land" and ""Hard Times Come Again No More."

O'Malley didn't eschew his musical career after he entered politics. That guitar was with him when he stumped. And he certainly wasn't the only office seeker to entertain supporters. One was Idahoan Glen Taylor back in the '40s, who earned the nickname, "The Singing Cowboy." He'd drive from town to backwater town and entertain from the back of a pickup truck. After several unsuccessful attempts, he finally made it to Washington as senator from the Gem State. But his singing didn't stop. Faced with the post-World War II housing shortage, in hopes of finding a place to rent, Taylor stood outside the Capitol building and sang, "O give us a home, near the Capitol dome, with a yard for two children to play . . ." It worked.

The Hart adventure inspired O'Malley to try his own hand at wooing voters. In 1990, he went for a state Senate seat without the support of the Dem bigwigs in Baltimore. No state Senate seat for O'Malley. A year later, the same bigwigs backed him for Baltimore City Council. This time he won.

He bided his time for eight years on the council before putting his name up for the mayorship. Think about this. Baltimore. Mostly black population. Highest violent-crime rate in the country. People fleeing by 1,000 per month. And a wonky, guitar-playing white guy thought he had a shot at the nomination? By promising to reduce crime, Marty got some key endorsements. When he won the primary (that meant, as a Dem, he won the office), The Washington Post headline read, "WHITE MAN GETS MAYORAL NOMINATION IN BALTIMORE."

Have to say one thing about O'Malley. When he promises something, he makes good on the promise. Crack down on crime, you say. How about 100,000 arrests in 1999 when Baltimore's population was 673,000? Obviously, some of those arrests were for minor violations like open carry. But Marty had brought in Jack Maple, who advised Rudy Giuliani on his broken-windows policy. It's a theory that argues coming down hard on minor crime will reduce major crime. We have criminologists George Kelling and James Wilson to thank for this. They believed crimes like vandalism led to more serious offenses. A variation of tokin' marijuana takes you down the path to shootin' up heroin.

O'Malley liked to recite a stat that violent crime dropped 41 percent. Critics claimed there was creative fiddling with the numbers. Maybe, maybe not.

This hard-nosed approach got the guitar picker lots of accolades. Esquire 2002: "The Best Young Mayor in the Country." Time magazine 2005: a "Top 5 Big City Mayors." Businessweek 2005: A "new star" in the Democratic Party, in the good company of Mark Warner, Ken Salazar, Rahm Emanuel and oh yeah, that guy with the big ears and funny name, Barack Obama.

Heady stuff for O'Malley. Heady enough to make him decide to move up the political food chain and run for governor in 2006. He got the endorsement of The Baltimore Sun, which wrote, "When he was first elected mayor in 1999, the former two-term city councilman inherited a city of rising crime, failing schools, and shrinking economic prospects. He was able to reverse course in all of these areas."

O'Malley ended up defeating Republican incumbent Bob Ehrlich 53 to 46 percent.

There was a slight blemish on the newly minted wunderkind's resume. A little something from his mayor days called "The Wire," a TV drama that presented Baltimore in all its muck-filled glory. Creator and writer David Simon was a former Sun police reporter. Once someone who seemed to like O'Malley, that ended when either a)

O'Malley wouldn't agree to a Simon-written bio, or b) Simon became disillusioned with Mayor O'Malley.

A rather unpleasant, dishonest mayor was written into the script. One who cheated on his wife. This led to rumors O'Malley was stepping out on wife Katie, whom he met in law school and went on to become a district judge. This led to an aide suggesting to the good mayor "the fooling around" rumor was given credence because of the band. O'Malley was advised to be home with his family, "not in a bar in a muscle shirt with 3,000 screaming 20-year-old girls." Girls screaming over Woody Guthrie?

Once he was governor, Marty brought in a data-tracking and management tool that had been very successful in Baltimore for improving the level of services—filling potholes quickly, reducing absenteeism in city departments, snow removal, illegal dumping—and the quality of life. O'Malley took the attitude that data would save the world. Maryland StateStat started slowly with a handful of public-safety and human-services agencies, but grew to encompass 20 statewide agencies. For a guy who was looking toward a better political address, the program got him good press.

So did a lot of other issues and laws that the Guv pushed through the state legislature. He got the death penalty outlawed. Passed a gun-registration law. Improved schools. Same-sex marriage? O'Malley supported a bill to legalize it despite the archbishop of Baltimore urging the good Catholic not to.

However, it was safe to say the governor wasn't a darling of environmentalists. What was he doing opposing a lawsuit against Maryland-based Perdue Farms? The company was accused of polluting Chesapeake Bay with run-off phosphorus. He stayed consistent when he threatened to veto the Poultry Fair Share Act that would have forced Perdue and other polluters to shell out money to clean up the bay.

There was also that little matter of fracking. In 2014, O'Malley said OK to the controversial oil extraction as long as it was tightly regulated. While many environmentalists wanted it banned outright, at least, this was a compromise.

When O'Malley left office in 2015, he looked in pretty solid shape to go after the Democratic presidential nomination. However, there were those in the party who still remembered his poorly received 2012 DNC speech. He was given a coveted prime-time spot. Alas, the reviews ran from "not very good TV" to he was "transparent in his desire to make the speech primarily an introduction for himself to the country . . . so Beaver Cleaver" to "O'Malley's enthusiasm and passion came across as manufactured not organic and the crowd seemed ready to love him but wound up just sort of liking him." Owwy. But his big spanking was yet to come.

Fate is a bitch. While in Ireland for some paid speeches (hey, Forbes put him as the poorest candidate, and he had four college tuitions to suffer), O'Malley got word of the death of Freddie Gray. He was the young black man who Baltimore police threw into the back of a paddy wagon for allegedly having an illegal switchblade. The cops may have used unnecessary force. What they definitely didn't do was properly secure Gray. Sometime during the "rough ride" to the precinct house, Gray hurt his spinal cord, fell into a coma and died.

O'Malley flew back to Baltimore where protests turned

into riots, and he was met with scathing criticism. He hadn't been mayor for eight years. So why was shit hitting his fan? His zero-tolerance approach to crime might have looked good on paper. And it may have lowered crime. But it also created a lot of anger in the black community. It was black young men who bore the brunt of his policies. And it created, it was argued, the climate that led to Gray's death.

This was not an auspicious start for Marty's presidential run. Undaunted, he formally announced his candidacy on May 30, 2015. More shit hit his fan. He was met with NOMALLEY and Black Lives Matter banners. He was pushed to defend his policing policies. Cracking down on crime was no longer popular—at least among Democrats. Probably saying he liked politicians didn't help his cause, either.

In the debates, O'Malley was unable to withstand the party favorite Clinton or the mighty tide of Bernie Sanders. Pulling out, he retreated to the safe academic confines of Carnegie Mellon and Georgetown universities.

At 53, O'Malley may rise again. And he can hope "The Wire" stays consigned to Netflix "only on DVD."

Randy the Magnificent

Love him or hate him, Rand Paul is a political wizard. No, not the kind who works magic to make the country a better place. He's the sort who was able to conjure up a career in politics seemingly out of thin air. He can make policy and legislation vanish like no one else. And it's impossible to deny that his father looks like a character who escaped from a Harry Potter novel.

Randal Howard Paul was born on Jan. 7, 1963, in

Pittsburgh, Pa. Of course you remember his father, Ron Paul, the Potter stand-in and libertarian who repeatedly, unsuccessfully, ran for president. Well it was undoubtedly some of the Paul magic that led to Rand's rise in politics.

Randy enrolled in the honors program at Baylor University in 1981. He was a member of the swim team, the Young Conservatives of Texas and a secret organization (that you can read all about on Wikipedia) called the NoZe Brotherhood. Sadly, it wasn't the type of secret brotherhood that practices occult spells. The NoZe are a satirical fraternity that pokes fun at other clubs, paints things pink and generally makes themselves into colossal nuisances (an ability Paul would later put to use on the Senate floor). He left Baylor just shy of graduating after being admitted to the Duke University School of Medicine, earning an M.D. in 1988.

That year marked another important milestone in Randy's life. He met Kelley Ashby while completing a surgical rotation at Georgia Baptist Hospital. The two began dating (after some initial confusion over whether Randy was a teenager or a 25-year old doctor) and married in 1990. It was Kelley who felt the name "Randy" sounded too immature. Presto, change! Now, he was Rand.

Rand completed his residency in ophthalmology in 1993 and moved to Bowling Green, Ky. While performing eye surgeries in Kentucky, he stayed active in his father's political career. Rand the Magnificent managed Ron's 1996 congressional campaign and spoke on his father's behalf during the 2008 presidential run.

At this point, Rand had been hanging around his father's campaigns since he was a teenager. He felt it was time to fully enter the magical world of politics, and in

2009, he pulled his greatest trick of all—"No experience up this sleeve . . . no political offices on the resume up the other sleeve, and . . . KAZAAAM! I'm a United States Senator!" Of course, like all magic, it was really just a sleight of hand. His father's supporters knew him well, and they had done the political version of Jewish grandmothering. "You know who we could fix up as a senator? Randy! I know he doesn't have any experience—like literally none at all—but he's such as nice boy!" They threw their support behind Rand—and more importantly their money. This allowed him to cruise through the Republican senatorial primary, winning by a 23-percent margin.

The general election did not go as smoothly. Why? Well, Rand happened to mention that if he had been a senator during the 1960s, he would have questioned the constitutionality of Title II of the Civil Rights Act of 1964. This is the part that outlaws "discrimination based on race, color, religion or national origin in hotels, motels, restaurants, theaters, and all other public accommodations." Obviously, Rand felt movie theaters should be able to keep black people from enjoying "Toy Story 3" if the owners saw fit. Somehow (somehow being that the election was in Kentucky), Paul still won with 56 percent of the vote. Later on, Paul would say, "I don't think there has been anybody who has been a bigger defender of minority rights in the Congress than myself." If he had been asked for comment, Georgia Congressman John Lewis, former chair of the Student Nonviolent Coordinating Committee and co-organizer of the historic 1963 March on Washington, would have undoubtedly laughed hysterically.

Paul was sworn in into the Senate on Jan. 5, 2011, and began a storied career of making legislation disappear, voicing his disapproval and doing little else. Let's examine some of the highlights, shall we?

- He voted against a stopgap bill that cut $4 billion from the budget and would have temporarily prevented a government shutdown. He wanted a bill that would cut even more and one week later, voted against both Democratic and Republican bills, saying they still didn't cut enough.
- He blocked a bill that would have provided $36 million in benefits for elderly and disabled refugees, fearing that some of the refugees could be terrorists.
- He, along with fellow gremlins Ted Cruz and Mike Lee, R-Utah, threatened to filibuster any legislation to expand federal gun-control measures. They attempted the filibuster, but it was dismissed by cloture, which is the political equivalent of "Talk to the hand because the face doesn't want to hear it."
- He said he would not allow the government to bail Detroit out of bankruptcy. "I basically say [Obama] is bailing them out over my dead body because we don't have any money in Washington," Paul added. When reached for comment, multiple community members of inner-city Detroit said they would gladly make that a reality if Paul ever visited their neighborhood.
- He had a habit of turning himself invisible. After missing a meeting on the Patriot Act, Republican Sen. Dan Coats said, "Anything that goes against anything he believes, he never comes. It's always helpful if you're in there working to have your po-

sition understood, and we all learn a lot, and we all try to come to a much better understanding of what we're trying to do."

Rand did make one other newsworthy splash during his career as a senator. In October 2013, television host Rachel Maddow pointed out that Paul lifted a line in one of his speeches from the Wikipedia page for the movie "Gattaca." The line reads, "In 'the not-too-distant future,' liberal eugenics is common, and DNA plays the primary role in determining social class." Obviously Paul is deeply troubled by the plot of "Gattaca" because if DNA engineering ever comes to pass, he and his fellow gingers will likely be eradicated. Quickly, more reports of Paul plagiarism came in, including the plagiarism of three pages in Paul's book "Government Bullies." In response, Paul said, "'I'm being unfairly targeted by a bunch of hacks and haters." Yes Rand, those stupid bullies think that having original thought is important and that a U.S. senator should at least be held to the same standard as an 18-year-old college freshman or a first-year at Hogwarts.

So, after gaining valuable experience vanishing bills and plagiarizing sci-fi movies, Rand felt he was ready to be president of the United States of America. He announced his candidacy on April 7, 2015. Unfortunately, Paul had yet to master the magic of mind control and received endorsements like "Senator Paul is the worst possible candidate of the 20 or so that are running on the most important issue, which is national security," from fellow Republican John McCain. After only placing fifth in the Iowa Caucus, Paul pulled his final disappearing act, dropping out of the race on Feb. 3, 2016.

What a Dick

In a more accurate world where soccer is called football and doughnuts are sugar bagels, Richard Santorum would be named Dick. "Can't I go by Richard?" young Santorum asks his parents. "No, you're definitely a Dick," they tell him. A Dick who would go on to lead a political career based around intolerance and being, well, a dick.

Richard John Santorum graced the world with his presence on May 10, 1958. He was the middle of three children, and his father, Aldo Santorum, was a clinical psychologist. One can only wonder if Aldo ever psychoanalyzed young Rick and identified the traits that would lead his son to literally make their family name synonymous with fecal matter.

Rick Santorum attended Penn State University and joined the Tau Epsilon Phi fraternity. Other notable TEPs include Larry King, Jerry Springer and Dwight Eisenhower (an honorary member). (TEP legend has it that President Eisenhower held King's legs during his first keg stand.) Santorum later received an MBA from the University of Pittsburgh's Joseph M. Katz Graduate School of Business and a Juris Doctorate from Dickinson School of Law.

Rick practiced law for four years at the Pittsburgh law firm, Kirkpatrick & Lockhart. It had a reputation for churning out political candidates and lobbyists. Notable alumni include Slade Gordon, Eric Schneiderman and Jack Abramoff. (K&L legend has it Schneiderman held Abramoff's legs during his first keg stand). While at K&L, Santorum successfully lobbied to deregulate professional wrestling, making it exempt from federal anabolic-steroid regulations. Pharmaceutical companies, rednecks and manufacturers of 4XL sequined tights rejoiced. In 1990, Santorum was elected to the U.S. House of Representatives from Pennsylvania's 18th district. He defeated six-time incumbent Doug Walgren by running an aggressive campaign. According to a Pittsburgh Press article, Santorum even went as far as going "Door-to-door, a daunting undertaking in a congressional district, where the population is set at about 500,000, to tell voters that Walgren does not own a home in the 18th District." We have to assume that much of Santorum's $200,000 campaign budget went toward hiring a small army of Santorum impersonators.

Santorum was elected as Pennsylvania's junior senator in 1995. He ran under the campaign slogan "Join the fight." Little did voters know that there was tiny sub-slogan reading, "Against gays, abortion, women and science."

In 2001, Santorum added a provision to the No Child Left Behind bill allowing schools to teach intelligent design alongside evolution. The bill passed the Senate 91–8. After taking criticism, Santorum defended it, calling intelligent design "a legitimate scientific theory that should be taught in science classes." That is like saying unicorns are a legitimate form of wildlife and should be featured more regularly in National Geographic. Of course, Santorum would never advocate for unicorns because as we all know all unicorns were homosexual (which is why they died out), and he fundamentally hates them. By 2005, Santorum had adopted the "Teach the Controversy" approach, a campaign championed by a conservative Christian think tank. The goal was to "poke holes in the theory of evolution." Shockingly, not a single member of the think tank possessed a scientific background.

Santorum also supported what President George W. Bush dubbed the "War on Terror." Naturally, fighting a war on an intangible emotion proved difficult, and subsequent wars on jealousy, depression and anxiety were also ineffective. Still, Santorum defended many aspects of the war calling the invasion of Afghanistan "a very winnable operation," which is like saying a head-on car crash is a "very survivable automobile-to-automobile interaction." In particular, Santorum defended the use of waterboarding in Guantanamo Bay. When Sen. John McCain, a former Vietnam prisoner of war, voiced his opposition, Santorum countered by saying that McCain "doesn't understand how enhanced interrogation works." This led many to suspect that Santorum doesn't understand how irony works.

Santorum ran for re-election for a third Senate term in 2006 amid a congregation of controversy. Apparently saying a slew of bigoted things can eventually catch up to you in politics. In his book, "It Takes a Family," he denounced 1960s "radical feminism," saying it made it "socially affirming to work outside the home" at the expense of child care. In Santorum's defense, this is slightly more politically correct than saying "women belong in the kitchen, barefoot and pregnant." He also compared pro-choice Americans to "German Nazis." There is no defense for that.

Believe it or not, comparing people who want women to have control over their bodies to the murderers who perpetuated one of the largest slaughters in history wasn't even Santorum's biggest problem. Back in 2003, he had compared homosexuality to bestiality and pedophilia, shades of Huckabee, saying the "definition of marriage" has never included "man on child, man on dog, or whatever the case may be." Syndicated sex columnist Dan Savage didn't take kindly to the slur. Savage started a contest encouraging his radio listeners to invent slang terms to "memorialize the scandal." The winner came up with this definition:

> Santorum (san-TOR-um) n.
> The frothy mixture of lube and fecal matter that is sometimes the by-product of anal sex.

Savage followed the contest by launching a website with the definition. Thanks to bloggers, it passed Santorum's own campaign site on the Google search rankings, and no doubt contributed to Santorum's crushing 18-point defeat in the 2006 election. It was the largest margin of loss for an incumbent senator since 1980 when Jacob Javits fell to Alfonse D'Amato in New York.

Unable to take a hint, in January 2010, Santorum sent an email to his supporters saying, "I'm convinced that conservatives need a candidate who will not only stand up for our views, but who can articulate a conservative vision for our country's future."

Santorum formally announced his run for the Republican presidential nomination on ABC's "Good Morning America" on June 6, 2011, saying he's "in it to win." Thankfully, Santorum did not "win it." He suspended his campaign on April 10, 2012, in Gettysburg, Pa. Ironically, this was where Abraham Lincoln delivered the Gettysburg Address, proclaiming, "All men are created equal." Santorum must have found a special asterisk everyone else missed that read "This does not include gay men."

Santorum briefly explored a second go-around saying, "I'm open to looking into a presidential race in 2016," on NBC's "Meet the Press" in 2013. The voters made it resoundingly clear that they were not open to this idea, and Santorum aborted his campaign on Feb. 3, 2016.

iCarly

Carly Fiorina is an example of how you can be hugely successful in the business world without having much success. Fiorina was named to the Forbes Top 10 list of the world's most powerful women in 2004. Over the years, that list has included such foreign leaders as Angela Merkel and unstoppable forces of nature like Ellen DeGeneres and T-Swizzle (aka Taylor Swift). So how can you say Fiorina hasn't had much success? Often results in the business world are murky, at best. Fortunately, political elections, at least outside the state of Florida, are not.

Cara Carleton (Carly) Sneed was born Sept. 6, 1954, in Austin, Texas, with a silver gavel in her mouth. For clarification, a silver gavel is the equivalent of a silver spoon for the daughters of conservative law professors from uber-wealthy families. Her father, Joseph Tyree Sneed III, was also bit of a teaching trollop. He got around. He was a professor at the University of Texas, Cornell, Yale, Harvard, Stanford, schools in London and Ghana, and finally he became dean of the Duke Law School. Later, President Richard Nixon appointed him deputy attorney general and then a federal judge. Carly's mother was an abstract painter, which is a polite way of saying unemployed.

Carly received a Bachelor of Arts in philosophy and medieval history at Stanford University in 1976. It is likely that she was strongly influenced by Joan of Arc, another powerful woman who crashed the figurative glass ceiling, then went out in a fiery ball of destruction. Carly enrolled at UCLA School of Law in 1976, but dropped out after one semester, prompting her father to say he "didn't think she'd amount to much." Perhaps she shouldn't have bought him that "World's Most Pessimistic Dad" mug for Christmas.

Carly spent several months working as a receptionist for real-estate company Marcus & Millichap, eventually moving up to a broker position. The journey of self-discovery continued when she married her first husband in 1977 and moved to Bologna, Italy. There, she tutored Italian businessmen in English, teaching them key phrases like "You will pay $2,000 for that suit and like it."

After ditching husband Number One, Carly joined AT&T as a management trainee in 1980. AT&T had reached a deal with the government to settle a sexual discrimination lawsuit and needed more female managers. While at AT&T, she met Frank Fiorina, an AT&T executive who quickly became husband Number Two. On their first date, he told Carly that he envisioned her as head of the company. "It was a good line. She loved it," Frank Fiorina said. Ladies' men take note: All you have to do to get a girl is work really hard to become an executive, put her career before yours, then retire at age 48 to perfect that art of making grilled-cheese sandwiches.

In 1990, Carly became AT&T's first female officer as senior vice president overseeing the company's hardware and systems division. In 1995, she took over corporate operations for Lucent Technologies. On paper, her time at Lucent was a huge success. Lucent added 22,000 jobs, and revenues increased from $19 billion to $38 billion. Good, right? Not exactly. According to Fortune, "In a neat bit of accounting magic, money from . . . loans began to appear on Lucent's income statement as new revenue while the dicey debt got stashed on its balance sheet as an allegedly solid asset." That's like giving your 16-year-old nephew a loan to buy an Escalade at your Cadillac dealership.

Apparently, Hewlett-Packard didn't pay much attention to bookkeeping, or resumes for that matter, because they named Fiorina CEO in July 1999. Yale School of Management's Jeffrey Sonnenfeld in Fortune magazine described the move as the result of "a dysfunctional HP board committee, filled with its own poisoned politics, [which] hired her with no CEO experience, nor interviews with the full board."

Fiorina immediately began flexing her management muscle. She streamlined departments. And she changed HP's work culture, which was roughly, "everyone love everyone," to her new mandate of "shape up or ship out," creating a horde of disgruntled vegan-hippie programmers. Then, in September 2001, Carly made her big move. She announced the acquisition of Compaq with its $25 billion in stock. The merger created the world's largest personal computer manufacturer.

"Hooray for Carly," everyone at HP must have cheered as they carried her around the office on their shoulders as unicorn-shaped confetti fell from the sky. Not so fast.

"The HP-Compaq merger was met with almost universal skepticism and cynicism," said Ben Rosen, former Compaq board member. Walter Hewlett, an HP board member and son of *the* Hewlett, even launched a proxy fight in an attempt to block the merger. (A proxy fight is the corporate equivalent of a Mad Max Thunderdome.) So, how did it all work out? Did Fiorina prove them all wrong, lead HP to become the most successful computer company in the 21st century and establish herself as the Steve Jobs of the tech world? Of course not. Why are you even asking that question? You live in the future and know Steve Jobs went on to become the Steve Jobs of the tech world. The company performed worse than Ben Carson at a slam-poetry reading. There were no gains in net income despite a 70-percent gain by other top companies during this period. HP's debt also rose from $4.25 billion to $6.75 billion, and its stock price fell by 50 percent. In 2004, the board forced Fiorina to resign. It is important to note that HP stock jumped 6.9 percent at the news of Fiorina getting the boot, instantly adding $3 billion to the company's value. This begs one of the more intriguing political "what ifs?" Could we erase the national debt if we elected Carly president and then immediately impeached her? The world will never know.

After taking a dump load of money from Hewlett-Packard on her way out, Fiorina joined numerous boards, organizations, nonprofits and wrote her autobiography. Eventually, she got bored of being a board member. So after working as an adviser on John McCain's campaign, she announced her candidacy for the California senatorial seat in November 2009. Despite donating $6.5 million of her own money to the campaign, incumbent Barbara Boxer won the general election 52.2 percent to Fiorina's 42.2 percent. It was a sad day for Fiorina, but on the bright side, perhaps the greatest campaign ad in the history of American politics was created as a result of her running.

The ad, which became known as "Demon Sheep,"

attacked primary Republican rival Tom Campbell and looks like the product of a Terry Gilliam and Andy Samberg acid trip. Words don't do it justice, though. Do yourself a favor, and search YouTube for "Fiorina Demon Sheep." You will laugh hysterically while simultaneously being weirded out that this was part of a U.S. Senate campaign.

On the strength of her failed run as HP CEO and her failed bid to become a senator, Fiorina announced her candidacy for president of the United Sates during a "Good Morning America" interview on May 4, 2015. Many saw her as the GOP's foil to Hillary Clinton. And Fiorina made a special point of going after Hillary any chance she got.

"Despite holding many positions, she has not accomplished much of anything in her life," Fiorina said of Clinton during one of the GOP undercard debates. "Now she's trying for the White House, but she's probably more qualified for the big house. She's escaped prosecution more times than El Chapo. Perhaps Sean Penn should be interviewing her."

Fiorina can count getting Larry the Cable Guy to write her debate material among her accomplishments. But unfortunately for Carly, being a successful CEO, winning a Senate bid or getting the 2016 Republican nomination are not among them.

The Little Engine That Couldn't

There are Delusionals, and then there are Uber Delusionals. Count Jim Gilmore as one of the latter. Jim who? you might wonder on your way to Google the name. You're not alone. When Donald Trump was asked about Gilmore in August 2015, he answered, "Him, I don't know."

Here is Gilmore's background check.

Gilmore first appeared Oct. 6, 1949, born to a church secretary and a meat cutter.

After graduating from the University of Virginia in 1971, Gilmore enlisted in the army where he was put in spook training at the Army Intelligence Center, then sent to Germany as a counterintelligence agent. Back in the States, he got a law degree from UVA and wended his way into politics. By 1994, he was living in the governor's executive mansion.

Gilmore had conservative credentials. He was a director of the NRA. He supported the privatization of Social Security. Getting rid of estate and capital-gains taxes. Banning abortion after eight weeks.

So, where does the Uber come in? This wasn't the first time Gilmore made a try for the White House. He went up against Romney in 2007. You might think that he had done so rousingly well that first time around, came so squeakingly close to routing Romney, that he would try it again. Nope. Gilmore had a terrible showing, in one quarter only raising $174,790.

This brings us to 2015 when he became the last to throw his somewhat bedraggled hat into the Republican ring. This is a guy who was once called a "charisma-free zone." Little wonder he made little impression on the Iowa voters. Only 12 of them gave him a nod. He did much better in the New Hampshire primary where he got a whopping 133 votes. Gilmore retrieved his hat three days later on Feb. 12.

What is it with these people? Do they think they are

the little engine that could, that all they have to do is keep repeating "I think I can. I think I can." Then they will miraculously make it up the hill and sit behind the desk in the Oval Office?

Gilmore, again, turned out to be the little engine who couldn't.

Chapter Three:
Candidates with Legs

T his was the deal. If you were a Republican and your poll numbers stunk, you were relegated to join the other Delusionals at the dinner-time debate. Carly Fiorina managed to sneak onto the main stage, but she still was a Delusional, hence her appearance in the previous chapter.

It was tidier on the Democratic side since there were initially only five candidates, so no need for a kiddy table. All five proudly marched onto the stage. Quickly, it was three and then there were two.

So here they are in all their glory, the prime-time Republicans.

Hurricane Christie

It would be easy to label Chris Christie a cartoon-ish character. He fans out over Bruce Springsteen like a 14-year-old girl at a Justin Bieber concert. He'll shout till he's red in the face like Chris Farley in an SNL sketch. But in truth, Chris Christie is much closer to Tony Soprano than Yosemite Sam. That is if Tony Soprano was only passive aggressive and sued people and whined instead of having them offed.

Christie was born Sept. 6, 1962, in Newark, N.J. To understand Christie and his family, you first have to understand his birth city. When you enter Newark, you are assailed by an almost indescribable funk. It's walking into a room with a hidden block of decaying Limburger cheese. It's gritty. It's visceral. And you're pretty sure that somewhere, something is rotten.

Things were especially bad in Newark in 1967 when Christie was 5 years old. The city was gripped by poverty, police brutality, and the large African-American population felt like their local politicians valued them only slightly more than the copious amounts of trash found on the side of I-95. So, when a black cabdriver, John DeSimone, was wrongfully arrested and beaten by Newark police, riots erupted. In short, they were "The Purge" in real life—six days of looting, rioting and violence.

This was the crucible in which the Christie family was forged. His parents came from large Newark clans. His mother, Sondra, was of Sicilian descent. And his father, Bill, was Irish-German. That's pretty much an ethnic recipe for human dynamite. They were no-nonsense people who argued constantly and felt the way to be heard was to shout louder. They taught Chris to never give an inch. It's like that old Newark saying, "You give someone an inch, and they'll steal your TV set."

Nobody stole the Christies' TV set during the Newark riots. Even so, Sondra and Bill decided Newark was no longer the place to be. So they relocated 12 miles away to the figuratively greener pastures of Livingston, N.J. It was here that Chris learned his first lessons about forcing your way into politics, suing people and corruption.

When Christie was 14, he heard local politician Thom-

as Kean speak at Livingston High School. Like most teenagers who can't get enough of city-level politics, the appearance intrigued Chris. You can picture him stalking
back and forth across his kitchen floor that night, like a
frenzied Chris Farley, before saying, "*Mom, I'm gonna be a
politician!*" So how did his mother counsel him to pursue
this dream? Check out a book at the local library or perhaps write a letter to Kean like a normal human being?
That's not how a hard-charging Sicilian who lived through
the Newark riots does business. She drove Chris directly to
Thomas Kean's home that night and made him knock on
the door.

"Sir, I want to get involved in politics, and I don't know
how to do it, and my mother says I gotta ask you,' " Christie
told Kean.

You can almost imagine Sondra standing behind Chris,
nodding her head while slowly drumming her palm with a
baseball bat. Kean, presumably out of abject terror, invited
the kid to accompany him to Bergen County as he geared
up to run for governor. Chris was hooked and volunteered
for Kean's campaign staff.

Chris's father also imparted important life lessons.
Even though "Dad was just a passenger, Mom was the driver," as Chris put it, old Wilbur, aka Bill, taught Chris the importance of using the legal system for personal gain. When
Chris' position as starting catcher for his high-school baseball team was threatened by a transfer student, Wilbur explored legal action to block the student's enrollment. Now
if you think that's absolutely ridiculous, then you share the
opinion of Christie's teammates, who talked him out of
it. The transfer student enrolled, and Chris Christie was
benched for the remainder of the season.

Don't feel too bad for Chris, though. He had plenty of other things to keep him occupied. He was class president for three straight years, and in his senior year, he was one of two students chosen to represent New Jersey in the Hearst Foundation's Senate Youth Program. The students were supposed to spend a week with their home-state senators, observing the legislative process from the inside out. Unfortunately, the day before Chris got to Washington, news broke of a massive FBI operation in which a federal agent posing as an Arab sheik had bribed elected officials with suitcases stuffed with cash

This became known as Abscam, a sting operation straight out of the movies (oh, it was in the movie, "American Hustle") that busted the mayor of Camden, six members of the House of Representatives and New Jersey's senior senator, Harrison Williams, among others. "It was an incredible embarrassment," Christie later recalled. "We were the butt of jokes all week" during the Senate Youth Program. In his telling, it was the defining moment that alerted him to "the problem of corruption in New Jersey."

After high school, Christie enrolled in the University of Delaware to study political science. He met his future wife, Mary Pat, in student government. It was undoubtedly love at first sight, as Mary Pat swoons describing her first impression of Christie, as "a student government geek." The two were married in 1986.

A year later, Christie graduated from Seton Hall University School of Law, passed the bar exam for the state of New Jersey and the United States district court, and began a middling law career. He joined the firm of Dughi, Hewit & Palatucci in Cranford. Granted, the firm sounds more like an all-Italian version of Donald Duck's nephews, but it got Christie going. He specialized in securities law, appellate practice, election law and government affairs. It wasn't enough for Christie, though. His long-harbored dreams of being a politician called to him like a pepperoni pizza calls to, well, Chris Christie.

In 1994, he ran for a seat on the Board of Chosen Free-holders in Morris County, the wealthy district where he and Mary Pat, now a Wall Street investment banker, had settled. Freeholders are unique to New Jersey. They are essentially a board of seven city councilmen who preside over a district. Christie ran on a platform of political reform. He was going to clean up the dirty politics and shady dealmaking. This is easier said than done in the Garden State.

New Jersey remains singular in its political twistedness. Unlike most states, it relies heavily on local politicians who rule over their districts like medieval English lords. True, they don't go so far as invoking Prima Noctae (taking a new bride into their bed on the night of her wedding). But they're not shy about fucking someone over, either. New Jersey politicians are famous for accepting contributions from everyone—political bosses to businesses to constit-uents—in exchange for all manner of favors. Ironically, Christie saw himself as the William Wallace (you know, Mel Gibson in "Braveheart") who would put an end to these dirty politics.

Even as Christie crusaded against New Jersey's cor-ruption, he didn't hesitate to use one of the uglier cam-paign tactics available. One afternoon, Ed Tamm Jr., a Re-publican he was running against, got a call from a friend who asked if he'd seen a Christie ad that had just aired. It said that Tamm and another board member were under investigation. They weren't. Not even a little. But it was the final weekend before the Republican primary, leaving no time to respond, and Christie and his running mate ousted Tamm and the other incumbent off the board to become a freeholder. They sued him successfully for defamation, marking the first of many lawsuits in Christie's political career. And Christie had to do something that didn't then and doesn't now come naturally to him. He had to publically apologize.

You'd think after winning an election under dubious circumstances, and then subsequently losing a lawsuit, Christie would keep his head down for a bit. Not our boy. Four weeks after taking office as freeholder, Christie announced that he was thinking of challenging a veteran Republican for the state assembly. As far as the entrenched New Jersey Republicans were concerned, Christie might as well have bought a billboard on the Garden State Parkway screaming they could all go screw themselves in flashing neon lights. They pushed back hard, and Christie lost the race by a landslide. Then two years later, they made sure he lost his freeholder position.

At this point, it was 1998. Christie was in his 30s, and all he had to show for his venture into New Jersey politics was an entire state of Republicans that hated him more than a feminist hates the cast of the "Jersey Shore." Incidentally, Christie is not a big fan of the show's cast member, The Situation, either. "They parachuted these losers into New Jersey."

Returning to his law firm, the next logical step was to become a lobbyist. This was a chance to be aggressive and abrasive in another arena. One of his biggest clients was the University of Phoenix in its quest to obtain a New

Jersey higher-education license and put tens of thousands
more students deep into debt. Still, this was not enough
for Christie. He wanted to be an aggressive and abrasive
politician, not an aggressive and abrasive lobbyist. So at
the suggestion of Rick Merkt, his former freeholder running mate, he tried a different avenue and sought a federal position.

Following the advice of Bill Palatucci, a partner at
his law firm and George W. Bush's driver when he campaigned for his dad in the state, Christie began fundraising for the 2000 Bush campaign. He and Palatucci proceeded to pull in an impressive $350,000. That qualified
Christie as a Bush "Pioneer," which is the equivalent of
a Monopoly card for a Bush administration favor. After
George W. was elected, it came time to appoint the New
Jersey U.S. Attorney. It was one of the biggest offices in the
country. Christie was about as qualified as a Jiffy Lube mechanic is to work on a NASA space shuttle. He had never
practiced criminal law or even filed a motion in federal
court. But Palatucci was buddies with Karl Rove from their
campaigning days and forwarded along Christie's resume.
Surprise, surprise. Christie got the position and was sworn
in Jan. 17, 2002.

Soon after taking office, Christie made it known that
he was again going after political corruption in New Jersey. Now, is it possible that he did this to divert attention
from some of his own shady dealmaking? Possibly. What's
not debatable is that the next seven years unfolded like a
season of "Law and Order Dirty Politicians Unit." Christie's office won guilty pleas from 130 public officials, Republicans and Democrats, at the state, county and local
levels. The convictions ranged from things like bribery,

mail and wire fraud. Granted, Christie also negotiated seven controversial deferred-prosecution agreements. They were controversial because they led to benefits like a $52-million contract for his former boss, John Ashcroft, George W.'s first attorney general. But, you're missing the point. Christie was building an image of himself as a no-nonsense reformer and becoming a major political player in the process.

On the wave of this newfound popularity, Christie filed as a candidate for the office of governor in 2009. Thomas Kean helped Christie campaign and raise money. Christie won the Republican nomination and went on to defeat incumbent Jon Corzine by a margin of 49 percent to 45 percent.

The New Jersey governorship is one of, if not the most powerful in the country. The governor nominates attorneys general and treasurers. He or she determines the size of the budget and fills hundreds of super-cushy, well-paying slots on the state's many commissions and authorities. And the governor doles out aid to hundreds of towns and cities. Christie played the system masterfully and built a reputation as someone who could straddle the partisan gap and get things done. He also endeared himself to the public, by playing up his gruffness and calling his detractors things like "stupid," "jerk," "idiot," "hack," "ignoramuses," "thugs," "big shot," "losers" and "numb-nuts." This brings us to Christie's brightest moment and his fall from grace.

In October 2012, Hurricane Sandy wreaked havoc on New Jersey like a bottle of tequila on one of the cast members of the "Jersey Shore." To put it mildly, the state was in a complete mess and needed serious help to get back on its feet. Christie took immediate action. He pushed hard for federal relief. He made personal appearances and gave his own time to those who had suffered losses. He told a heckler at one of his speeches for relief effort to ""Sit down, and shut up."

When his re-election came up in 2013, Christie was super popular in New Jersey. Still, he wanted more. He started going after Democratic endorsements. There were major incentives for Democrats who jumped onboard. For example, the Orthodox Jewish community in Lakewood had endorsed Corzine in 2009. In March, 2013, a coalition of the town's rabbis and businessmen announced it would be backing Christie. Two months after the endorsement, the state gave $10.6 million to fund an Orthodox rabbinical school in the township. By Election Day, Christie had the endorsements of more than 50 elected Democratic officials. He won re-election with a ridiculous 60 percent of the vote, doing well with women and Hispanics. "I know that if we can do this in Trenton, N.J., then maybe the folks in Washington, D.C., should tune in their TVs right now and see how it's done," he crowed. A Christie run for the White House had begun.

Then came what can be described as Christie's Icarus moment. If you recall, Icarus is a Greek mythological figure who flew too close to the sun and fell from the sky. In Christie's case, he crawled a little too close to the scum and couldn't wipe off the stink.

A few months before Christie's re-election, three access lanes from Fort Lee to the George Washington Bridge's toll plaza were inexplicably closed. They stayed that way from Sept. 9 through Sept. 13, plunging Fort Lee into gridlock. It was later revealed that Christie's deputy chief of staff, Bridget Anne Kelly, had sent an email to Port Authority official David Wildstein, a Christie appointee, stating, "Time for some traffic problems." Wildstein replied with "Got it." It just so happened, the Democratic mayor of Fort Lee, Mark Sokolich, had not endorsed Christie, as if the guv needed the endorsement. This looked like dirty politics at its slimiest.

Initially, Christie said, "The fact is that mistakes were made, and I'm responsible for those mistakes." Then he quickly back-pedaled saying, "I had no knowledge or involvement in this issue, in its planning or its execution, and I am stunned by the abject stupidity that was shown here." He even quipped, "I moved the cones, actually, unbeknownst to everybody," in an attempt to make the accusations sound ludicrous. The people of New Jersey didn't buy it, and as the story caught the national media's attention, Christie's approval ratings plummeted to just 29 percent.

By the time Christie announced his bid for the 2016 Republican candidacy, it was too late. The myth he had built of himself as a reformer was shattered. People no longer saw him as Braveheart against corruption, someone who could cross party lines and was straight to the point. Now, he just looked like an overweight bully. He dropped out of the presidential race on Feb. 10, 2016, after receiving just 7.4 percent of the vote in the New Hampshire primary.

"How could I lose to Donald Trump?" Christie must have thought. "I can be loud and obnoxious. I can bully people. I can become embattled in lawsuits and controversy. But I actually have experience and success in politics." In truth, Christie probably would have made a better president than The Donald, which isn't saying much. But the real tragedy isn't his failure to secure the Republican nomination. The real tragedy is that Chris Farley died too early to portray Christie, stalking back and forth in front of a podium in a too-tight suit, shouting at a reporter to, "Sit down, and shut up."

Jeb!

Now you probably thought Jeb was the namesake of some famous country singer-turned business tycoon-turned politician- turned arctic moose hunter. Not so. Jeb is actually an acronym of John Ellis Bush. Born Feb. 11, 1953, in Midland, Texas, he is the son of George H.W., 41st president of the United States, and grandson of Prescott Bush, U.S. Senator and big-bucks Wall Street banker. From early on, it was clear Jeb was headed for greatness because if not, he'd be kicked out of the family.

Jeb has an older brother George (43rd president of the United States and unintentional spoken-word poet), as well as a younger sister and two younger brothers. Now you may be thinking, "Oh my God, there are more Bushes out there, waiting like a dormant case of syphilis to erupt onto the face of politics." It's OK. Take a deep breath. At the very least, it is unlikely we will see a Neil Bush For President. While Neil had shown an interest in politics, joining the Ted Cruz campaign as a fundraiser, he was also involved in defrauding U.S. taxpayers out of $1.5 billion in a savings-and-loan scam. Later, he mongered influence for the Chinese government, who in turn provided him with Chinese prostitutes. Unless your last name rhymes with "Dump," it's nearly impossible to survive that kind of a past running for office.

Jeb's bad-boy days were considerably tamer and shorter lived. They took place during his time at Phillips Academy, starting when he enrolled in 1967. Of course, Phillips is an elite boarding school, so being a bad boy there is like being the most energetic person at a meeting of Narcoleptics Anonymous (of which Ben Carson is a member). "I drank alcohol, and I smoked marijuana when I was at Andover, both of which could have led to expulsion," Jeb admitted. His grades were also so bad he probably would have been expelled if he weren't a Bush with a father on the school's board of trustees. So, what changed? Why didn't this slippery slope continue to fraudulent business deals and Chinese hookers? Jeb met a girl.

In 1970, he went on a study abroad trip to help build a school in Ibarrilla, a small village outside León, Guanajuato, Mexico. After finishing work for the day, students would hang out and socialize in the small-town square. It was there one of Jeb's classmates met Lucila Gallo, a local, and needed someone to accompany her younger sister on a double date. That someone was to be Lawrence Bump. Except Lawrence was sick with a fever, so Jeb got the nod and met Columba Gallo. "I fell madly in love with her—literally love at first sight," Jeb recounted. "Whatever I was doing beforehand, I vaguely remember. But my life got really organized after that." Upon returning to the States, Jeb wrote to Columba constantly and stopped smoking so much pot, which accounts for the improvement in his memory.

After returning from Mexico, Jeb's academics improved dramatically, and he made honor roll for the first time. However, things weren't all sunshine and taco-flavored kisses at Phillips. The social climate was trending much closer to napalm and picket signs. The Vietnam War was still in full swing, and protests erupted around campus. However, Jeb took an approach that very much said, "Can you guys leave me out of this, please? I just want to play tennis and fantasize about my long-distance Mexican girlfriend." He couldn't escape the war altogether, though. After graduating high school in 1971, Jeb registered for the draft, but no draft orders were issued.

Jeb then made a big break in family tradition. Instead of enrolling at Yale like most of his family had, he went to the University of Texas. While there, he majored in Latin American studies (to better understand and communicate with his long-distance Mexican girlfriend) and received his B.A. in 1974.

He then married Columba. The Bushes were thoroughly confused by her, mainly because she didn't speak English. "It came as no surprise to us as Columba was the only girl he had ever dated," Barbara Bush wrote in her memoir, no doubt contemplating the likelihood of Mexican grandchildren. Keep in mind, the Bushies weren't true Texans. Had they been, the thought of a Hispanic daughter-in-law would have been appalling since Hispanics were considered lower on the social scale than blacks. After the wedding, Jeb accepted a position at an international division of Texas Commerce Bank. In November 1977, he went to Caracas to serve as branch manager and vice president.

Jeb returned to the States in 1980 to campaign for his father in Florida. By this point, Jeb was fluent in Spanish, and with a Mexican wife. His Hispanic street cred was at a level never thought achievable for a Bush. After the election, Jeb and family moved to Miami-Dade County, Fla. He took a job at a real-estate firm that focused on finding tenants for commercial developments. The firm quickly became one of Florida's most successful, and when Jeb made partner, he put a dent in one of the non-negotiable items on every Bush's bucket list. "I want to be very wealthy, and I'll be glad to tell you when I've accomplished that goal," Jeb explained. Other Jeb bucket-list items included being able to tango dance, portraying Chewbacca in a future "Star Wars" movie and finally, beating George W. in a game of "Warcraft." Or not.

Jeb took his first political office as chairman of the Dade County Republican Party. He then looked to up the ante in 1994 by running for Florida governor. Unfortunately, he lost the election because he hadn't mastered the "art" of being a politician. For example, when asked what he would do for African Americans, Jeb said, "It's time to strive for a society where there's equality of opportunity, not equality of results. So I'm going to answer your question by saying—probably nothing." Jeb, what the hell? You're supposed to respond with vague euphemisms that sound encouraging, but you had no plan to act on. Meanwhile, George W. successfully won his bid to become governor of Texas.

In 1998, Jeb's euphemism game was on point as he ran for governor again as a "consensus-building pragmatist." That roughly translates to "someone who gets people to agree with them by saying mind-numbingly obvious things." He defeated Democrat Buddy MacKay, and George W. won re-election, making them the first siblings to govern two states simultaneously since Nelson and Winthrop Rockefeller in New York and Arkansas from 1967 to 1971.

During his eight years as governor, Jeb initiated environmental improvements such as conservation in the Everglades. He supported caps on medical-malpractice litigation and reduced taxes by $19 billion. That $19 billion accounted for an annual savings of $140 per person. Meaning every Florida citizen could buy an extra 56 packages of Ham and Cheese Hot Pockets per year. That's a total of 112 flakiness of hammy goodness for the people of the Sunshine State, all thanks to Jeb. However, the one place Jeb's administration was highly questionable was in its sweeping education reform.

Jeb enacted the "A+ Plan" that established higher standards for public schools. The better the schools performed on government-issued standardized tests, the more government funding they would receive, with hefty penalties for underperforming schools. That's makes as much sense as feeding Spud Webb an all-lettuce diet because he isn't growing tall enough, but giving Shaq human-growth hormones. Jeb was also a proponent of school vouchers and charter schools. This led to the opening of several hundred for-profit charter schools in Florida. They were largely owned by real-estate companies, staffed by inexperienced teachers and spent less per student and performed worse academically than their public-school counterparts. Yes, Jeb had University of Phoenixed education in Florida.

Despite some questionable policies, he did practice very practical politics compared to his objectively insane Tea Party counterparts. In particular, he supported positions on immigration reform and suspended all executions in Florida on Dec. 15, 2006, after a botched execution took 37 minutes and two lethal injections to complete. How the idea of not publicly executing people must have horrified Tea Party enthusiast and closeted serial killer Ted Cruz. In 2012, Jeb also publicly criticized the national Republican Party for "an orthodoxy that doesn't allow for disagreement."

As his second term as Florida governor drew to a close, John Ellis had many exciting job prospects. In May 2006, he was approached to become the next commissioner of the National Football League. This would have been a significant step up from a paltry position like president of the United States in Jeb's native Texas. Instead, he went on to make piles of cash. According to Fox Business, that amounted to almost half of his $29 million between 2007 and 2014 coming from Wall Street companies. He had finally accomplished that important Bush bucket-list item — making piles of money.

On Dec. 16, 2014, Bush announced via Facebook that "I have decided to actively explore the possibility of running for President of the United States." The announcement read like an awkward 14-year-old trying to ask a girl out on a first date. "If you're not doing anything this 2016 campaign season, would you maybe want to run with me for president, if you're, you know, not busy and stuff?" Everyone knew what amounted to a formal proclamation was coming. The Bushies had a dynasty, and Jeb was next in line to assume the throne. And there was little doubt he would do so.

His wishy-washy announcement served another function. By not officially declaring, Jeb was able to circumnavigate several campaign-finance laws that limit donations and prohibit coordinating with Super PACs. By May 2015, he had already raised close to $100 million. Everyone knew the proclamation was coming.

Jeb officially announced his candidacy on June 15, 2015, at the multicultural campus of Miami Dade College. "Our country is on a very bad course," Jeb said. "And the question is: What are we going to do about it?" His answer was to make a very awkward, stumbling run for the presidency. And little did Jeb know just how bad a course the country was on.

After a series of poor results in Iowa and New Hampshire, Jeb dumped his remaining money into the South Carolina primary on Feb. 20. He placed fourth with less than 8 percent of the vote. That night he suspended his campaign. Jeb had lost to a Tea Party "Wacko Bird" and an orange reality TV-show star with a laundry list of scandals. The Bush presidential legacy died that night. But who knows, maybe Neil Bush will revive it, like a majestic Chinese prostitute, dressed as a phoenix, rising from the ashes.

Ben SMASH!

By outward appearances, Ben Carson is just a mild-mannered neurosurgeon and evolution denier. But if Carson is to be believed, and virtually no one does, underneath that tranquil exterior exists a monster of rage and blind anger. So, don't make Ben Carson angry. Because you wouldn't like him when he's angry. And probably not when he's calm, either.

The good doctor came from an impoverished background in Detroit, where he was born Sept. 18, 1951. Growing up, his mother held down three jobs, and the family relied on food stamps. In his biography, "Gifted Hands," Ben claimed to have had a violent temper. He said he bashed his mother on the head with a hammer. He hit a student with a school combination lock. And one fateful day, according to Ben, he nearly stabbed a friend. The two were arguing over what radio station to listen to. What did Ben want to hear? Who knows? Let's say it was an Icelandic flute percussion duo he really dug. Then, his friend changed the station, and the monster inside Carson erupted. Ben attacked, violently stabbing at the offender with a knife. The blade struck his friend, but miraculously, it deflected off a belt buckle, snapped, narrowly averting a murder.

Horrified by what he had almost done, Ben retreated to the bathroom in his family's tiny home. We can envision him squatting on the porcelain throne, praying for deliverance. Just then, as if sent by an angel (or sold by Rick Perry), Ben found a Bible. He opened it to the Book of Proverbs and read a passage on the importance of controlling one's temper. "Lord," Ben said, speaking directly to the heavenly father, "despite what all the experts tell me, You can change me. You can free me forever from this destructive personality trait." It worked. Two miracles in one day. "When I left that bathroom," he later told voters at the September Commonwealth Club event in San Francisco, "I was a different person."

The only problem with this dramatic scenario is collaboration couldn't be found. Like literally no one believes it. Not Carson's former neighbors, kids from his school, none of them. One of Carson's high-school classmates said this alleged violent streak came as news to him. "I don't know nothing about that. It would have been all over the whole school." OK, before we go pointing fingers, let's take a step back and analyze Ben's story.

First, take into account that Ben Carson has incredible dexterity and hand-eye coordination. It is the God-gifted ability that let him make the most precise of incisions later as a neurosurgeon. Second, understand that in order for a strike, it would need to be delivered at an almost perpendicular angle to the stabee's waistline. Otherwise, it would just glance off the buckle. So, best-case scenario for Ben and he's telling the truth, then he tried to stab his friend in the dick. That's messed up, even by a hulking, green rage-monster's standards.

Be that as it may, the stabbing event led to a calmer Ben (one so calm you often can't be sure if he's awake). This new sloth-like Carson went on to Yale, then the University of Michigan Medical School. In another memory lapse, Carson said he was offered a full scholarship to attend West Point. Only thing, West Point had no record of him applying nor is anyone given a full scholarship since everyone admitted to military academies automatically gets free tuition.

Carson did make it to Johns Hopkins, though, where he took his residency in neurosurgery. After a year in Australia, he returned to Hopkins as director of pediatric neurosurgery. By all accounts, he was an outstanding surgeon, even separating German twins conjoined at the head. This miracle surgery was often cited to prove Carson's brilliance. Unfortunately, it was one of those instances where two separated heads were not better than a conjoined one. In this case, neither boy would ever walk or be capable of feeding himself. One did not speak. A few years after the operation, their mother said, "I will never get over this. ... Why did I have them separated? I will feel guilty forever." Carson concurred saying, "In a technological 'star wars' sort of way, the operation was a fantastic success. But as far as having normal children, I don't think it was all that successful."

Successful or not, that surgery made Ben Carson's career. He walked out of the operating room that day directly into a post-surgery news conference covered worldwide. Speaking engagements and book deals followed, as well as many effective surgeries, such as operating on babies in utero.

Except for the poor German brothers, all this sounds like something out of Hollywood—which it became when "Gifted Hands" was made into a TV movie starring Cuba Gooding Jr. The movie received decent reviews, although critics kept panning Gooding for a flat performance. Variety added, "Gooding appears constrained by his limited screen time and the narrow demands of the part." He gave a narrow, flat performance with low energy? Sounds like he nailed Ben Carson.

Many honorary degrees and awards followed, including the Presidential Medal of Freedom.

Still, all this would not have made Ben a darling of the conservatives. No, that love fest came from things like Carson saying that the devil made Charles Darwin come up with the theory of evolution. He explained, "My personal theory is that there was no room for these dinosaurs on the Ark. It's a big boat, but these are big guys." OK. Let's take a look at Ben's theory for a second.

God was angry. He tells Noah he's making a great flood to wipe out all the evil, and then God turns into a general contractor. "The ark," God said as he removed his hard hat, "is to be 300 cubits long, 50 cubits wide and 30 cubits high." For those of you wondering, a cubit is about

18 inches, making the ark 450 feet long by 75 feet wide. So perhaps a pair of massive brontosauruses could not fit on a 450-foot boat along with all the other creatures of the world, as Carson suggests. Fine. But then where are the velociraptors today? There would have been plenty of room for them, although the Old Testament would end like this—"At the Lord's bidding, Noah shepherded two of every animal onto the great ark. And thusly the velociraptors ate everyone in a frenzy of blood and carnage. Did you not see 'Jurassic Park'! Why would you bring those killing machines on a boat? Amen."

Always a favorite stand for many conservatives, Ben supported a bill banning abortions starting at 20 weeks. Although he was once on a board that gave money to Planned Parenthood, he later decried the group's "abhorrent practices." Same-sex marriage? "Marriage is between a man and a woman. No group, be they gays, be they NAMBLA, be they people who believe in bestiality [what is it with these guys and their fascination with bestiality?], it doesn't matter what they are. They don't get to change the definition." For those not familiar with NAMBLA, it stands for the North American Man/Boy Love Association. That's like disagreeing with transvestites for their fashion choices and lumping them in with Buffalo Bill from "Silence of the Lambs"—"Men should wear conservative slacks. No alternative, be it a sequined skirt, be it the skin of a human female, is acceptable."

However, what sealed his far-right credentials was his speech at the 2013 National Prayer Breakfast, where he said, "Moral decay, fiscal irresponsibility. [Ancient Romans] destroyed themselves. If you don't think that can happen to America, you get out your books, and you start reading." President Obama, who was sitting front and center, didn't look too happy.

The learned doctor later characterized the Affordable Care Act as the "worst thing to have happened in this nation since slavery." In case you're compiling a list of American worsts, you can add the Native American genocide, Pearl Harbor, Japanese internment camps, 9/11, the Bay of Pigs invasion and "Baywatch" getting canceled ahead of the Affordable Care Act.

Now Carson had backing of big-bucks types. He had led surgical teams. Wasn't that credentials enough to be the leader of the free world? His hat went into the ring on May 4, 2015. His hat got pulled out of the ring the following March 2. What happened that changed this rising star to falling dud?

Put yourself out as someone deserving of the Oval Office and you should expect to go under a harsh and exacting microscope. There was the violent-boy story. Debunked pretty much. Then there were foreign-policy nuttiness. Shouldn't he have known that Baltic countries were members of NATO?

Part of Carson's fall from campaign grace might be attributed to staff upheavals and not getting endorsements from evangelical biggies like Jerry Falwell Jr. and Tony Perkins. His performance on the debate stage sealed his fate. During the first debate, he barely spoke. After the second, a commentator said Carson was "shockingly weak" and "lame."

Despite that, he managed to move ahead of Donald Trump by four points in one national poll, was beating him in Iowa and pulled even in South Carolina.

After the first two GOP debates, Dr. Ben Carson steadily surged until he was the co-frontrunner. He was filling rally halls. Then the momentum stalled. Two weeks before the Iowa caucuses, his staff was scrambling to get seats filled at events. Carson boldly—OK, maybe "boldly" is too strong a word—predicted that prognosticators would be surprised after the votes were tallied. And the winner was . . . not Ben Carson, though he did come in fourth.

Carson made staff changes before Iowa. "He's soft-spoken and sometimes people confuse soft-spokenness with not being strong enough," his new campaign manager said, promising "more fire in his belly."

Ben did show a spark, if not quite a fire, when he feebly pushed back against Ted Cruz for his staff spreading the rumor on the day of the Iowa vote that the neurosurgeon was dropping out of the race. A recorded message urged Carson backers to switch to Cruz. "It's clear that there were people who tried to take advantage of a situation," Carson said in the dulcet tones that did more to put voters to sleep than inspire them. In the end, maybe Ben became too good at controlling his rage-monster.

Little Marco

Donald Trump dubbed Marco Rubio, "Little Marco." It was a schoolyard taunt. Trump might as well have called him "Marco Butthead-Face," but something about Little Marco fit. Like most of the candidates, Marco has some skeletons in his closet. But they were small skeletons, figuratively a couple of gerbils that escaped from their plastic habitat and died of malnourishment. He had a less-than-large betrayal of his political big brother. There was a minor scandal with a credit card. And of course, who could forget the tiny fudging of family history?

Marco Rubio was born in Miami on May 28, 1971, the little brother to three older siblings. His parents, Mario and Oriales, emigrated from Cuba in 1956. Here's where there is a little coloring of the facts. In Rubio's biography, he claimed his parents left Cuba to escape the terrible, no-good Fidel Castro. Only Castro didn't rise to power until three years later in 1959. As it was later revealed, the Rubios left for economic reasons and actually made trips back to Cuba after the emigration. That's not nearly as captivating origin story.

Marco, if you are going to fudge the truth, take a cue from Donald Trump and go *big*. Or in Donald's parlance, go *yuge*. Your parents were both secret spies. Your mother was deep undercover for Castro, who was launching guerilla attacks from the Sierra Maestra mountains. Your father, meanwhile, was the top secret agent for the dictator of Cuba, Fulgencio Batista. Married, neither knew of the other's double life, until they were each tasked to assassinate the other. It was Romeo and Juliet with guns, cigars and a happy ending. They saw the oppressiveness of Cuba, put aside their differences and escaped to America to sire a son who would one day become president of the United States. OK, is that even remotely true? No. Is it roughly the plot of the film, "Mr. and Mrs. Smith," in which Brad Pitt and Angelina Jolie famously met and started a torrid affair? Pretty much. Would it almost instantly be fact-checked and proven wrong? Absolutely. But that's never stopped The Donald, he was one day of mass temporary insanity away from becoming president.

Rubio's father was a bartender in Miami, his mother held various jobs in the service industry, and both were Roman Catholic. Rubio was a star football player in high school.

He met his wife at a high-school party, and she later became a Miami Dolphins cheerleader. This is the storybook beginning fitting a Disney movie. A first-generation American of humble origins embarks on a journey across streets made of gold. Here's where things get a little off-kilter.

The family moved to Las Vegas in 1979. His father landed a job at Sam's Town, an Old West-style casino. His mother was a maid at the Imperial Palace. So, as Cuban immigrants struggling to get by in an even more foreign place than Miami, they did the only sensible thing. They joined the Church of Latter-Day Saints. Yes, for six years, Marco Rubio was a Mormon.

No amount of investigative digging could confirm if Rubio ever donned the Mormon's magic underwear. But perhaps even higher on the Mormon-stuff scale, he was a massive fan of the Osmonds. You remember the Osmonds, right? They were the family musical group that was equal parts saccharine sweet and cult creepy. At the time, they were the most visible Mormons in America, and Marco idolized them. In attempt to follow in Donny Osmond's platform-shoed footsteps, Rubio formed an Osmond tribute group with his sister and cousins.

Try to picture Little Marco at a family function, in front of all his relatives, belting out the words to the Osmonds' "Go Away Little Girl."

> I love the little wiggle in your walk . . .
> But you're too young to know the score
> So come back when you're older

Apparently the Osmonds were counseling their listeners on the dangers of jailbait and were early adopters of

the "Wait till she's eighteen" motto used by responsible pe-
dophiles everywhere. Upon returning to Miami in 1985,
the Rubios rejoined the Catholic Church.

Marco graduated from South Miami Senior High
School in 1989 and enrolled at Tarkio College in Missouri on a football scholarship. He left a year later, which
is probably for the best as Tarkio, an NAIA athletic school,
went out of business in 1992. If you're wondering what the
NAIA is, it's an alternate governing body to the NCAA.
Basically, the NCAA is to the NAIA as Steve Wynn (real-
estate mogul and one-time owner of the Frontier, Golden
Nugget, Mirage, Treasure Island, Bellagio, Wynn Las Vegas and Encore hotels) is to Donald Trump. That is to say
the NCAA is calculating, cutthroat and a financial gold
mine while the NAIA is a hot mess that will do anything
for attention.

Rubio transferred to Santa Fe Community College
in Gainesville, Fla., and then to the University of Florida
where he earned a B.A. in political science in 1993. He
rounded out his education graduating cum laude from
the University of Miami School of Law three years later.

While studying law, Rubio interned for U.S. Representative Ileana Ros-Lehtinen. He also played a relatively
big role in Republican Sen. Bob Dole's 1996 presidential
campaign. Rubio wasn't a gofer running to get coffee,
Centrum Silver, prune juice, Bengay or whatever else Dole
staffers might have needed. Instead, he was the general-
election campaign leader in Miami-Dade and Monroe
counties. Granted, Dole lost Florida 37 percent to Bill
Clinton's 57 percent. Still, Rubio's efforts caught the eye
of some of Florida's major political players.

When he ran for the city commission in West Miami,

Rubio received a $50 check. No, it was not for services rendered while moonlighting as a cabana boy/personal masseur on the side. It was from soon-to-be governor of Florida Jeb Bush. As they said in the film, "Casablanca," this was the beginning of a beautiful . . . mutually beneficial arrangement.

Dan Gelber, a Democrat who served in the Florida House when Rubio and Bush were in state government, dubbed Jeb, Marco's "Frenementor." The Frenementorship continued in 1999 when Rubio successfully ran for the Florida House of Representatives. Jeb provided Marco with guidance and financial donors. Marco provided Jeb with an ally in the state legislature and a colleague that made him look slightly less awkward (which is still very, very awkward). Rubio won re-election in 1999, 2002, 2004, running unopposed in the last two. And again, things get a little weird.

In 2005, Rubio became the first Cuban-American speaker of the Florida House of Representatives at age 34. To honor the new speaker, Jeb presided over an induction ceremony held in Tallahassee. A plane was even chartered so hundreds of Miami-based well-wishers could attend. Rubio gave an impassioned speech promising a bright future with sugarplum gumdrops and rainbows for all. (Not the gay kind of rainbow, because as Rubio later said, he would make gay marriage illegal again if elected president.) And Jeb, Jeb gave Rubio a sword.

"I can't think back on a time when I've ever been prouder to be a Republican, Marco," Jeb said. Then things got even weirder as Jeb explained about Chang.

"Chang is a mystical warrior. Chang is somebody who believes in conservative principles, believes in entrepreneurial capitalism, believes in moral values that underpin a free society. I rely on Chang with great regularity in my public life. He has been by my side, and sometimes, I let him down. But Chang, this mystical warrior, has never let me down."

He then handed Marco a golden sword. Bush only had two years left in his last term as governor. Many saw this as a symbolic changing of the guard, a token that Rubio would carry on Bush's legacy in Florida. But as Sigmund Freud said, "Sometimes a sword is just a sword." Besides, it wasn't much of a sword.

Rubio served as speaker from 2005 to 2008. This is the time of Marco's little scandal. He had a Republican Party of Florida American Express card for work-related expenses. In three years, Rubio racked up $100,000 in charges, with an estimated $22,000 of it being personal. These included things like lavish dinners, airplane flights and a trip to Disney World. The account also incurred more than $1,700 in delinquency and late fees. So, why is this a little scandal, again?

Rubio did make $13,900 in payments to American Express to reimburse the party for his personal expenses. Sure, things like the following charges were still covered by the Republican Party:

- $765 at Apple's online store for "computer supplies"
- $25.76 from Everglades Lumber for "supplies"
- $53.49 at Winn-Dixie in Miami for "food"
- $68.33 at Happy Wine in Miami for "beverages" and "meal"
- $78.10 for two purchases at Farm Stores groceries in suburban Miami

No biggie. Rubio's campaign was able to explain most of these away. The $765 dollars at the Apple Store was for a new hard drive that was needed for backing up important government files and stuff. The truth is that using the card the way Rubio did was messy and irresponsible, but it probably seemed the best of several bad options. He could have held up a liquor store, after all.

The one part of Rubio's origin story that is 100-percent accurate is that he was the son of poor Cuban immigrants. They couldn't pay for his education. So according to financial disclosures, by the time he was elected to the Florida legislature, Rubio had $150,000 in student-loan debt, $30,000 in other debt and a net worth of zero. It's hard for someone to be good with money when they have never had any. And let's be honest, running up a huge debt might be one of the most presidential things Rubio had ever done.

In 2009, he ran against former Florida Republican Gov. Charlie Crist for a U.S. Senate seat. Crist had been Jeb's successor. As a moderate Republican, many of Crist's ideas clashed with Jeb's. In an effort to keep his legacy alive, Jeb made moves. "Everyone knew behind the scenes, Jeb was pushing Marco," Florida Senate President Mike Haridopolos said. "He didn't endorse until late, but everyone knew Jeb was giving him encouragement." It didn't hurt that the ultra-conservative Tea Party was pushing for Rubio, too.

Initially, it didn't look like it would make a difference. Rubio trailed by double digits in the polls, and all the pundits expected him to get crushed. Then in a Disneyesque turn of events (if Disney made animated movies about two men figuratively trying to claw each other's eyes out in a political election), Rubio made a dramatic come-from-behind win.

It was Jeb who introduced Rubio at his victory celebration. "I'm so proud of Marco," he gushed. "I'm so proud of his high-voltage energy. I'm so proud of his enthusiasm. I'm so proud of his eloquence. And I'm so proud that he will be a part of a next generation of leaders that will restore America. Marco Rubio is the right man at the right time."

Then Jeb did his impression of the infamous soap-star Susan Lucci "I promised myself I wouldn't do this" acceptance speech at the Emmys.

"Bushes get emotional," Jeb started, already misty eyed. "So I'm going to try my hardest . . . My wife has told me, 'Don't cry. Don't cry.' But Marco Rubio makes me cry for joy!" It wouldn't be too long before Rubio would make Jeb cry for an entirely different reason.

As Jeb geared up for a 2016 presidential run, rumors of a Rubio candidacy started to surface. Jeb's camp thought, "Well, there's no way he'd do that," said Steve Schale, the Democratic strategist who ran Obama's Florida campaign. "Their response was, 'Well, he wouldn't do that.' They were almost indignant about the idea that he'd get in. How dare he?" But dare he did.

Rubio announced his candidacy on April 13, 2015, two months ahead of Jeb. Those who knew Rubio weren't surprised. "It's just how Marco is," said Jose Fuentes, his former spokesman. "There's no intent to betray—it's just that he has a plan in his head, and he's not going to wait. He'll do what's best for him." It was betrayal of sorts, just a little one in the grand scheme of things. They were never actual friends. Marco didn't attend the Bush family Christmas party and hunt polar bears on horseback, or whatever the Bushes do at Christmas. Jeb was just Marco's "frenementor."

As the campaign progressed, Jeb and Rubio took frequent digs at each other. Most were indirect, then as Jeb trailed in the polls, things heated up. Their Super PACs warred, each putting out negative ads. Their supporters in Florida were split, and the attacks got personal. It was actually Jeb who fired the first shot at Rubio's height on MSNBC's "Morning Joe." There had been much tittering over Marco wearing expensive boots with high heels.

"Yeah, but Jeb, do you own any platform boots that make you taller?" co-host Joe Scarborough asked, to which Bush responded, "I got my cowboy boots on, big Joe." (Bush is 6'3".)

"Do they make you three inches taller, or are they just normal cowboy boots?" Scarborough asked. "I don't have a height issue," Bush quipped. Jeb was never much of a quipper.

The big problem for Rubio was he had no future as president without the Bush family backing and his home state, which was heavily behind Jeb. On March, 15, 2016, Rubio only managed to win 27 percent of the Florida primary vote, while Trump took 45.7 percent and all of Florida's delegates.

"I think the general consensus at the time was that Marco was, you know, being a little too big for his britches," said a lobbyist in Tallahassee and a Bush backer. The britches were undoubtedly too big, probably sized for someone close to 6'3".

Rubio suspended his campaign immediately after the Florida result came out, saying he would go back to being a private citizen. Back to being Little Marco. That didn't last long, as he then did a "never mind" and ran for his Senate seat.

Darth Ted

There have been many great villains that can make your skin crawl. Darth Vader is at the top of the list, and now you can add Ted Cruz. Cruz even has some Vader parallels. He's highly intelligent and persuasive. He's despised across the Galaxy. He views himself as the chosen one, meant to restore balance to the forces of American politics. And he can choke people with his mind. All right, maybe he can't literally choke someone with his mind. But you'd be hard pressed to prove Cruz doesn't have some kind of strange powers after seeing John McCain sputtering on the Senate floor after Cruz theatrics.

Like Darth Vader, Cruz was born in an alien land under a different name. Rafael Edward Cruz, the unlikely infant to transform into Darth Ted, emerged from the womb in Calgary, Canada, on Dec. 22, 1970. His mother, Eleanor, came from Delaware. His father, Rafael, was born in a place universally reviled by Republicans called Cuba. This is the point to cue the record-scratch sound effect.

If Ted wasn't born in the U.S. and his father was an immigrant from Cuba, how in the name of Donald Trump's comb-over was he running for president? Aren't these the exact set of circumstance that led Trump and the birthers to relentlessly hound Obama? Yes, but as it turns out, you don't have to be born stateside to become president. (Even though Hawaii may be in the Pacific, it has been a state since 1959.) What the Constitution actually says is

"No Person except a natural born Citizen, or a Citizen of the United States, at the time of the Adoption of this Constitution, shall be eligible to the Office of President." This means you need to be a citizen at birth and do not have to go through the naturalization process. Anyone with one American parent qualifies. Neither Trump nor his comb-over were ever one for facts.

Rafael says he fought for Fidel Castro in the Cuban Revolution, and after being imprisoned and beaten, he fled to the U.S. on a student visa. By the time he graduated from the University of Texas in 1961 with a degree in mathematics and chemical engineering, he had already been married and divorced. He met Eleanor in 1969. A year later, the couple moved to Canada, started a seismic-data processing firm for oil drillers, presumably had sex (although you cannot rule out some kind of perverse ritual involving pentagrams and weasel blood) and created Ted.

The happy times in Canada were short lived. In 1974, Rafael left the family and returned to Texas. It was there, after attending a Bible study with a colleague, he found God. And if you think about it, God probably was hiding in Texas during that century. It's the only way to explain the 1990s Dallas Cowboys. Now that Rafael was born again, the couple reconciled, and Eleanor and Ted moved to Texas.

Here we see the foreshadowing of the rise of Darth Ted. Ted was valedictorian of his class at Houston's Second Baptist High School, an admirable accomplishment. But he also joined an after-school program run by the Free Enterprise Institute. Part of the program was for Ted and his fellow "Constitutional Corroborators" to give speeches around Texas preaching conservative issues. He was a disciple in training.

Cruz enrolled in Princeton University, and it was here that the dark side first emerged. Ted continued his stellar academic performance, as well as becoming a master debater. He won the top speaker award at both the 1992 U.S. National Debating Championship and the 1992 North American Debating Championship. Despite the accomplishments, he was hated by everyone. You think "everyone" is hyperbole? It is not.

Craig Mazin, Ted's Princeton roommate, said, "When I met Ted in 1988, I had no word to describe him, but only because I didn't speak German. Thank you, Germans for 'Backpfeifengesicht.'" "Backpfeifengesicht roughly translates to "a face that needs punching." In case you didn't completely grasp how much Mazin loathes Cruz, he added, "I have plenty of problems with his politics, but truthfully, his personality is so awful that 99 percent of why I hate him is just his personality." Several fellow classmates who asked that their names not be used corroborated Mazin's account, using words like "abrasive," "intense," "strident," "crank" and "arrogant." Four independently offered the word "creepy."

Darth Ted had awakened.

Cruz graduated from Princeton in 1992, armed with his Force-power of debate and enrolled in Harvard Law School. He graduated magna cum laude in 1995 with a Juris Doctor degree. He was a primary editor of the Harvard Law Review, and Harvard Law professor Alan Dershowitz said, "Cruz was off-the-charts brilliant." But in Cruz's case, with great brilliance comes even greater creepiness.

While at Harvard, Cruz founded a study group, but said he only wanted to let those who had graduated from Harvard, Princeton or Yale join, referring to the other schools as the "minor Ivies." A classmate who agreed to carpool with Cruz revealed, "We hadn't left Manhattan before he asked my IQ."

After leaving a wave of people who despised him at Harvard Law in his wake, Cruz worked as a law clerk for several judges, including Supreme Court Justice William Rehnquist from 1996 to 1997. This is where he completely gave himself over to the dark side. While clerking for Rehnquist, Cruz became obsessed with the death penalty.

"That I think was a special interest of his," said former clerk Renée Lerner. Lerner also noted that Cruz paid special attention to the details of murders in his memos. Instead of summarizing them and moving on to the legal merits, like a normal, well-adjusted human being, he went full Sith. He described every grisly detail like he was writing the screenplay for a Wes Craven movie. "It was unusual for a Supreme Court clerk to do that," Lerner said. But it is not unusual for a Sith Lord (or a serial killer).

After Cruz finished his clerkships, he took a position with Cooper, Carvin & Rosenthal. Ted would like you to remember his service for the National Rifle Association, helping prepare testimony for the impeachment proceedings against President Bill Clinton and working pro bono for a veterans group to preserve a cross that had been erected on federal land. What Ted does not want you to remember is the moral flexibility he demonstrated in many of his cases.

In 1999, Cruz joined the George W. Bush presidential campaign. He was supposed to advise then-Gov. George W. on policy and legal matters. But being so close to the throne was too much for Darth Ted.

Cruz was notorious for sending many emails expressing his opinions on virtually everything in the campaign.

He also had a penchant for sending them in the middle of the night, as well as regular updates on his personal accomplishments. Everyone in the Bush campaign grew to despise him. In fact, one Bush campaign alum recalls, "The quickest way for a meeting to end would be for Ted to come in. People would want out of that meeting. People wouldn't go to a meeting if they knew he would be there. It was his inability to be part of the team. That's exactly what he was—a big asshole."

Perhaps one of the few people who did not despise Cruz was Heidi Nelson. They met while working on the campaign and married in 2001. Now you may be skeptical than an actual human woman would fall in love with Darth Ted. Take comfort. Much like Cruz's assertion that we do not have conclusive evidence that climate change is real, we also do not conclusive evidence that Heidi Nelson is human. Still, Cruz counsels, "If you want to meet your spouse, go join a political campaign," proving Ted knows as much about courtship as he does about climate change.

After Bush's victory, many of Cruz's campaign colleagues headed to the White House. However, neither they, nor President Bush, wanted Cruz anywhere near them. Bush has disdain for Cruz to this day, saying, "I just don't like the guy" at a 2016 fundraiser for his brother, Jeb. So, they exiled Darth Ted to the frigid wasteland that is the Federal Trade Commission.

Ted escaped two years later and was appointed to the office of Texas solicitor general by the state's attorney general, Greg Abbott, in 2003. Abbott wanted to use the office as a platform for advancing conservative legal theories on issues like religion and states' rights. Cruz was the perfect tool for such a mission. Cruz argued nine cases before the U.S. Supreme Court including the landmark Medellín v. Texas in defiance of an international court ruling, as well as an order from President Bush. Cruz successfully defended the state's right to execute a Mexican citizen who'd participated in the gang rape and murder of two teenage girls in Houston.

Not nearly as widely publicized, Cruz also fought to uphold a ban on dildos in the state of Texas. No, that is not a typo. A ban on dildos. Two undercover cops arrested a Texas mother who was a sales rep for Passion for selling them. Uneasy about the arrest, the adult-toy industry challenged the Texas law forbidding the sale and promotion of "obscene devices." Under the law, a person who violated the statute could go to jail for up to two years. Despite filing a 76-page legal brief, the appeals court told Cruz and his team to forget it. One can only imagine what was in that brief— "Now if your honor will turn to page 56, subheading, Pulse-Pounding Kitty Tickler . . ." Just another day for Darth Ted in his never-ending battle to banish joy and pleasure from the galaxy.

But even so, this is another instance of Cruz championing good Christian values.

Because of his work on the landmark Dildo Case, among others, Cruz was being talked up for a federal judgeship. That's not what he wanted, though. He wanted to become Emperor. So in December 2010, he journeyed to Washington for the annual meeting of the Federalist Society, a conservative legal group. It was here he hoped to uncover a path to power. He met Utah Sen.-elect Mike Lee. Like Cruz, Lee had left Washington to become a government lawyer. And like Cruz, he had never run for office. But Lee triumphed by going full dark side and championing the Tea Party. Cruz saw opportunity.

Now, if you're confused by what the Tea Party is, you're not alone. First, it's not a political party. The name refers to the Boston Tea Party, where colonials dumped tons of British tea into the Boston Harbor in protest of lacking representation when it came to British taxation. They were not against taxes per se. The modern movement, which became known as the Tea Party, is basically all the most conservative of conservative Republican views kicked into hyper-drive and sprinkled with uber-Christian rhetoric. No taxes. Small government. Abortion is a sin. Obama must be thrown into the rancor pit to be devoured whole. Many Tea Party loyalists refer to themselves as "tea baggers," which incidentally, is the slang term for a sexual act in which the male puts his scrotum into his partner's mouth over and over. The moniker fits.

After scanning Lee's brain, Cruz launched his rebel Senate campaign the following January and aimed his Death Star at GOP frontrunner David Dewhurst. Cruz went after him from the right, a classic Tea Party battle tactic. He used his Supreme Court victories, from Medellín to his successful defense of a Ten Commandments statue on the grounds of the Texas State Capitol, to cast himself as a conservative crusader. "He made the solicitor general's job sound like a combination of Rocky and Rambo," said Texas GOP consultant Matt Mackowiak. Cruz forced a primary runoff with Dewhurst. He then throttled Dewhurst by 15 points and blasted his Democratic opponent in the general election.

Darth Ted was now a United States senator. Let that sink in. But surely now he would abandon his creepy behavior and stop being an "asshole." If only that were so.

Cruz wasted no time in offending practically the entire Senate. That includes Democrats and Republicans alike.

Bob Dole said Cruz would be an ineffective president because "nobody likes him. He doesn't have any friends in Congress. He called the leader of the Republicans [Mitch McConnell] a liar on the Senate floor. If you want to call somebody a liar in the Senate, you go to their office—you don't go on the Senate floor and make it public."

John Boehner, the former speaker of the House, called Cruz "that jackass" and a "false prophet." Sen. Lindsey Graham added, "He is an opportunist, he's a libertarian when it is hot." But no one hates him more than Sen. John McCain. Perhaps it's because Cruz insulted McCain's run for presidency along with Romney and Dole.

Cruz said, "We need to look to history and what works and what doesn't, and the one thing is clear is if Republicans run another candidate in the mold of a Bob Dole, or a John McCain, or a Mitt Romney—and let me be clear, all three of those are good, honorable men. They're decent men. They're patriots, but if we run another candidate in the mold of a Bob Dole, or a John McCain, or a Mitt Romney, we will end up with the same result, which is millions of people will stay home on Election Day."

McCain did not take kindly to the slight. "He fucking hates Cruz," a McCain adviser said. "He's just offended by his style." McCain went on to famously dub Cruz a "wacko bird."

Cruz's defining wacko-bird moment came in October 2013. Darth Ted, drawing on all his power, orchestrated a government shutdown during which he gave a 21-hour speech on the Senate floor in an attempt to hold up a federal budget bill and defund Obamacare. So what did he talk about for almost a full day? There was plenty of railing against Obama as the ultimate evil. But there was some filler, too. In particular, Cruz read Dr. Seuss' "Green Eggs and Ham" in its entirety. Of course, Obamacare stayed, but thanks to Cruz, the eternal words of Dr. Seuss are now printed in the Congressional Record. It seemed like there was no stopping his rise to power.

Cruz announced his presidential candidacy on March 23, 2015. Despite a majority of Washington hating him, Cruz did surprisingly well in the primaries. He won 12 states and earned 559 delegates. He also raised nearly $92 million, a record for a GOP primary candidate. So what went wrong? Why couldn't Darth Ted use his considerable mind-control powers to crush his foes during the Republican debates? The answer: He ran into an even more powerful Sith Lord. The force is strong with Darth Donald.

Shortly after losing overwhelmingly to Trump in the Indiana primary on May 3, 2016, Cruz suspended his campaign.

So is this the end of Darth Ted, or will he majestically rise again like a wacko bird from the ashes? It's likely we haven't heard the last of him. As Cruz said himself in one of his many bizarre digressions during the 21-hour filibuster, "Just like in the 'Star Wars' movies, the empire will strike back."

Cranky Pope Kasich

If you were a nice Catholic boy in McKees Rocks, Pa., in the early '50s, then you wanted to be a priest. Unless you were John Richard Kasich. Then you wanted to be pope.

McKees Rocks was a steel-manufacturing town near

Pittsburgh, best known for a bloody strike in 1909. By the time Pope John was born on May 13, 1952, the town had started a population decline going to 16,000 from a high of 18,000 in 1940, closing today at 6,000.

As Kasich over the years *often* mentioned, his father was a postal carrier, though back then the occupation was postman. David Cercone, a boyhood friend, recalled John Sr. was the type of guy "who if you wanted to mail a letter, but didn't have a stamp, you could tape a nickel on it, and he would put a stamp on it once he got back to the post office at the end of his route."

Little John was an altar boy, who when Cercone expressed interest in joining him, Kasich said his friend was too fat. "They didn't have a cassock big enough to fit him."

Some people drift into politics. Others are born into it. Kasich bulled his way in. By the time he got to Ohio State, the Pope gave up his boyhood dream of becoming a priest, having realized celibacy was not for him. College campuses will do that. Instead, he converted to conservatism.

This was 1970, days of sex, drugs, rock and roll—and campus unrest. So what did Kasich, all 18 years of him, do? He wrested 20 minutes with Richard Nixon, in the White House, no less, to offer the president some friendly advice. Maybe Nixon thought the kid was Elvis in disguise.

The close personal relationship with Nixon didn't help Kasich win the student-government presidency in his senior year. After that, Kid Kasich blossomed politically.

After graduation, he passed on law school, which would have put his political career on a three-year hold. Instead, he opted to toil at the Ohio Legislative Service Commission, then for state Sen. Buz Lukens, famous for being charged with "contributing to the delinquency of a minor." These were baby steps toward becoming a state senator himself at 26, beating an incumbent. In 1983, he took on another incumbent, U.S. Congressman Bob Shamansky—and won and won eight more times.

It was in the House that Kasich furthered his much-deserved reputation of being a loud-mouthed, hyperkinetic churl, ready to pick a fight with a fellow Republican or the Grateful Dead's manager who denied him onstage access. John McCain, with some anger issues of his own, slammed Pope Kasich for his "hair-trigger temper."

Nor were constituents spared. After Kasich made fun of Jane Fonda, Sissy Spacek and Jessica Lange testifying before a congressional hearing, snarkily calling them "noted agricultural experts," he got called out by a woman whose vote he might court later. A "backwoodsy redneck," she labeled him. In the fine tradition of Donald Trump, Kasich couldn't ignore the insult. "I would recommend you enroll in a remedial course on protocol before writing any more advisory letters to your elected officials. Or better yet, refrain from writing." He was obviously not material for the diplomatic corps.

An extreme budget hawk, Kasich teamed up with Congressman Tim Penny, a Democratic-Farmer-Labor party member. As a way to stop the government from hemorrhaging money, they proposed the Penny-Kasich Common Cents Spending Cuts plan. The cents was in there because a penny would be slashed from every outgoing federal dollar. Didn't pass, though it came close.

Another Kasich crusade that went kaput was his attack on the movie, "Fargo." He got a copy from Blockbuster and was outraged that it wasn't funny as billed. It was the wood-chipper scene that got him. He was outraged. Conservative columnist George Will wrote, "The people who distribute Academy Award nominations like that movie, but the congressman from Columbus, Ohio, emphatically— all his judgments are emphatic—does not. The Blockbuster fellow tried a Nuremberg defense—'I'm just the store manager'—but Kasich would have none of it, telling him that at least the movie should be labeled for gratuitous violence." Will went on to call Kasich "effervescent," but got around to "hyperactive."

By 1999, the Pope had been in the House for more than 15 years when ambition overwhelmed him. He had already set up the obligatory Super PAC. He would be the Jolt Cola, "just a little different and a little fresher" than the Pepsi and Coke of Elizabeth Dole and George W. Bush, who were in the hunt for the presidency, as well.

Kasich's campaign soon fizzled out. If he didn't get the proper respect he deserved in politics, why, he would retire from the House and go make some real money—at the then-thriving Lehman Brothers. And he would have a platform for his rantings. Where else than the young Fox News, which gave him a segment called "Outrage of the Week"?

It was back to his true calling in 2010 when he ran for governor of Ohio. This would be a much better path to 1600 Pennsylvania Avenue. Starting with Thomas Jefferson and ending with George the Younger, 17 governors had successfully made the move up. (Don't bother Googling, yes, Thomas Jefferson did live in the White House, the first president to do so.)

Kasich did it again. He beat an incumbent, this time Democrat Ted Strickland. And Kasich did whatever it took to win. He didn't care that he had raged against corporate welfare. Now, he charged Strickland with not being friendly enough to business. And the Tea Party? Once a proponent of "passionate conservatism" (Bush co-opted the term), Kasich shamelessly converted and was embracing these frothing extremists. "I think I was in the Tea Party before there was a Tea Party," he announced.

Still, linking Strickland to the hard economic times was what clinched the victory, winning by 2 percent of the vote.

Now that Kasich was bishop-in-charge, it was time for the snarling to amp up, time to push his extreme anti-choice views and union-busting agenda. Given his Catholic background, anti-choice was no surprise, even though he had long since left the close embrace of the Holy Mother Church. And for heaven's sake, those public workers shouldn't be allowed to strike. "They've got good jobs, they've got high pay, they get good benefits, a great retirement. What are they striking for?" And throw out collective bargaining, giving these ingrates higher wages and benefits was an unacceptable drain on taxpayer money. That and Kasich appeared to be holding a grudge against a police officer who ticketed him three years earlier for passing too close to an emergency vehicle. In the guv's estimation, the cop was an "idiot," making the guv look like the true idiot.

The taxpayers begged to differ in a 2011 referendum, and collective bargaining stayed.

It was more politically expedient for a chastised Kasich to come across as more moderate. When he first took office, he was criticized for having all-white, all-male administrators. A black Democratic lawmaker said she would introduce him to qualified blacks. Kasich's response? No hiring "your people." When that didn't play well, the poor, misunderstood governor explained he meant Democrats. Doesn't that sound reasonable? Some African Americans were subsequently hired.

But Kasich, whose favorable ratings were in the toilet, try 30 percent in his first year, needed some moderate credentials if he were ever to reach the White House. So, good Christian that he professed to be, he saw the need to take fed money for Medicaid. Suddenly, Obamacare wasn't the work of the devil. The poor must be healed.

Good move, as his approval rating doubled. Not with the Tea Party morons, but they could carry the Pope's ambitions only so far.

He also acknowledged climate change, the need for nonviolent offenders getting shorter sentences, education-funding reforms that would funnel additional money into poor schools, letting undocumented immigrants legally stay in the country, slapping a tax on fracking. Ohio is a big fracking state.

Man, how much more moderate can this guy get? Putting aside the "let's cut taxes" cries, there was one area that threw him into the uber right-wing column. Abortion.

He spent his years in the gubernatorial office attacking the rights of women to choose from as many sides he could find. "Hardliner" is too soft a word for this defender of a sperm and egg that could develop into a baby, but were still nothing more than a collection of cells.

From 2011 to 2015, the Pope signed 16 of the most stringent anti-abortion laws in the country. How about rape counselors being forbidden from sending victims to where they might get an abortion? Or taking away 1.4-million federal dollars from Planned Parenthood, money earmarked for family planning?

Kellie Copeland, executive director of NARAL Pro-Choice Ohio, an abortion-rights advocacy group, for one, took a jaundiced view of Kasich trying pass himself off as a middle-of-the-roader.

"Kasich is a wolf in sheep's clothing. He's going out there trying to sell himself as a moderate, he's no moderate. He is an extremist. He is—if not the worst—among the worst of anti-choice governors in this country's history."

You have to wonder with 50 percent of Americans in 2016 being pro-choice and 45 percent anti whether Kasich might have had a cynically pragmatic change of political heart at some point.

Come the 2016 campaign and suddenly a new, upbeat guy who cast aside his cranky nastiness appeared. I'm a likable guy. Vote for me. But as Steve Koczela, president of a Massachusetts polling company, presciently pointed out, the 2016 election wasn't 2000 when people voted for teetotaling Bush as the candidate with whom they'd like to have a beer. "These days, you don't have to be well liked by everyone." The case in point being Donald Trump, a fiercely unapologetic trash talker who was an equal-opportunity denigrator. Trumpistas lapped up this nastiness. How was the poor Pope to know this before he chose to become the grown-up in the room and not Trump down and dirty?

His mistake. He's limited to two terms, which means he's out of office after the 2018 election. At 64, does he have enough time to reinvent himself for 2020? The overriding question is does anyone care? He was gone, the next-to-last man standing, on May 4. Which left Donald John Trump.

The Inner Donald

Think back to the last time you were in line at the grocery with a cantankerous 1st-grader in front of you. His father is busy fiddling with his phone. The kid head-butts his distracted dad's leg and screams, "Look at me!" Like red porches, Facebook posts that begin with "I hate pictures of myself" and Kanye West's entire wardrobe, it's an obvious cry for attention. The father glances down, nods and goes back to the phone. The kid scowls and swipes a low-hanging candy bar from the shelf, stuffing it in his pocket.

"Hey, I saw that!" the cashier cries.

"I didn't do it," the kid fires back without batting an eyelash.

"You put that candy bar in your pocket," the cashier stammers, flustered by the kid's unwavering confidence.

"You're a liar," the kid screams. "You're a liar and a stupid loser."

This flaxen-haired miscreant hasn't developed the part of his brain that handles impulse control. He wants attention, instant gratification, and he isn't bound by the moral conscience of a full-grown adult. The scary part is that also describes Donald Trump in an insult-slinging, pussy-grabbing nutshell. To understand why Trump is this way, we need to go all the way back to Germany in late 1880s.

Although Donald Trump once claimed to be of Swedish descent, he is actually German and Scottish. His grandfather, Friedrich Trump, immigrated to the United States in 1885. By the end of the century, Friedrich had made it all the way to Canada's Yukon Territory, following the

Gold Rush. He wasn't a gold-pan handler, though. Even back then, toiling on your knees in a filthy stream was beneath a Trump. Instead, Friedrich built an establishment called New Arctic Restaurant and Hotel. The Arctic catered to the hundreds of gold miners and was part bar and grill, and part whorehouse. Yes, the origin of the Trump fortune, not unlike many of Donald Trump's business dealings, revolved around instant gratification and people getting screwed.

After a side trip to his native Bavaria and during which he married, Friedrich moved to New York where Donald's father, Fred, was born in Queens in 1905. Friedrich continued to amass wealth, and when he died in 1918, Fred took over. Soon after that, Fred started a residential-garage building company. He called it Elizabeth Trump and Son because he was too young to sign off on checks. Fred continued his business ventures and expanded into real estate. By the time Donald Trump was born on June 14, 1946, in Jamaica, Queens, Fred owned thousands of apartment buildings and was a multimillionaire.

Now to understand Donald, you need two things. The first is a copy of the movie, "American Psycho." The scene where Patrick Bateman has sex with a beautiful young woman while focusing completely on himself flexing in a mirror is very informative. The second is an understanding of who Fred Trump was as a man.

In short, Fred was old school. Not old school like he enjoyed smoking a pipe and saying, "Gosh golly!" He was old school like, "My business will be passed down to my first born, women belong in the kitchen, and blacks belong somewhere I'm not." Yes, in 1927, a brawl erupted, led by the Ku Klux Klan, and Fred Trump was among those arrested. When asked to comment on the arrest, Donald Trump did not deny his father's Klan affiliation, only saying, "There were no charges, no nothing. It's unfair to mention it, to be honest, because there were no charges." Just like the kid in the grocery line, Donald has always been more concerned with getting away with something than right or wrong.

Fred Trump was also addicted to work the way sharks are addicted to swimming. He would spend all day managing his growing empire, come home for dinner, then immediately go back to making business calls. Fred was frugal and not known as a particularly good landlord. He bought the cheapest materials to build more than 27,000 subsidized apartments and row houses. Donald recalled that Fred Trump would even "walk through a construction site picking up loose nails and things. He'd use everything. He'd sell it."

Donald absolutely idolized his father. Meanwhile, Fred wanted nothing to do with raising his kids other than lobbing criticism their way like mental grenades. This resulted in Donald lashing out for attention. Fred Trump told an interviewer, Donald "was a pretty rough fellow when he was small." That is similar to calling Hannibal Lecter a pretty unconventional cook. According to neighbors, Donald was a notorious bully. Once, Martha Burnham left her son in a playpen in a backyard adjoining the Trumps' property, only to return to find Donald throwing rocks, "using the playpen for target practice." Trump corroborates some of this behavior in "The Art of the Deal," saying, "I actually gave a teacher a black eye. I punched my music teacher because I didn't think he knew anything about music, and I almost got expelled." Fred Trump found Donald's antics embarrassing. So he did the parental equivalent of dropping the nuclear bomb. He sent Donald to military school.

Donald enrolled at New York Military Academy in Cornwall, N.Y., in 1959 at age 13. The place was essentially "Lord of the Flies" meets "A Few Good Men." Hazing was rampant across campus and not the fun kind of hazing where you pound a bottle of Jack Daniels and attempt to write the lyrics to Will Smith's "Gettin' Jiggy Wit It" in freshly fallen snow. Boys fled the NYMA campus regularly to escape being brutalized by older cadets. Being exiled by your father into this harsh environment is the sort of thing that could leave a person emotionally frozen like a bad line of credit. But according to Donald, he liked it. "Thinking back, it was a very positive influence," Trump said. "You had to learn how to survive, essentially, with some of these guys. I learned discipline—how to dish it out and otherwise." Exacting revenge would be a big theme for the rest of Trump's life.

Donald attended Fordham University for two years after NYMA. He then transferred to the Wharton School of Finance at the University of Pennsylvania where he received a bachelor's degree in finance in 1968. "I was a really good student at the best school. I'm like a smart guy," Trump told Barbara Walters on "The View." Incidentally, "I'm like a smart guy" ranks as one of the worst phrases to convince someone you're intelligent along with "I wonder what that fish is thinking," and "Do electric sockets taste like cinnamon?" Trump also claimed he graduated top in his class. Of course, there is no record of Trump receiving honors in his graduating class yearbook, and he refuses to release his transcripts. Not shocking. As Tony Schwartz puts it, "Lying is second nature to him. More than anyone else I have ever met, Trump has the ability to convince himself that whatever he is saying at any given moment is true, or sort of true, or at least ought to be true." Schwartz was the "with" writer on "The Art of the Deal" and spent months shadowing Donald and listening in on all his phone calls.

As it turns out, Trump's claims about his business knowledge may be an exaggeration, too. Trump filed a lawsuit against journalist Timothy L. O'Brien for writing that Trump's net worth might have been far less than a billion dollars. During the proceedings, Trump was questioned by a lawyer about his knowledge of finance and how he determined his net worth. He told the lawyer that one of the main factors in determining his net worth are his personal feelings at any given moment.

"Let's talk about net worth for a second. You said that the net worth goes up and down based upon your own feelings?" the lawyer asked dumbfounded.

"Yes," Trump answered. "Even my own feelings, as to where the world is, where the world is going, and that can change rapidly from day to day. Then you have a September 11th, and you don't feel so good about yourself." In this exchange, Trump demonstrated a complete lack of basic financial concepts, not to mention the empathy of a little kid who thinks the world revolves around him.

Not long after college, Donald inherited his father's business. Donald's older brother, Fred Jr., had clashed with Fred Sr. He didn't agree with the way the business was being run and didn't enjoy the lifestyle. As a result, Donald took over Elizabeth Trump and Son in 1971, putting him in charge of a multi-million-dollar network of apartments and condominiums. His first act was to rename it

The Trump Organization, which his advisers unanimously agreed was better than his first choice of "Donald Is The Greatest Incorporated." OK, so maybe Trump didn't suggest that, but might have if he had thought of it.

It was around this time Donald began frequenting Le Club and other hotspots of New York City nightlife. He was looking to meet powerful men and beautiful women to hustle and screw, not specifically in that order. It was there he met Roy Cohn. Cohn was an attorney who became famous for aiding Sen. Joseph McCarthy during the Red Scare. Cohn was also a well-known consigliere for the Mafia. In other words, Cohn was about as upstanding as a paraplegic weasel. "I don't kid myself about Roy," Trump wrote in "The Art of the Deal." "He was no Boy Scout. He once told me he'd spent more than two-thirds of his adult life under indictment on one charge or another." This would have sent someone with a fully developed set of morals running. Instead, Cohn became Donald's most lasting business associate and closest adviser.

Trump first hired Cohn in 1972. In July of that year, the federal government authorized a series of field tests for compliance with the 1968 Fair Housing Act. A black woman was sent to ask about renting an apartment at Trump's Shore Haven apartments. She was told none were available. However, shortly after, the superintendent told a white woman with the same employment record that she could have her pick of two units. In response, the government filed a discrimination lawsuit against Trump. Donald didn't like the idea of settling, though. He told Cohn, "I don't like lawyers" because they delay deals, say no and "are always looking to settle instead of fight." Donald doesn't like waiting or being told "no." He doesn't have the attention span for that. Tony Schwartz was especially struck by this trait saying, "It's impossible to keep him focused on any topic, other than his own self-aggrandizement, for more than a few minutes." So, Donald heeded Roy Cohn's advice and filed a countersuit against the federal government.

Not surprisingly, Trump's countersuit was dismissed, and the government proceeded with its investigation. Trump folded like a house of cards (one where all the clubs and spades had previously been forced to stay in the box). A government press release said the Trump settlement was "one of the most far reaching ever" to end racial discrimination in housing. Trump was required to run advertisements to solicit non-white tenants, submit to monitoring and end all discriminatory practices. Of course, Trump still claims the settlement was a victory, saying, "We settled the suit with zero—no admission of guilt." As Schwartz has said, "Trump only takes two positions. Either you're a scummy loser, liar, whatever, or you're the greatest." In Donald's world, settling means you didn't get caught, and you're still the greatest.

The common folk in the boroughs were wearing on Donald. As he said, "You have to think anyway, so why not think big?" He wanted more attention. He wanted to see his name in lights. Which is why in 1978, he partnered with the Hyatt Hotel Corporation and bought The Commodore Hotel. The Commodore was hemorrhaging money, losing 1.5 million dollars the previous year, but it had an excellent location adjacent to Grand Central Station. The deal and extensive remodeling was largely funded by a $70-million construction loan jointly guaranteed by Fred Trump and the Hyatt hotel chain. Thus The Commodore was renamed The Grand Hyatt. It was a very successful deal, but in Donald's world, you are a loser if you don't have your name on the building.

In 1979, Trump leased a site on Fifth Avenue next to the famous Tiffany & Company. This was to be the location for the monument to his personal greatness, Trump Tower. But before construction could begin, he had to demolish the Bonwit Teller department store.

Instead of hiring an experienced demolition contractor, Donald followed in his father's footsteps and chose the cheapest option, Kaszycki & Sons Contractors. K&S was a window-washing business whose labor force was comprised of many illegal Polish immigrants. That's like having your toilet back up and hiring a bathroom attendant to fix the plumbing. Like, "Here you, go Marcin, you clean up all this shit."

When they began the demolition of Bonwit Teller in January 1980, the immigrants worked without hard hats, goggles or face masks to prevent breathing in the asbestos. They stripped electrical wires with their bare hands. The only way the job site could have been less safe is if they had Ted Kaczynski as their foreman. To make matters worse, they weren't being paid the $4 or $5 an hour they had been promised. By July, the unpaid wages came to almost $104,000. One day, the workers cornered one of Trump's representatives and threatened to throw him off the building. Donald placed a frantic phone call to labor consultant Daniel Sullivan.

"Donald told me he was having some difficulties," Sullivan later testified, "and he admitted to me that—seeking my advice—he had some illegal Polish employees on the job. I reacted by saying to Donald that 'I think you are nuts.' I told him to fire them promptly if he had any brains." This is perhaps one of the few times Trump did not jump at the chance to fire someone. Demolition was completed, but the workers were still owed thousands of dollars. They successfully sued Trump, and Judge Charles E. Stewart ruled that Trump had engaged in a conspiracy to cheat the workers of their pay. At the core was Trump's violation of his fiduciary duty to the workers and the union. Stewart said the "breach involved fraud and the Trump defendants knowingly participated in this breach." The workers were awarded $325,000 in damages plus interest. Trump appealed with his customary "I didn't know" defense. He later settled, allowing him to maintain his "greatest" status.

With Bonwit Teller demolished, construction on Trump Tower could begin. Trump made the unusual choice of using ready-mix concrete as the primary building material. At the time, the concrete industry was controlled by the mob, and most builders were avoiding it like a vegan avoids Trump-brand steaks. Even so, Donald bought his ready-mix from S&A, a concrete company that was owned by Mafia bosses Anthony "Fat Tony" Salerno and Paul Castellano. This put him at the mercy of racketeers who routinely jacked up prices and called work stoppages to extort more money out of builders. But Donald had his mob fixer in Roy Cohn to smooth things over. When the cement workers went on strike in the summer of 1982, the concrete continued to be poured at Trump Tower.

Years later, Trump Tower still stands as an edifice to Trump's ego. Every detail from the shining brass accents to pink-veined marbled walls scream, "Look at me! Look how great I am!" But those things, like much of Trump's success, are a façade. The building was raised on the strength of fraud, exploitation and skirting more laws than New York City cabdrivers at rush hour. Trump Tower foreshadowed the many twisted and bizarre exploits Donald would go on to have.

Let's explore some of the most telling ones.

- In 1983, Trump purchased the New Jersey Generals, a member of the United States Football League. It was a fledgling organization, and the USFL played games in the spring to avoid competing with the NFL, giving fans an additional football fix. However, in typical Trump fashion, he didn't want to wait for the business to grow organically. He wanted the league to play in the fall. He convinced his fellow owners to sue the NFL in a high-stakes, antitrust case. This was only a slightly better decision than wearing corduroy pants in a marathon. Though the jurors found that the NFL was a monopoly, they only awarded the USFL $1 in damages. Four days later, the league went out of business.

- Donald went into the casino business in 1984 when he partnered with the Holiday Inn Corporation to open Harrah's at Trump Plaza. Shortly thereafter, he bought out Holiday Inn and renamed the casino Trump Plaza Hotel and Casino to avoid being a loser. Trump's Castle and the Trump Taj Mahal followed. (Incidentally, it is widely believed that Trump's Castle is also what Donald calls his underwear). Over the years, there were at least 60 lawsuits and 200 liens from contractors who had not been paid as much as $75,000 for the work they did on Trump casinos. It also became clear that Donald was like a child with a shiny new bicycle he didn't know how to ride, crashing his casino business into a metaphorical telephone pole. There were six bankruptcies between 1991 and 2009. In 1991, finances were so bad that Trump stopped paying his personal bills, and several big New York banks had to loan him $60 million to avoid a fire sale of his assets.

- When Fred Trump Sr. died in 1999, Fred Trump Jr.'s lineage was largely cut out of the will. In response, they filed a lawsuit. Meanwhile, Fred Jr.'s son and wife just had a baby who was suffering seizures. In the months ahead, the baby had many complications, and their medical bills ran to nearly a third of a million dollars. Fortunately, Fred Trump Sr.'s company supplied medical coverage to all his children and grandchildren. However, after learning about the lawsuit, Donald arranged for the couple's medical benefits to cease. When a New York Daily news reporter asked Donald Trump about this, he said, "Why should we give him medical coverage?" When the reporter noted that this was colder than a polar bear's nut sack in December, Donald countered with, "I can't help that. It's cold when someone sues my father."

- Donald started Trump University LLC in 2005. It was a for-profit real-estate education company that was supposed to teach the secrets of how to get as wealthy as Monopoly's Rich Uncle Pennybags. Among other things, the literature claimed Donald Trump personally selected the instructors. He did not. In fact, many of the instructors had no previous experience in real estate, while courses cost anywhere from $1,500 to $35,000. Eventually, people realized Trump University was a bigger scam than Nigerian prince emails and fat-free ice cream combined, and lawsuits were filed. Trump was also found personally liable for failing to obtain a business license. In a settlement, Trump forked over $25 million, but did not admit to any wrongdoing. He was still the greatest, in his own mind.

- The Donald J. Trump Foundation was initially established in 1988 to give proceeds from "The Art of the Deal" to charity. It eventually turned into the philanthropic branch of Donald's empire, even though he had not given personally to the charity since 2008. Then in 2016, The Washington Post discovered that Trump spent more than a quarter-million dollars of the foundation's money to settle lawsuits from his for-profit businesses. The Trump Foundation also spent $20,000 to buy a six-foot-tall portrait of The Donald and $12,000 for an autographed Tim Tebow football helmet.

- Donald owned part or all of the Miss Universe, Miss USA and Miss Teen USA beauty pageants from 1996 until 2015. Miss USA contestant Tasha Dixon recounts, "Our first introduction to him was when we were at the dress rehearsal and half-naked changing into our bikini. He just came strolling right in. There was no second to put a robe on or any sort of clothing or anything." She was only 18 years old at the time. Donald corroborated this on the Howard Stern Show saying, "You know, they're standing there with no clothes. Is everybody OK? And you see these incredible-looking women. And so I sort of get away with things like that." He was still the little boy playing peeping Tom in the girl's locker room.

- In 2003, Donald became the executive producer and host of the NBC show, "The Apprentice." He got to be on TV. He had people clamoring for his attention and approval. And he got a star on the Walk of Fame (that was later vandalized). It was a dream come true and validation that the rules do not apply to Donald Trump. Nothing was more telling of this mindset than Trump's 2005 conversation with TV host Billy Bush (George H. W.'s nephew). Donald said, "I'm automatically attracted to beautiful women—I just start kissing them, it's like a magnet. Just kiss. I don't even wait. And when you're a star, they let you do it. You can do anything. Grab 'em by the pussy." Instant gratification at its creepiest. Trump later defended himself saying, "Nobody has more respect for women than me," which is like saying no one treated Muslims better than the guards at Abu Ghraib. In many ways being on "The Apprentice" was what Donald always wanted. Maximum attention, everything revolving around him. Perhaps the only way he could get more attention than the 20.7 million viewers from the show's peak was to become president of the United States.

Trump officially announced his candidacy for president on June 16, 2015, on the grand escalator of Trump Tower, with adoring paid extras in the crowd below. He had flirted with running in the past, but it's been speculated that the 2011 White House Correspondents' dinner was a turning point for his political ambitions. At the dinner comedian, Seth Meyers quipped, "Donald Trump has been saying that he will run for president as a Republican, which is surprising since I just assumed he was running as a joke." Many believe this is when Trump decided to take his candidacy seriously, including The New York Times, which noted, "That evening of public abasement, rather than sending Mr. Trump away, accelerated his ferocious efforts to gain stature within the political world." Donald was still that angry little kid, shaking his fist, defiantly while shouting, "I'll show those stupid losers."

Now perhaps you disagree with this assessment of Trump as an emotionally stunted 1st-grader. Perhaps you believe behind all the bluster and bragging, there is a deeper, more compassionate human being. Tony Schwartz disagrees, insisting. "There isn't. There is no private Trump. All he is is 'stomp, stomp, stomp' — recognition from outside, bigger, more, a whole series of things that go nowhere in particular." New Yorker writer Mark Singer put it more eloquently in a 1997 profile where he described Trump as leading "an existence unmolested by the rumbling of a soul."

But don't take the word of those biased loser liars. Go right to the source, The Donald himself. "When I look at myself in the first grade and I look at myself now," Trump said, "I'm basically the same. The temperament is not that different."

That, ladies and gentlemen, is the man who will have the nuclear codes. That is your 45th president of the United States of America. But we jump ahead.

The Democrats had Bernie and Hillary. So different,

so liked and so disliked. Pundits pronounced that even if Sanders somehow got the nomination, that no how would he win the general election. Others less punditry pointed out that the same thing was said about Barack Obama. Both Sanders and Clinton were long-time pols, but with strikingly different styles, temperaments and agendas.

Bernie and the Boulder

Recall the story of the ancient Greek King Sisyphus who, for his treachery, was punished by the gods to roll an immense boulder up a hill every day, only to have it come tumbling back down. But what if Sisyphus wasn't rolling the boulder because he was being punished? What if he was doing it because he believed the very existence of Greek civilization depended on getting the boulder to the top of the hill? So instead of gloomily going about his task, every morning, he attacks the giant rock with unbridled enthusiasm. You pass him on your way to work, and he looks almost joyful in his toil.

"Hey, Sisyphus how's it going?" you ask when he catches your eye. His face is already beet red from strain, and his wispy white hair blows spastically in the wind.

"It'd be going a lot better if you got off ya butt and helped me with this boulda," he barks in a thick Brooklyn accent, which is weird because you're in ancient Greece and Brooklyn doesn't exist yet.

"Um, maybe later," you tell him. "I'm going to go to work. Pay my electric bill, that sort of thing."

"When," he gasps, "are you going to get it through your thick skull that this boulda needs to get to the top of that hill? No if ands or buts!"

You can't help but admire his singular focus. His head might be even harder than the boulder itself. This incarnation of Sisyphus was born for boulder rolling, and Bernie Sanders was born to roll an entirely different type of boulder. Instead of ancient Greece, his story began in a poor part of Brooklyn on Sept. 8, 1941.

Bernie grew up in the Flatbush section of Brooklyn. It was a working-class neighborhood populated mostly by Irish, Italians and Jews. His family was Jewish and had emigrated from Poland. They were poor. His father sold paint, and Bernie said he was "very conscious as a kid that my father's whole family was killed by Hitler." Forget about finding out there's no Santa Claus, that's a hell of thing to shape your worldview as a kid.

"Dad, don't I have a grandma and grandpa?"

"Well son . . . once upon a time, there was this mass murdering fuckhead . . ."

It's not surprising Bernie took it upon himself to look out for those he perceived as the downtrodden (like impoverished, minorities and New York Mets fans). This was Bernie's boulder right from the start. He even ran for high-school class president, unsuccessfully, on the promise of granting scholarships to Korean refugees.

Bernie graduated from James Madison High School in 1959 and attended Brooklyn College for a year before transferring to the University of Chicago. There he continued to fight for the little guy, joining the Congress of Racial Equality, the Student Nonviolent Coordinating Committee, the Student Peace Union and the Young People's Socialist League. Among his chief exploits were attending the 1963 March on Washington, organizing a sit-in to end segregation in university-owned apartments and helping freshman co-eds get laid.

Yes, in addition to sticking up for African Americans, Bernie wrote a 2,000-word manifesto railing against the administration's impositions on the sexual freedom of students. He concluded the article by saying, "If people cannot have the privacy to do what they think is good, and right, they will do it without privacy. They will do it in motels, in cars, on the Midway, or behind the Chancellor's house, but they will do it." So if you happen to pass behind the chancellor's house at the University of Chicago, take a moment to reflect that Bernie Sanders probably got lucky right where you are standing.

Bernie graduated in 1964 (without honors, because he found the classroom "boring and irrelevant") and married Deborah Schiling. His father had died, leaving him $2,500, and the two used it to buy 85 acres in Vermont. They spent a couple summers living in a sugar shack, the only structure on the property. For clarification, "sugar shack" is not a euphemism for a cozy love nest in the woods. It is literally a shack where maple sap is processed, without electricity or running water. So while Bernie successfully added "a shack in Vermont" alongside "behind the Chancellor's house" on his list of peculiar lovemaking spots, it's not a shock that the couple divorced in the late 1960s.

Bernie spent the next few years bumming around. He bounced between New York and Vermont. He worked as an aide at a psychiatric hospital, which probably helped prepare him for the 2016 campaign. He taught preschoolers for Head Start. He researched property taxation for the Vermont Department of Taxes and registered people for food stamps for a nonprofit. He dabbled in carpentry and freelance journalism. It was a resume that would give a Jewish grandmother fits and make The Dude from "The Big Lebowski" proud (although Bernie wasn't a hippie, as he was "the only person who did not get high in the '60s").

Then, on March 17, 1969, Bernie bought another property in tiny Stannard, Vt. Four days later, his son, Levi Noah Sanders, was born. But what of the mother, you ask? Was she some truck-stop floozy, a free-love hippie who admired Bernie's college writing, or was Levi motherless, springing into existence like Athena directly from Zeus' head? According to Levi's birth certificate, his mother was a woman named Susan Campbell Mott. Bernie lived with Mott in Stannard before moving to Burlington, Vermont's largest city. The two worked out an informal custody arrangement. This is when Bernie's battle with the boulder began in earnest.

It was in Burlington that Bernie discovered Liberty Union. Liberty was a political party that rose out of the anti-war movement, akin to a psychedelic mushroom from a pile of cow excrement. It existed only in Vermont, and the party hoped to capitalize on the influx of uber-liberal voters. Surprisingly, a demographic that is perpetually stoned didn't prove to be the most reliable, and by 1971, Liberty Union was dissolving like a tab of acid on a hippie's tongue. They couldn't even find a candidate to run for the 1972 Senate special election. Not until Sanders, holding his 2-year-old son in his lap, piped up.

"I'll do it," Sanders said. "What do I have to do?'"

It's probably not a good sign when your candidate literally doesn't know the first thing about running for office. Still, Liberty Union was like, "What do we have to lose?" The answer—many, many elections.

Bernie ran on the Liberty Union ticket for the U.S. Senate in a special election and later for governor in 1972. He lost badly both times. Then he ran for the Senate again in 1974 and for governor again in 1976. He never got more than 6 percent of the vote, as the boulder came crashing back after each campaign. But he was tireless in his effort, like a wound-up Scottish Terrier that refuses to let go of its bone. Bernie crisscrossed the state campaigning in a beat-up Volkswagen with no windshield wipers. He showed up at newspapers and demanded to be interviewed. He spoke at rallies and radio shows. He even went doorstep to doorstep. Can you imagine opening your door and being barraged by a young Bernie Sanders with his curly black hair and Buddy Holly glasses?

"The rich are getting richer, and the poor are getting poorer, and the vast majority in the middle are having a harder and harder time!" Bernie's message has been as unflinching as Ann Coulter after a fresh round of Botox.

When Bernie said, "The poor are getting poorer," he might have been talking about himself. Nancy Barnett, one of his neighbors, recalled, "He was living in the back of an old brick building, and when he couldn't pay the electric bill, he would take extension cords and run down to the basement and plug them into the landlord's outlet." Perhaps Bernie's signature rumpled suits and disheveled hair are a product of a non-functional iron and hair dryer. He was eventually evicted. As it turns out, being a "shitty carpenter" only pays the bills when your Tim Allen's character on the sitcom, "Home Improvement." Something had to change.

Bernie left Liberty Union in 1977, and his big break came in 1980 when Richard Sugarman, a friend and religion professor at the University of Vermont, showed Bernie a breakdown of his Liberty Union vote tallies. As a whole, they were less encouraging than a weight-loss speech given by Chris Christie. But Bernie had done much better in Burlington than anywhere else. So, in 1981, he ran as an independent for mayor of Burlington on a hyper-local platform, championing causes like preserving a hill for sledding and pushing to bring a minor-league baseball team to town. He campaigned hardest in the city's poor neighborhoods. No one gave him a chance against five-time Democratic mayor Gordon Paquette. But improbably, Bernie won the election by just 10 votes out of 8,650. The job came with a $33,800-a-year salary. "It's so strange," Bernie told the Associated Press, "just having money."

Bernie's mayoral election caught national attention. He was a self-described socialist in the midst of the Reagan era. He was interviewed by Phil Donahue on NBC. He was on Canadian TV. He was on British TV. He was in The Boston Globe and the San Francisco Chronicle and The Philadelphia Inquirer and The New York Times and Newsweek and The Irish Evening Post.

"Yeah, OK, I'm a socialist," he told The Globe. "We'll charge $10 a head to come see the freak mayor of Burlington." It would have been an innovative way to raise campaign funds. Somehow, Bernie would almost fit standing between Bertha the Bearded Lady and Cornelius the Lizard-man, barking about corruption on Wall Street.

Despite Bernie's freak-show appeal and a city council stacked with Republicans, he was an incredibly effective mayor. Allen Gear, a Republican member of the Board of Aldermen since 1979, said, "He's done things I don't think we Republicans could have done. . . . He's taken a lot of very Republican ideas and put them in place. Such as combining all of the garages of the various city departments and putting them into a single public-works department, initially a Republican proposal, to gain efficiency in handling city rolling stock . . . He's put a lot of modern accounting practices and money-management practices into place that are good Republican business practices . . . And he has surrounded himself with some very talented, vigorous people."

Bernie was re-elected three times, defeating both Democratic and Republican candidates in 1983, 1985 and 1987. But after serving four two-year terms, he chose not to run again in 1989 and set his sights on a congressional seat. He ran unsuccessfully in 1989, but by this point, losing elections didn't faze Bernie. He ran for the seat again and defeated the incumbent, Peter Plympton Smith, by a margin of 56 percent to 39 percent in 1991. Thus making Bernie the first socialist congressman.

Early on, Bernie often alienated both Democrats and Republicans with his criticism of each political party. It's funny how that can happen when someone is berating you in a thick Brooklyn accent for being in cahoots with Wall Street and not looking out for the little guys. He also frustrated both parties with votes against their interests.

For instance, he irked Democrats in 2005 by voting for the Protection of Lawful Commerce in Arms Act. It was supposed to prevent firearms manufacturers from being held liable for negligence when crimes were committed with their weapons. Bernie defended his vote, saying, "If somebody has a gun and it falls into the hands of a murderer and the murderer kills somebody with a gun, do you hold the gun manufacturer responsible? Not any more than you would hold a hammer company responsible if somebody beats somebody over the head with a hammer." Conversely, Republicans weren't happy with Bernie when he vehemently opposed both wars in Iraq. Prior to the 1991 invasion, Bernie said, "We should make no mistake about it, today is a tragic day for humanity, for the people of Iraq, for the people of the United States and for the United Nations as an institution. It is also a tragic day for the future of our planet and for the children, 30,000 of whom in the Third World will starve to death today as we spend billions to wage this war—and 25 percent of whom in our own country live in poverty because we apparently lack the funds to provide them with a minimal standard of living." Even in times of war, Bernie was still pushing that boulder.

On April 21, 2005, Bernie entered the race for the U.S. Senate. Even though he was running as an independent, he received endorsements from Chuck Schumer, chairman of the Democratic Senatorial Campaign Committee; Senate Minority Leader Harry Reid and Democratic National Committee chairman Howard Dean. Even then-Sen. Barack Obama briefly hit the campaign trail for Bernie. He won by an approximately 2-to-1 margin and was re-elected in 2012 with 71 percent of the vote.

So what changed, why were Democrats suddenly taking such a shine to Bernie? For starters, he did vote with them the vast majority of the time. But more importantly, they realized what voters in Vermont had known for years. "Wow, this isn't an act. This guy really, deeply believes what he's saying, and despite his frequent inability to control the volume of his voice . . . We really like him." Polling conducted in August 2011 by Public Policy Polling backs up

Back in happier times. Governor Bush congratulating his protégé after Rubio won the speakership of the Florida House of Representatives (2006).

Governor Chris Christie of New Jersey.

Proving John Kasich has been around politics for a long time. He's on the right, by the way.

Bernie, Jane and Sanders supporters
Berning it up.

Bernie showing, despite losing the nomination,
his fervor had not diminished as he addressed the DNC.

At the DNC in Philadelphia

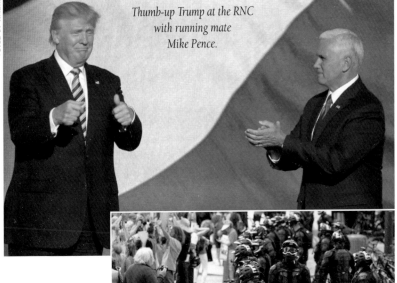

Thumb-up Trump at the RNC with running mate Mike Pence.

GOP Convention Cleveland.

The nominees celebrating at the DNC

Hillary and Donald at the first presidential debate.

Vice President Biden swears in Secretary of State Hillary Rodham Clinton. Joining Secretary Clinton is her husband, former President Bill Clinton, their daughter Chelsea Clinton, and Secretary Clinton's mother Dorothy Rodham.

The Bushies in the early 1960s. Front row, left to right, Neil, Marvin, Jeb. Back row, Doro, George W., Barbara and George H.W.

Chris Christie sure looked like he was BFF with Obama after the president surveyed Hurricane Sandy damage in New Jersey.

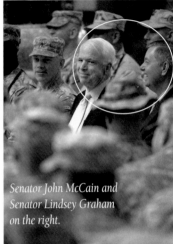

Senator John McCain and Senator Lindsey Graham on the right.

A sex scandal rocked Grover Cleveland's bid for president in 1884 after claims surfaced he had fathered an illegitimate child.

Sen. Elizabeth Warren (D-Mass) got into a fiery tweet war with Trump.

Mike Pence scoping out the Oval Office with its then-occupant, George W. Bush (2007).

At the DNC, former N.Y.C. Mayor Mike Bloomberg called Trump a "dangerous demagogue" and suggested he wasn't sane.

Melania and Trump at a Jets-Patriots game in MetLife Stadium, Nov. 13, 2011. Pats trounced Jets 37-16.

Ivanka's husband, Jared Kushner, Ivanka and Melania were celebrating Trump's New York primary victory, though they don't look like they are celebrating much.

Another Trump supporter.

Santa might want to learn how to spell "elves."

SANTA'S ELVS FOR TRUMP TODAY

A Trump Supporter.

Back in 2010, Tim Kaine having lunch with President Obama in the Oval Office Private Dining Room.

Michelle Obama campaigning for Hillary in Phoenix Oct. 20, 2016.

Michelle Obama's speech at the DNC.

Hillary accepting the nomination in Philadelphia.

Hillary with President Obama.

this sentiment. It found that Sanders' approval rating was 67 percent and his disapproval rating 28 percent, making him then the third-most popular senator in the country. And in a 2015 Morning Consult poll, Sanders had an approval rating of 83 percent among his constituents, making him the most popular senator in the country

Bernie started generating presidential buzz after he delivered a rather lengthy speech against the Tax Relief, Unemployment Insurance Reauthorization, and Job Creation Act of 2010, which was a proposed extension of the Bush-era tax rates. "You can call what I am doing today whatever you want. You can call it a filibuster," he said. "You can call it a very long speech. I'm not here to set any great records, to make a spectacle. I am simply here today to take as long as I can to explain to the American people the fact that we have got to do a lot better than this agreement provides."

He spoke for eight-and-a-half hours straight. The subject matter was familiar, and he concluded with "If the American people stand up and say we can do better than this, that we don't need to drive up the national debt by giving tax breaks to millionaires and billionaires. If the American people stand and we are prepared to follow them, I believe we can defeat this proposal. I believe we can come up with a better proposal that better meets the need of this country, and in particular, the children of this country. I believe we can do that. And with that, ladies and gentlemen, I yield the podium."

Not once did he mention green eggs or ham, showing his lack of understanding of how filibusters work. (Perhaps Ted Cruz can give him some pointers.) The bill passed, and the boulder came crashing back down. But a lot of people, including progressive activists such as Rabbi Michael Lerner and economist David Korten took note, and publicly voiced their support for a Bernie run against Obama in the 2012 presidential election.

It wasn't until April 30, 2015, that Bernie announced his intention to seek the Democratic Party's nomination. His campaign officially launched on May 26, 2015. The rest, as they say, is history. Bernie generated fervent support and an adoration among his constituency usually reserved for boy bands. He even had a group who called themselves "Bernie Sanders' Dank Tinder Convos," independently campaigning for him on the popular dating app, Tinder. It wasn't quite enough. Following the final primary election in the District of Columbia, on June 14, Hillary Clinton became the presumptive Democratic nominee.

The Pant-suited Crusader

Many of the would-be presidents of 2016 were near-cartoon figures. Ted Cruz a Darth Vader in the making. Mike Huckabee a homophobic Mr. Rogers. But Hillary is more nuanced, not so easily cast as hero or villain. Hillary Rodman Clinton is Batman.

The Dark Knight and Hillary are both fiercely committed to helping others. They both adopted austere masks to hide their dual identities. On occasion, they both have walked in what many consider moral gray areas. And finally, like all great heroes or anti-heroes, at their core, they were shaped by their origin stories.

Hillary Diane Rodham was born Oct. 26, 1947, into a seemingly cookie-cutter, middle-class Chicago family. Her father owned a small business that made drapes for ho-

tels, offices and airlines. They lived in the leafy, white, cul-
turally sheltered suburb of Park Ridge. But despite what
looked like a charmed upbringing, there were dark forces
in young Hillary's life — granted, not "having your parents
killed in cold blood in front of you in an alley" dark forces
like Batman, but dark, nonetheless.

The main source of conflict was Hillary's father. To say
he was a difficult man is like saying getting kicked in the
nuts is an undesirable groin adjustment. For reference,
picture a toned-down version of Drill Sergeant Hartman
from the movie, "Full Metal Jacket." Hartman is the character who famously screamed, "Were you born a fat, slimy,
scumbag puke piece o' shit, Private Pyle, or did you have
to work on it?"

Hugh Rodham had, indeed, been a drill sergeant in
World War II. If Hillary or one of her two younger brothers left the toothpaste cap off the tube, he would throw it
outside, even into the snow in the dead of a Chicago win-
ter, and tell them to get down on their hands and knees
and find it. No infraction was too small to avoid a spanking. In grade school, he would wake Hillary at 4 a.m. to review her multiplication tables. When she received an A on
her test, he would say something like, "Well I guess you go
to an easy school." Hugh acted like he was conducting his
own Comedy Central Roast of Hillary's mother, constantly
putting her down and diminishing her. In short, he was a
verbally abusive asshole.

Why didn't Dorothy Rodham tell him to go fuck himself and leave? Religious sensibilities aside, Dorothy had
her own backstory that would make Oliver Twist pee his
adorable little knickers. When Dorothy was 8 years old,
her parents went through a messy divorce. Her father

won the legal battle, but had no interest in the kids. So he shipped off Dorothy and her younger sister alone on a cross-country train to unwelcoming grandparents in California. At 14, Dorothy ran away and found work as a live-in nanny in the midst of the Great Depression. Her takeaway from this Dickensian childhood was that "You do not get divorced. You find a way to make it work."

It wasn't all bad. Hillary's parents taught her many invaluable lessons. From her father, Hillary got her steely reserve and the ability to remain emotionless, military style, in the face of adversity. He taught her a woman could do anything a man could. "He was such a force in the family, and there's a lot of him in Hillary," said former White House press aide Lisa Caputo. "The discipline, the tenacity, the work ethic, a lot of that's from him." Meanwhile, her mother passed on the independent spark that would let a 14-year-old girl set out on her own. She told Hillary, "If the boys knock you down, you get up, dust yourself off, and, and you go back up to bat." And they both made Hillary believe she was destined to do something great.

A piece of Hillary's origin that is often missed is that she is deeply religious. The family was Methodist, and to this day, Hillary still carries a Bible, riddled with underlined passages and notes. The church was a place of solace for Hillary, and it was through a youth minister who took his charges from neat and green Park Hill to inner-city Chicago that her eyes were opened to the world around her.

And so Hillary set off for college with these dual sides of her personality. On the one hand, she was a dedicated student with a track record of overachieving. On the other, she was a drill sergeant's daughter with icy resolve who could curse you like a drunken sailor if she wanted to. And, like most girls with daddy issues, she was a little screwed up when it came to boys. Hillary was already becoming like Bruce Wayne and the Batman.

Hillary arrived at Wellesley College, a tree-shaded and tony enclave in suburban Boston and one of the country's elite women's colleges, in the fall of 1965. A political-science major, she was elected student-government president during her senior year in 1969, and in an attempt to mollify campus protests, she was chosen the first student speaker ever at commencement. No one imagined that she would grab a national spotlight.

Sen. Edward Brooke of Massachusetts was the commencement speaker. He was the first black senator since Reconstruction and a Republican. Hillary, who had been a staunch Republican herself, had worked as a volunteer in his campaign.

"The waves of protests passing over the United States both mirror and create deep social tension," Brooke lectured with all the joie de vivre of a clinically depressed Charlie Brown shortly after losing his Prozac prescription. "In some cases, one finds it extremely difficult, if not totally impossible, to determine which protests are based on just grievances and which are merely exploiting issues for the sake of some ulterior purpose."

Hillary was incensed. She threw out her carefully prepared speech and improvised. This was tantamount to Bruce Wayne turning on his former mentor, Ra's al Ghul and the League of Shadows. (As far as we know, Hillary was not on any mind-altering substances like Bruce, but it was the '60s, so you never know). Though Hillary refrained from burning Wellesley to the ground, this was the moment she became the Batman.

"For too long our leaders have viewed politics as the art of the possible," she told him. "And the challenge now is to practice politics as the art of making what appears to be impossible possible." This became her mantra, akin to Batman's, "It's not who I am underneath, but what I do that defines me." The speech got her ink in Life Magazine.

Hillary enrolled at Yale Law School in 1969. While there, she volunteered for political campaigns, did charity work, assisted in pivotal research studies and many more things that sound important and lofty. But let's be honest, who really cares about that? Yale is also where she met Bill Clinton. The two began dating in 1971, and by all accounts, it was love at first prolonged, awkward stare.

Hillary was in the library when she noticed Bill across the room in a study group, staring at her like a puppy dog eyeing a bag of treats on a counter it can't quite reach. In other words, he was transfixed, and there may have been drool involved. When the awkwardness finally reached critical levels, Hillary went into alpha-mode and walked over to him.

"Well if we're going to stare at each other across the library, we should at least know each other's names," she said. "I'm Hillary Rodham."

After that initial introduction, Bill was smitten. Several days later, he saw Hillary on her way to register for classes and asked if he could accompany her, saying he needed to register, too. They waited together in the long registration line, Bill spitting game like a southern Cyrano de Bergerac. But when they finally made it to the front of the line, a confused registration clerk asked, "Bill, what are you doing here? You registered yesterday."

While there are reports that Hillary had a boyfriend

while she was at Wellesley, let's do some simple mathematics: Drill sergeant father + all-girls college + no makeup and a wardrobe that looked it was selected blindfolded from the floor of Janis Joplin's closet = limited romantic male attention. Bill was likely Hillary's first intense romance. Batman's romances were always dicey, too.

After graduation in 1973, Bill made the first of what would be several marriage proposals to Hillary. He wanted her to come with him to the cultural and political mecca that was Fayetteville, Ark. Hillary declined. She had a job with the high-profile Congressional committee looking into President Richard Nixon and the Watergate break-in. Afterward, she was to go to work for a big-time Washington law firm.

Then the unthinkable (at least for Hillary) happened. She failed the D.C. bar exam, but passed in Arkansas. To put this into context, picture that one girl in high school with her perfectly organized binder, immaculate handwriting and unending questions for the teacher. Now picture her flunking a test, and multiply that by 10,000. Hillary didn't tell anyone about failing the bar and left Washington to be with Bill.

"I took it as a sign," Hillary said many years later. "I chose to follow my heart instead of my head." If only Bill could have followed his heart more instead of his little head, the next few decades would have played out less like the movie, "Indecent Proposal."

After moving to Fayetteville, they taught law at the University of Arkansas. In 1974, Bill made his first run at office, challenging Republican incumbent John Paul Hammerschmidt for his seat in the U.S. House of Representatives. It was a much closer race than anyone expected, but Bill ended up on the losing end. He did, however, manage to have an affair with a student campaign volunteer. Hillary found out and went into a Dark Knightish rage. We can imagine Bill cowering in a poorly lit interrogation room as Hillary slams his head into a table yelling, "WHO IS SHE?" in a gritty voice. Hillary kicked the student out of campaign headquarters and tore into the staffers for letting the affair happen. It's likely Bill said, in the same slow, forlorn drawl he would later use during his impeachment, "I promise . . . it will never happen again."

Hillary must have believed him because the couple married in 1975 after Bill surprised her by buying a house.

In 1978, Bill, at age 32, was elected governor of Arkansas and then two years later was defeated in a re-election bid. Following the loss, the Clintons had to move out of the governor's mansion and into a small apartment. Bill went into a fit of depression, but Batman came to his rescue, as she would many times in the future. Hillary took over managing his political career, and he was re-elected governor in 1982. He held the position for 10 years with Hillary serving as the chief decision-maker in the administration.

By 1982, Hillary had made partner at the Rose Law Firm, the biggest in Arkansas and the third-oldest law firm in the nation. They had their first and only child, Chelsea.

The Clinton dynasty almost came to screeching halt near the end of Bill's governorship. The affairs had not ended with that first student, and Bill, it seems, was attracted to a particular look—rejected extras from a casting call for "The Dukes of Hazzard." Then Bill met a woman named Marilyn Jo Jenkins, with whom he actually fell in love. MJJ was different, a successful businesswoman with an MBA. Reading between the lines, we can infer that she told Bill something like "All those Big Macs are clogging your brainstem if you think I'm going to be your side chick. Pick her or me."

Bill picked Marilyn Jo and asked Hillary for a divorce. Hillary took some time to think about it. She reflected. She prayed. She most likely thought, "Why the fuck did I move to Arkansas to be with this giant, sentient phallus?" In the end, it was likely the voice and experience of her mother and her faith that set her path. "And why do we fall, Master Hillary? So we can learn to pick ourselves up," as Alfred the butler once counseled Bruce Wayne.

She decided that she "had put too much of her own heart and mind and soul into their partnership to abandon it," according to her biographer, Carl Bernstein. She told Bill she would fight to keep the marriage and that they were not getting a divorce. Bill broke it off with MJJ. Many point to Hillary's political aspirations as the reason she stayed. That may be part of it. But Hillary was also the daughter of Dorothy Rodham. With a daughter of her own, she was determined to make it work, even if it meant putting up with Bill and his wandering penis.

For Bill, a man of political passions as great as his sexual ones, the governorship of Arkansas was just a steppingstone to becoming president of the United States. During the 1992 presidential campaign, allegations of a 12-year affair between Bill and Gennifer Flowers surfaced in the supermarket tabloid Star. Gennifer was a mistress of the "Dukes of Hazzard" variety, and the story threatened Bill's candidacy. As a response, the Clintons went on a special edition of "60 Minutes" that aired after the Super Bowl.

"Who was Gennifer Flowers?" Steve Kroft asked. "How would you describe your relationship?" "Very limited," said Bill. Technically, this was true. Only seeing someone a few times a month at a Motel 6 does constitute limited interaction. The pant-suited crusader sprang to action, adding, "You know, I'm not sitting here—some little woman standing by my man like Tammy Wynette. I'm sitting here because I love him, and I respect him." This part was 100 percent true. Bill and Hillary legitimately love each other, but likely more in the way a physicist would love Stephen Hawking. The "60 Minutes" appearance worked. Bill won the election and took office in January 1993.

Now there are two ways to view Hillary's tenure as First Lady. One is as a sweeping tour de force for feminism, where Hillary assumed the largest role of any First Lady in the history of the country. The second is as a highway collision between a sedan and a truck transporting live poultry. That is to say it was a disaster with a lot of broken eggs and angry cocks.

The disaster began when Bill put Hillary in charge of the Task Force on National Health Care Reform. Her mistake, her personality failure, was to rely on her instinct as a lone vigilante. It is an approach that might work in rounding up the Joker's minions, but Congress, which is filled with as many as 535 clowns, is another story. And so when she gave a speech to the members of Congress that very much said, "I'm smarter than all of you, and I will figure this out," she was in trouble. Hillary continued to piss off the established policymakers by holding closed-door meetings and even going so far as keeping under wraps the names of the people working on the new healthcare plan. Only letting a select few into the Batcave is great for keeping your secret identity, but shitty for passing laws. The initiative failed to gather enough support for a floor vote in either the House or Senate even though the Democrats controlled both chambers. The proposal was abandoned in September 1994. The failure became a huge campaign issue in the 1994 election, so much so that Hillary was all, but exiled from the White House's West Wing.

There are also many reports running from aides to Secret Service agents of Hillary being an absolute nightmare to deal with. According to Ronald Kessler, conservative author of "First Family Detail," Secret Service agents "consider being assigned to her detail a form of punishment." How much of this is true is unclear especially when you consider Kessler was known for "National Enquirer-style gossip" filled with "innuendo and secondary sources."

The Clinton presidency essentially ended with the Monica Lewinsky scandal. According to one major Democratic player, Bill Clinton said, "I think that the cry for my resignation is going to be such that I will have to resign before the end of the week." But he didn't resign. Once again, the Bill-Signal was shining brightly in the night sky. Hillary appeared on the "Today Show" and went on the attack, blaming "a vast right wing conspiracy" and portraying Lewinsky as a predatory Harley Quinn. It was a strange dynamic that played out over and over again in Bill and Hillary's relationship. Bill would fuck up, and Hillary would charge in to the rescue. In a masochistic, Dark Knight way, she almost liked it. She and Bill would actually grow closer during those times, and he would show her more affection. And as one of her aides said, "She would much rather play the woman warrior—whether it's against the bimbos, the press, the other party, the other candidate, the right wing. She's happiest when she's fighting, when she has identified the enemy and goes into attack mode."

In 1999, Hillary decided to run for the U.S. Senate seat from New York being relinquished by Daniel Patrick Moynihan. It was a big step for her. Since the Arkansas days, she struggled with having a separate identity from Bill, so much so that initially she had kept her maiden name saying, "It showed that I was still me." She only took the Clinton last name when it appeared that not doing so hurt Bill's gubernatorial re-election effort. This was a chance to do something separate from Bill and in some ways, redeem the tarnished Clinton legacy.

In typical Clinton fashion, Hillary ran a polished, expensive campaign, winning the election on Nov. 7, 2000, with 55 percent of the vote. Hillary's time as a senator was relatively uneventful. She realized she had managed to royally infuriate the majority of Congress as First Lady, so mostly, she just kept her head down. The two things she will be remembered for most as a senator was successfully securing government funding to help rebuild New York after the Sept. 11 attacks and voting for the invasion of Iraq—along with 76 other senators.

After winning a second term, spending $36 million to do it, Hillary shifted gears toward a presidential bid. She announced her candidacy in January 2007, saying, "I'm in, and I'm in to win." Initially, she led all candidates for the Democratic nomination in opinion polls. However, Sen. Barack Obama's sweeping grassroots movement and message of change eventually tipped the primaries in his favor.

On Dec. 1, 2008, President-elect Obama announced that Clinton would be his nominee for secretary of state.

Hillary expected to be a real policymaker who would help shape the Obama administration foreign policy. No dice. She was shut out of the West Wing very early in the presidency. Instead, she became a kind of ambassador-at-large, successfully gaining goodwill around the world for the United States and Obama. Unfortunately for Hillary, she will be remembered most from her time as secretary of state for her email scandal.

Again, as in the case of the healthcare task force, the dark side of being Batman surfaced. The desire to be the lone vigilante, cloaked in secrecy, did her in. Instead of the government email system, Hillary used a private server that was located not in the Batcave, but the basement of her home in Chappaqua, N.Y. Actually maybe that is the Batcave. So instead of using @us.gov, she used @clintonemail.com.

At the time, this was not illegal. Colin Powell had used a similar setup when he served as secretary of state. But hers mixed official and personal emails, and some of the official emails, emails that she ended up forwarding, were eventually changed to classified status. In other words, it was a mess.

Setting up the private server was done out of a desire for secrecy. Anyone who buys Clinton's excuse of "only wanting to carry one phone" should probably never watch The Home Shopping Network or open any emails from Nigeria. You can track this secrecy all the way from early questionable escapades like the Clintons' Whitewater real-estate deals to the closed-door meetings on healthcare reform.

When the scandal broke, you could see her pulling her cowl over her face and her steely eyes staring out. She tried to dismiss it. She tried to joke about it. She downplayed it. She said most of the emails were personal dealing with things like yoga classes. What she didn't do, couldn't bring herself to do, was say, "This was a terrible idea, and I messed up. I will make sure my communications are more transparent in the future." Why couldn't she just own up to it? Because illegal or not, this reflected poorly on her, and Hillary Clinton struggles with the truth in these situations. Even now, there is much of the 26-year-old who couldn't bear to tell anyone that she failed the D.C. bar exam.

By the time Hillary announced she was a candidate for the presidency in the 2016 election, people trusted her less than the Gotham City Police trust Catwoman in a jewelry store. Instead, they elected Donald Trump, because even though he is staggeringly full of shit, at least, he's honest about it. It's a shame. Because she's not the president that America deserves, but in the 2016 election, she's the one it needed.

In some ways, our world is much darker than Gotham City. In our world, Batman was defeated by the Joker.

Chapter Four:
Debate Jabs, Kicks and Knockouts

The primary debates were filled with high comedy, low blows and ridiculous rhetoric. At least on the Republican side. The Dems were remarkably substance- and policy-oriented with little or no name calling. Oh yes, the name calling. The Donald channeled his inner id and turned large sections of the debates into schoolyard dis sessions.

There were nine debates for the Dems, 12 Republican. A 13th got cancelled because the last two standing candidates, Trump and Kasich, declined to attend. The RNC should have asked Clint Eastwood to take the floor with two empty chairs. It worked out so-o-o well when he addressed an empty chair at the RNC 2012 convention. He was talking to an invisible Obama . . . or he was having a stroke. No one is really sure which.

Anyway, here is a recap of the good, bad and ugly of the debates beginning with the Grand Old Party.

Debate One.
Quicken Loans Arena, Cleveland.
Aug. 6, 2015.

It started out simply enough when moderator Bret Baier of Fox News asked for a show of hands, simple yes or no, will you pledge to support whomever gets the nomination and not run as an independent? (Trump had threatened to do just that if he wasn't the anointed one.) Up went the yes hands. One, two, three . . . nine. Nine? That was one short. After a little back and forth, Trump took what should have been a one-word answer and stretched it to a tortuous 83.

"I cannot say [he would support the nominee]. I have to respect the person that, if it's not me, the person that wins, if I do win, and I'm leading by quite a bit, that's what I want to do. I can totally make that pledge. If I'm the nominee, I will pledge I will not run as an independent. But—and I am discussing it with everybody, but I'm, you know, talking about a lot of leverage. We want to win, and we will win. But I want to win as the Republican. I want to run as the Republican nominee."

SOURCE: DONKEYHOTEY, DONKEYHOTEY.WORDPRESS.COM

And so began Trump's mic hogging and gibberish. If he does get the party nod, he wouldn't run as an independent. Huh? That's like saying if someone receives a shipment of Trump-brand steaks, they're not going to go to the butcher store afterward. OK, maybe that's a bad example, being almost all reviews on the steaks read something like "Trump steaks are way too greasy and tasteless." At least, the product reflects the owner.

The debate meandered around Marco Rubio's finances and Jeb Bush not being a daddy, mommy or brother boy. Then it got to co-moderator Megyn Kelly bringing up a touchy Trump question. That being the unfortunate downside of speaking his "mind" about women.

"You've called women you don't like 'fat pigs, dogs, slobs, and disgusting animals.'"

Oh no, demurred the champion of women, only actress and comedian Rosie O'Donnell. No, no said Kelly, he had tweeted disparaging remarks about how women look and telling an "Apprentice" contestant it would be nice to see her on her knees. In his defense, Trump could have simply been encouraging her to take up yoga so he could teach her his favorite pose, "The Downward Douchebag."

The debate continued on the budget, abortion, ISIS. What might be considered important issues. The Great Wall of Trump came up, which The Donald used to go after Jeb Bush. The third moderator, Chris Wallace, asked Trump if he had evidence that the Mexican government was dumping criminals across the border into the U.S. Please, Donald had talked with border-patrol types, and they told him that was what was happening. ". . . our leaders are stupid. Our politicians are stupid. And the Mexican government is much smarter, much sharper, much more cunning." Forget that Rubio tried to "clear the record . . . that the majority of people coming across the border are not from Mexico. They're coming from Guatemala, El Salvador, Honduras."

Take a guess. What were the debate's headlines? You won if you said Trump's attack on Megyn Kelly for her questioning his misogyny. "There was blood coming out of her eyes, blood coming out of her wherever." It's as if Trump had forgotten the entire point of the exchange was to establish whether he's a misogynist. Kelly might as well have asked, "Mr. Trump can you comment on your excessive swearing?" with Donald responding, "I sure as shit do not fucking swear excessively, and you're an ass-punching thundercunt for even suggesting it." After being roundly criticized, Trump backpedaled and said he was referring to her nose when he said "wherever." Kelly much later revealed Trump had been given her question beforehand. Maybe he didn't have time to read it.

Debate Two.
The Reagan Library.
Sept. 16, 2015.

Eleven candidates took the main stage. Carly Fiorina's strong showing in the Debate One undercard pulled her polling numbers up enough to rate the honor. Her departure from the kiddy table added to the number of those in the early-hour debate dropping from seven to four as Rick Perry bowed out. Maybe he wanted to start practicing bows for his appearance on "Dancing with the Stars" the following year. (No, that is not a joke. He lasted three weeks after introducing himself as the governor of

Texas. Realizing his gaffe, he corrected that to "former" governor.) Jim Gilmore hadn't managed to poll 1 percent, thus got left off even the undercard. His numbers improved, and he did make it to the seventh go-round on Jan 28, the last one with a kiddy table. You got to hand it to the guy. He was an optimist, hanging in until Feb. 12, when he pulled the plug on his less-than-stellar performance.

Scott Walker got off to an early two-for-one zinger aimed at Trump and Obama. "We don't need an apprentice in the White House. We have one there right now."

Chris Christie treated the viewers to how many bills he vetoed. Donald reminded people that he didn't declare personal bankruptcy. He also said he never attacked Rand Paul's looks, even though there was "plenty of subject matter right there." Remember Carly Fiorina was on the stage, the very same Carly Fiorina about whom Trump said, "Look at that face! Would anyone vote for that? Can you imagine that, the face of our next president." In this Rolling Stone interview, Trump added, "I mean, she's a woman, and I'm not s'posed ta say bad things, but really, folks, come on. Are we serious?" This coming from a man who looks a giant Cheeto with a post-coital cat perching on top of it.

On the debate stage, Trump suddenly found Carly's face "beautiful." Carly didn't crack a smile, clearly indicating The Donald shouldn't expect an invitation to Thanksgiving dinner at her place.

Jeb Bush tried to counter his "I'm self-funding" opponent's attacks that the Florida governor was a donor puppet. "The one guy that had some special interests that I know of that tried to get me to change my views on something — that was generous and gave me money — was Donald Trump. He wanted casino gambling in Florida." And the Trumpmeister's response? No, no, didn't happen. And if he had wanted to get casino gambling in the state, he would have.

Then came a long Trump pause as the others talked about Putin and Kurds and serious stuff.

Mike Huckabee managed camera time as he defended the Kentucky county clerk who blatantly defied the law by not allowing same-sex marriages. His take was she was being persecuted as part of the criminalization of Christianity. Mike didn't seem to understand the concept of forcing your religious beliefs on others.

On and on. Ted Cruz would veto any budget that included funds for Planned Parenthood. Carly claimed to have seen a video that didn't exist. "I dare Hillary Clinton, Barack Obama to watch these tapes. Watch a fully formed fetus on the table, its heart beating, its legs kicking while someone says we have to keep it alive to harvest its brain." There is no such video, period, but we learned Carly needs to stay away from LSD and the movie, "Alien."

Then there was the question of speaking Spanish on the campaign trail. Trump had questioned Bush's immigration stance because Jeb's wife is of Hispanic heritage. It degenerated into Trump declaring, "This is a country where we speak English, not Spanish." And Rubio going on about his Cuban grandfather before getting to his sort of point that "I do give interviews in Spanish, and here's why — because I believe that free enterprise and limited government is the best way to help people who are trying to achieve upward mobility. And if they get their news in

Spanish, I want them to hear that directly from me. Not from a translator at Univision."

And the end of the night, some commentators gave the winner's cup to Fiorina. One wrote, "(She) successfully challenged Trump — criticizing his wisecracks about her personal appearance and challenging his credentials as a global businessman by deftly ticking off hotspots around the world and suggesting ways she would tackle them."

Marco got high marks. Trump not so much.

Debate Three.
The University of Colorado.
Oct. 28, 2015.

The Republicans bravely marched into The People's Republic of Boulder, still a strong liberal bastion, even though you have to be a rich liberal to live there. No Scott Walker. He had turned out the lights in campaign offices the month before.

A dopey opening question that sounded like it belonged in a Miss Universe contest — what is your greatest weakness? — elicited some howlers in response.

Mike Huckabee: "I don't really have any weaknesses that I can think of. But my wife is down here in the front, and I'm sure, if you'd like to talk to her later, she can give you more than you'll ever be able to take care of." Apparently, Huckabee's weakness is insipid, bad jokes.

Jeb Bush: "I can't fake anger." And don't forget he's also impatient.

Carly Fiorina: "Well, gee, after the last debate, I was told that I didn't smile enough."

And the best of all? Donald Trump: "I think maybe my greatest weakness is that I trust people too much. I'm too trusting." Now lest his supporters interpret this as his being a wimp, he followed up with "And when they let me down, if they let me down, I never forgive. I find it very, very hard to forgive people that deceived me."

When it got to taxes and the deficit, all kinds of numbers were thrown around. Moderator John Harwood of CNBC probably earned a permanent spot on Trump's shit list by first asking him if he was running a "comic-book version of a presidential campaign." The Great Pouter was not amused. "No, not a comic book, and it's not a very nicely asked question the way you say that." If it was a comic book, and Trump was the cover hero, it would undoubtedly be an orange version of "The Incredible Hulk," who needs to hear ego-stroking compliments to transform back from his rage. Harwood kept pressing on how much Trump's tax plan would add to the deficit. It wasn't pretty. Yet, Trump, uncharacteristically, stayed fairly cool.

Marco Rubio made it clear that no matter how much Jeb Bush and family had mentored and helped his political career, all bets were off. Jeb brought Rubio's sorry record of not showing up for Senate votes, asking if he was working on a French workweek. (An aside. The French work five days a week. However, they, lucky people, get five weeks of paid vacation.) Rubio slammed back with "I don't remember you ever complaining about John McCain's vote record. The only reason why you're doing it now is because we're running for the same position, and someone has convinced you that attacking me is going to help you." That symbolic sword Jeb had given Rubio was now being used to stab Bush in the back or maybe more accurately, the groin.

One thing the candidates agreed on was their dislike of

the moderators. Ted Cruz took the opportunity to lash out at all media, though he surely didn't mean Fox News and Breitbart. "The questions that have been asked so far in this debate illustrate why the American people don't trust the media. This is not a cage match." Oh, and the questioners had been so-o-o "fawning" at the Dem debate. He even managed to get in a reference to Colorado brownies.

Debate Four.
Milwaukee Theatre.
Nov. 10, 2015.

At this point, Trump and Carson were leading in the polls, something that must have confounded Bush supporters. The guy had the Super PACs, the family name, a solid performance as governor (as long as you overlooked the healthy economic numbers came on the back of the housing bubble—which burst after he left office).

This debate leaned more toward economic policies than personalities, though there were scuffles, to be sure.

Right out of the gate, Trump proclaimed he was against raising the minimum wage to $10 an hour. He explained, as only he could, that the U.S. isn't winning anymore because "taxes [are] too high, wages too high, we're not going to be able to compete against the world. I hate to say it, but we have to leave [the minimum wage] the way it is. People have to go out, they have to work really hard and have to get into that upper stratum." This is the Trump talking who had a massive trust fund since the day he was born. The hypocrisy in this statement is so colossal and thick that you could mix it with water, fire it in a kiln and use the resulting bricks to build a 1,000-mile wall you'd have no other way to pay for.

Carson was a no to a wage raise, too. Rubio went off on a favorite tangent about his father being a bartender and mother a maid. He somehow managed to steer the issue of wages to getting rid of Obamacare and making "higher education faster and easier to access, especially vocational training." Which led to one of his memorable, if inaccurate, riffs. "Welders make more money than philosophers. We need more welders and less philosophers." Forget that grammatically it should be "fewer" philosophers, fact-checkers pounced on it. It turns out that according to the Bureau of Labor Statistics, the median wage of welders is $37,420 and $63,630 for philosophy teachers. On the upside, these debates answered an age-old philosophical question. If a politician lies in a public forum and everybody hears it, does it make them unsound as a candidate? Apparently not.

As for balancing the budget, John Kasich would step on toes and reduce the growth of Medicare. (He's an innovator.) Economic growth? Ted Cruz would institute a flat tax of 10 percent for every American that, he said, would produce "booming growth and 4.9 million new jobs within a decade." Four point nine, mind you. Not 4.85 or 5.2. Four point nine.

When Kasich tried to horn into Bush's time, Jeb tried to show some moxie. "I got about four minutes in the last debate. I'm going to get my question right now." The question got him going on his promise to get the economy growing at 4 percent. Something that might be possible, but not probable. Even in the Clinton dot-com bonanza years, growth only hit 3.8. And because more businesses were closing than starting up—a "fact" Rubio cited in Debate Three—get rid of all those nasty Obama regulations.

Why the quotes around "fact"? The statement was based on out-of-date data. For two years, the opposite had been true—more open-ups than closed-downs.

Fiorina talked of her grand plan of reducing the tax code from 504 pages to three, thereby saving a lot of trees—see, she's an environmentalist. Cruz chimed in saying, "There are more words in the IRS code than there are in the Bible—and not a one of them is as good."

Predictably, Trump railed about immigrants in the country illegally hurting the economy, and he would build that beautiful wall. When pressed about whether deporting millions might, instead, cause harm, he replied, "We're a country of laws. We either have a country or we don't have a country. . . . Going to have to go out, and they will come back, but they are going to have to go out and hopefully they get back. But we have no choice if we're going to run our country properly and if we're going to be a country." This does not sound like immigration policy. This sounded like a sympathetic bouncer who just kicked a couple of underage kids out of a nightclub. "You're going to have to go out, hopefully, you get back." Ted's two cents was that these immigrants were pushing down wages and that the media would cover the issue differently if the undocumenteds were seeking jobs in journalism, as if they would in a collapsing industry. "Then we would see stories about the economic calamity that is befalling our nation," he said.

Rand Paul blamed income inequality on the Federal Reserve, but came off pretty well trying to explain his Libertarian philosophy on foreign policy. Rubio begged to differ, calling his opponent an "isolationist." The New York Times felt Rubio gave a "sharp," performance though probably too late to do any good.

Bush got in a good one during his closing, saying the country didn't need "an agitator-in-chief or a divider-in-chief." To whom do you think he was referring? Rubio gave his website address, and Trump took a dig at him with "I don't have to give you a website because I'm self-funding my campaign. I'm putting up my own money." Self-funding if you didn't count the reported four million in donations during the third-quarter of 2015.

On to . . .

Debate Five.
Fabulous Las Vegas.
Dec. 15, 2015.

Same list of usual suspects, Trump, Carson, Rubio, Cruz, Bush, Kasich, Fiorina, Paul—plus one, Chris Christie, who had risen in the polls high enough to join the big guys and one gal.

Going into the debate that was to focus on defense and foreign policy, Trump was leading in the polls with Cruz looking strong in Iowa, having won some key endorsements. Rubio was trying to stay relevant, and Carson had lost a lot of his luster.

Where to begin? Ted Cruz would carpet bomb ISIS bad guys without killing civilians. Christie would shoot down Russian jets over Syria—an action that could lead to World War III. Rubio and Bush decried the decimation of military funding, overlooking the fact that the U.S. spends twice as much as its enemies combined. Trump didn't have a clue as to how nuclear bombs are delivered, you know, the nuclear triad of plane, missile and submarine. It's bad enough when your senile grandpa is in charge of the remote control.

Since the Iowa caucuses were getting closer, the candidates took the opportunity to go tooth and pile driver at each other.

Bush called Trump a chaos candidate, strong words for Jeb. Oh yeah, came back Trump, "Jeb doesn't really believe I'm unhinged. He said that very simply because he has failed in this campaign. It's been a total disaster. Nobody cares." Then in case anyone had forgotten, Trump said he built a "tremendous" company. And when asked how intentionally killing terrorist families would set us apart from ISIS, Trump responded, "We have to be much tougher. We have to be much stronger than we've been." He would be "very, very firm with families. Frankly, that will make people think because they may not care much about their lives, but they do care, believe it or not, about their families' lives." This was one of the most truly terrifying statements in the debates. In addition to violating a host of international laws, it sounded very familiar to another outsider politician. He once echoed Trump's sentiments, saying that, "A single blow must destroy the enemy . . . without regard of losses . . . a gigantic all-destroying blow." That outsider was Adolf Hitler. Being "very, very firm with families" is the signpost at the top of a slippery slope that ends with "We're going to kill all the brown people."

Lots of argument about NSA surveillance. Fiorina vaguely claimed to have helped the agency after 9/11 while running HP.

The bottom line was the true villain was Barack Obama for not keeping the country safe. For goodness sake, he refused to use the term "radical Islamic terrorism." What more proof do you need?

Winners? Some felt Trump and Cruz, only because

they didn't skewer each other. Few felt that would last since Cruz was becoming a stronger opponent. Loser? Ben Who. He had dropped in polling because he didn't show much understanding of foreign policy. That was only strengthened by this night's non-performance. When he did talk, his voice sounded like it was putting his face to sleep. And then there those discrepancies in his bio. He really stabbed someone and then had an epiphany to become Gentle Ben?

Debate 6.
North Charleston (South Carolina) Coliseum.
Jan. 14, 2016.

(Rand Paul was relegated to the undercard and declined to participate.)

Ahh, Six was a slugfest between Ted Cruz and Donald Trump, with Marco Rubio getting some jabs in at Cruz.

The fight started over Trump and his assertions that Cruz was ineligible to be president because he was born in *Canada*. Trump had never given up his birther fight against Obama, perhaps believing Hawaii was actually part of Kenya and not the 50th state. This had Cruz giving a lecture on how someone could be born off American soil and still qualify. Look at John McCain, giving his first peep in Panama where his father was stationed. And what about George Romney, born overseas to American missionary parents? Trump did his best bristle when Cruz suggested that by The Donald's reasoning, the business guy wasn't an American citizen because Mama Trump was born in Scotland.

Did Trump bring up the birther business, moderator Neil Cavuto wanted to know because perhaps, maybe, because Ted was ahead of him in the Iowa polls? Does the Terminator have a sheet-metal cock? The answer is no because like the birther conspiracy, the Terminator is a work of fiction. Trump used birther claims the same way all conspiracy theorists do—to distract from the truth. "I'm broke and living in my mom's basement because the Illuminati is in control of all government and industry, not because I spend 19 hours a day playing 'Call of Duty' and searching for Japanese anime porn."

After a bit of blathering, Trump claimed he was trying to save the party from a suit by the Dems over Cruz' eligibility. Why, a lot of constitutional lawyers say the Canadian Texan can't run. To which Ted pulled his "I'm a Harvard Law School graduate who everyone hated" card. He would not take legal advice from the billionaire, not when he, Cruz, had argued before the Supreme Court.

They were like two fighters jawing at each other before weigh-in. "I don't get angry often. But you mess with my wife, you mess with my kids, that'll do it every time. Donald, you're a sniveling coward!" Marco Rubio saw it more like an episode of "Court TV."

Cruz later went after Trump for his "New York values." Not a good move since that gave the lifelong New Yorker (except for all the time he spends at Mar-a-Lago in Florida and golf courses here and there) a great rebuttal. "When the World Trade Center came down, I saw something that no place on earth could have handled more beautifully, more humanely, than New York. That was a very insulting statement that Ted made." Not that Darth Ted had a snowball's chance in his Southern Baptist hell of winning that state had he captured the nomination.

There was a lot of back and forth on tax plans—vat, flat, reduced rates. Leave it to Ben Carson to come up with one of his "say whats?" His mother "would drive a car until it wouldn't make a sound, and then gather up all her coins and buy a new car. In fact, if my mother were secretary of treasury, we would not be in a deficit situation." Let's set aside the fact that the secretary of treasury has little to do with the deficit. What was Carson even trying to say with that metaphor? If his mother was driving the vehicle that is the federal government, she would just ride it until it died, then get a new one? Someone needs to tell Carson that you can't find "Federal Governments" in the "For Sale" section of craigslist.

Rubio, trying to show he could be as tough as the big guys, went after Cruz especially on immigration. "Ted Cruz, you used to say you supported doubling the number of green cards. Now you say that you're against it. You used to support a 500-percent increase in the number of guest workers, now you say that you're against it. You used to support legalizing people that were here illegally, now you say you're against it. You used to say that you were in favor of birthright citizenship, now you say that you are against it." Yes Marco, if you're going to stay in politics, you need to get used to people being hypocritical.

And what about Cruz saying he would abolish the IRS? Rubio would have none of that. "You may rename the IRS, but you're not going to abolish the IRS, because there has to be some agency that's going to collect your VAT tax." Abolish . . . rename . . . like Shakespeare said, "What's in a name? That which we call the IRS by any other name would still be a giant pain in the ass."

Debate Seven.
Iowa Events Center.
Jan. 28, 2016.

You know what? We're not going to highlight much of Seven. If Donald Trump could skip it, so can we.

Trump the Courageous was outraged that he would be questioned by that blood-spewing Megyn Kelly again. He took his ratings to his very own rally to raise money for vets. Ah yes, money for vets. The Donald, who felt attending a high-school military academy was the equivalent of serving in the armed forces, claimed to have raised $6 million, $1 million of which came from his pocket. Of course, Trump never actually donated the $1 million, at least not right away. It took four months and a Washington Post story before that million was wrenched from his wallet. When a Post reporter asked if Trump had only made the donation because the media was asking about it, Trump responded, "You know, you're a nasty guy. You're really a nasty guy."

Before moving on to Debate Eight, Cruz did a masterful imitation of his closest rival. "I'm a maniac, and everyone on this stage is stupid, fat and ugly. And Ben, you're a terrible surgeon. Now that we've gotten the Donald Trump portion out of the way . . ." It's good to know that if, heaven forbid, Trump chokes on one of his "tasteless and greasy" steaks, we've got a Trump clone ready to go.

Debate Eight.
Saint Anselm College (New Hampshire).
Feb. 6, 2016.

Marco Rubio learned a tough political lesson. Start to surge and you will be attacked.

Rubio came in third in the Feb. 1 Iowa caucus with 23.1 percent of the vote behind Ted Cruz' 27.6 and Trump's 24.3. The rest of the field had pretty miserable showings. Carly Fiorina was in a snit because her barely measuring on the Richter scale 1.9 was still better than Kasich and Christie. Yet, she wasn't invited to the debate. She was like a 15-year-old girl, angry she didn't get an invite to the Spring Fling dance. "I wouldn't have gone anyway, but it *would* have been nice to be asked!" She pulled out four days later.

With New Hampshire looming, it behooved all the candidates on the stage to make a strong showing. Not a good time to stumble. Not a good time to be Marco Rubio. He and Christie got down and dirty when the governor questioned the first-term senator's experience, suggesting the country would be better off without a novice senator in the White House again. And that's when it got bizarre. In his response, Rubio worked in "Let's dispel with this fiction that Barack Obama doesn't know what he's doing. He knows exactly what he's doing. He is trying to change this country. . . . when I'm elected president, this will become once again, the single greatest nation in the history of the world."

Christie was having none of Rubio's "memorized 25-second speech." And then, seconds later, Rubio used the "Obama knows exactly what he's doing" line again and again and again. No wonder he picked up the nickname "Robo Marco," who was "cringe worthy," "badly programmed and robotic," "so rehearsed he comes off as inauthentic" and "exposed at last for the wind-up doll he is." If Rubio is a robot, his AI was probably upgraded from the ALGORE-2000 model, which allows him to appear slightly more lifelike and human.

Christie continued to pile on, again going after Rubio's less-than-perfect Senate attendance record for votes. "That's not leadership. That's truancy." Ouch again.

Jeb polled sixth in Iowa, better than Christie, and was the only one to go after Trump. The businessman defended the use of eminent domain, which he had taken full advantage of to get property from owners who didn't want to sell. Bush called The Big Builder "downright wrong" for trotting out eminent domain to seize lots for an Atlantic City casino. "The difference between eminent domain for public purpose—as Donald said, roads and infrastructure, pipelines and all that—that's for public purpose. But what Donald Trump did was use eminent domain to try to take the property of an elderly woman on the strip in Atlantic City. That is not public purpose. That is downright wrong." However, this does dispel the myth that Trump only screws younger women.

Oh, now Jeb wants to talk tough? Donald scoffed. Trump said he had walked away from the property a woman in her 70s had owned for 37 years, which would have been turned into limousine parking lot. Bush correctly pointed out that Trump walked away only after he lost in court. "How tough it is to take away property from an elderly woman?" The fact that they were even debating this is kind of horrifying in of itself. On the villain scale, stealing an old woman's house is right behind poisoning apples and killing kittens. But at this point, would anyone have been shocked if Trump kitten-killing allegations surfaced? You can easily picture him saying, "Look, some people prefer caviar, I like kittens. When you're extremely rich like I am, you can kind of get away with these sorts of things."

It was felt that the big loser of the night was Rubio, followed by Carson.

Debate Nine.
Peace Center, Greenville, S.C.
Feb. 13, 2016.

The New Hampshire primary had come and gone and the winner was: Donald Trump. Next up was the important South Carolina primary in seven days, hence the choice of The Peace Center. If people thought earlier debates had been contentious, they hadn't seen nuthin' yet, which would have made Philadelphia's First Union Center (FU Center for short) a more appropriate choice for Nine.

Because of the recent death of Justice Antonin Scalia, the Supreme Court took over center stage initially. Only Jeb Bush argued that Obama should nominate a new jurist. Nope, nope, nope, said the other five. "It's up to Mitch McConnell and everybody else to stop it," Donald Trump said. "It's called delay, delay, delay." Unfortunately for this position, Trump's delay tactic in dealing with his numerous fraud trials is not applicable to the Constitution.

Despite that, Trump's conservative credentials were called into question. Trump would nominate (shudder) *liberal* justices. And how did Cruz know? Because Trump had contributed to John Kerry, Hillary Clinton, Chuck Schumer and Harry Reid. And he had supported Jimmy Carter.

This did not sit well with Trump. As Frank Bruni of The New York Times described it, "Trump tried to talk over him, his face going from ruby to crimson, then crimson practically to magenta. Crayola doesn't have as many shades of red as Trump's cheeks and jowls."

Nor was he happy when Cruz tut-tutted him for breaking in and talking over. "Adults learn not to interrupt people." "Yeah, yeah, I know, you're an adult," Donald responded. As it has been well documented here, Donald is not an adult, but rather that sullen 1st-grader, and he continued to jump in whenever he felt like it.

If you want to talk about unhappy, look no further than Jeb Bush. He was big-time annoyed that Trump was going after George W. for being asleep at the switch before 9/11 and invading Iraq. Bush didn't like that from a trust-fund baby who beat the draft with student deferments and said John McCain wasn't a war hero. Nor did the former governor think much of Trump's attitude toward women and minorities. But Trump went way too far when he disparaged Barbara Bush. "Wow, Jeb Bush, whose campaign is a total disaster, had to bring in mommy to take a slap at me. Not nice!" Jeb countered with "I won the lottery when I was born 63 years ago, looked up and I saw my mom. My mom is the strongest woman I know." The Donald, who isn't known for restraint, retorted with "She should be running."

Marco may have sighed in relief that he wouldn't have to face Attack Dog Christie, who had transformed into Lap Dog Chrissy endorsing Trump, the guy he once called unsuited to be president. However, Ted Cruz was still on the stage. Rubio called him out on lies. Cruz brought up the "Rubio-Schumer amnesty plan," with the intimation that the boy from Florida was a closet liberal. "Marco went on Univision in Spanish and said he would not rescind President Obama's illegal executive amnesty on his first day in office." That got a rise out of Rubio, who wanted to know how Cruz knew what he said since the Canadian didn't speak Spanish.

All very entertaining as long as you could stay awake through the "my tax plan is better than your tax plan." In the end, Rubio was put in the Winners column for not sounding like a mechanical man. Bush did well, but not in time to further his cause.

Trump, on the other hand, did not do well. As Chris Cillizza of The Washington Post put it, "Trump, who often comes across as tough yet good-natured, came across on Saturday night as downright mean in several exchanges with Bush and Cruz. (And, as any politician will tell you, it's tough to make Cruz into an empathetic figure.)" In a way, it was almost impressive Trump could produce sympathy for Cruz, who even Ann Coulter described as a "sleazy, Rovian liar." That quote by Coulter is like Cruella de Vil admonishing someone for animal cruelty.

Debate 10 (would this never end?).
University of Houston.
Feb. 25, 2016.

And then there were five (though for a lot of the debate, it seemed like three). Even though Bush polled higher (7.8 percent) than John Kasich (7.6) and Ben Carson (7.2), his tango dance was over.

Rubio had fun swinging at Trump's hiring illegal Polish workers, with Trump, naturally, denying it and finally telling Rubio to be quiet. Curiously, the billionaire harped on his having hired tens of thousands of people. In typical Trump fashion, it was a complete breakdown in logic. Just because you hired people (and then in many cases didn't pay them) doesn't mean you will be able to handle a complex, often unpredictable system like the economy. It's not as if paying $10,000 for snow machines and $300 for Cuba

Gooding Jr. (because Ivanka wanted a Snow Dogs-themed sweet sixteen party) means you can control the weather.

Rubio wasn't done. In the healthcare segment, Trump said his solution was to sell insurance across state lines, something he said again and again when Rubio pressed him about his plan. Rubio jumped on him. "Now he's repeating himself." Trump countered with Rubio having repeated himself five times in one debate. Rubio came back with "I just watched you repeat yourself five times five seconds ago." Why let up when you're on a roll? "I see him repeat himself every night, he says five things, every one's dumb, he's gonna make America great again . . . We're going to win, win, win, he's winning in the polls." He brought up the bogus Trump University and said without Fred Trump's money, Donald would be selling watches. This reduced scion to quibbling over whether he got an inheritance or took a loan.

As long as Rubio was having so much fun, Cruz stepped into the fray. He questioned his opponent's immigration credentials. "I really find it amazing that Donald believes that he is the one who discovered the issue of illegal immigration. I can tell you, when I ran for Senate here in the state of Texas, I ran promising to lead the fight against amnesty, promising to fight to build a wall. And in 2013, when I was fighting against the 'gang of eight' amnesty bill, where was Donald? He was firing Dennis Rodman on 'Celebrity Apprentice.'" To be fair, if anyone needs to be deported from the United States, it's Dennis Rodman.

Were viewers hoping for yelling? They got it when Cruz had the effrontery of pointing out Trump had a history of contributing to Democrats. Wait a darn second. Trump had contributed to Cruz, and he had a signed book to prove it.

Poor Ben Carson, if only someone would attack him.

Winner: Rubio

Loser: Trump. It didn't help him when he said he couldn't release his tax returns because he was being audited, a statement that continued to haunt him throughout the campaign.

Debate Eleven.
Fox Theatre, Detroit.
March 3, 2016.

This debate was prefaced by Mitt Romney's extraordinary attack on Trump earlier in the day, going after him on many fronts. Economic policies? Trump's economic policies would lead to a long-lasting recession, Romney blasted. "Isn't he a huge business success and doesn't he know what he's talking about?" he asked mockingly. "No, he isn't, and no he doesn't."

"He inherited his business. He didn't create it," Romney said. "And what ever happened to Trump Airlines? How about Trump University? And then there's Trump Magazine and Trump Vodka and Trump Steaks and Trump Mortgage? A business genius he is not."

As if that weren't enough body-slamming, Romney called Trump "a phony" and "a fraud" who is "playing the American public for suckers. . . . His promises are as worthless as a degree from Trump University." You get the drift. Who knew Romney had it in him? Trump dismissed the former governor with—what else?—he's a loser.

As for the debate, Ben finally woke up and declined to attend. It was down to Trump, Cruz, Rubio and bless his unrealistic heart, John Kasich. It was do-or-die time, though death already seemed certain for Donald's opponents.

Undeterred, Rubio and Cruz attacked. And yes, this was the infamous penis powwow.

It was also the debate where Fox News, for whatever reason—but it was so much fun they did—decided to do instant, on-camera fact-checks. And guess whose facts didn't check. When asked by Chris Wallace to be specific about cutting the deficit, Trump said he would eliminate the Department of Education and Environmental Protection Agency. Bing. Bing. Bing. Fact-check thrown up on the screen showed that would only amount to a paltry $86 billion. The deficit is $544 billion. Getting rid of Education and the EPA wouldn't make a dent in the deficit. It would barely register a highway-pebble ding.

Quickly switching gears, Trump pulled out his old saw about how much Medicare would save by negotiating drug prices. He was talking $300 million a year. Bing. Bing. Bing. Medicare only spends $78 million on drugs annually. Well, what Trump really *meant* was saving tons by negotiating lots and lots of things.

Later, Megyn Kelly played clips of Trump's wandering positions. Was the war in Afghanistan a mistake? A terrible mistake. No, I never said that. How about accepting Syrian refugees? For humanitarian reasons, you have to. Of course, Trump later changed his mind. Those refugees could be a Trojan horse for terrorists. George W. Bush was a big fat liar about invading Iraq. Cue the tape. "I don't know if he lied or not. He could have lied. Maybe he did. Maybe he didn't. I guess you'd have to ask him."

While as entertaining as all this was, the real fun came

with the Rubio-Cruz pile on of Trump. "Wake up, wake up," Rubio and Cruz seemed to admonish Republicans. Perhaps the more accurate call to arms would have been, "Sober up, sober up."

So finally, in the 11th go-round, Trump gets a full-frontal attack. (Sorry, no penis allusion intended.)

Rubio had brought up The Donald's small hands, something that editor Graydon Carter mentioned years before. In case you don't know, teeny hands are supposed to indicate small genitalia. Well, Donald would have none of that. "And he referred to my hands, if they are small, something else must be small. I guarantee you there is no problem. I guarantee." If Hillary Clinton was trying to break through the glass ceiling in politics, it appeared Trump was trying to break through the concrete floor. "Mr. Trump, this is the basement of an underground missile silo, we promise you can't get any lower." You must remember that Trump called the celebrity-gossip show, TMZ, crowing that feminist lawyer Gloria Allred would be impressed with his penis if she saw it. And yet somehow, he jack-hammered further into a sub-basement.

Rubio also hit Trump on his fake university. Which gave Kelly the opening to jump in and point out that despite Trump saying the Better Business Bureau gave his esteemed university an A rating, it was actually a D. How much uglier could this get? Trying to inject fact and logic into Trump's nonsense is like trying to blow as hard as you can to stop a hurricane. No one blows harder than Donald, but Kelly is to be commended for trying. She started talking about "victims of con artists often sing the praises of their victimizers until they realize they have been fleeced."

Rubio or some of his people had done homework. He said that Trump U. students had "signed up for this course because they believed Mr. Trump was this fantastic businessman, that Donald is going to teach them the tricks of the trade. . . . They signed up. They paid $15,000 for this course. They were asked for additional money for this course. If they really wanted the real secrets of success, they had to pay even more money, and so they did. And you know what they got in these courses? Stuff you can pull off of Zillow. When they finally realized what a scam it was, they asked for their money back. And you refused to give them their money back."

Oh yes, this was also the debate of Trump name calling. Rubio became Little Marco and Cruz Lyin' Ted. Could someone have gotten Trump a better writer than the angry gnome that lives inside his head?

Amusingly, Lyin' Ted tried to act as a Trump whisperer. "Count to 10, Donald—count to 10," he said at one point. Later, it was "Breathe, breathe, breathe—you can do it."

Cruz was considered a winner because he didn't come across as totally crazy. Losers? Trump, Marco and the American voters.

Debate Twelve.
University of Miami.
March 10, 2016.

This was more subdued than Eleven. Sure Little Marco said Trump's Social Security numbers didn't add up. Cruz chided Trump for not being supportive enough of Israel. But you know what, the fat lady (who Trump would like to fire and replace with a younger, more attractive soprano) had sung. It was over. Fini. The last two in the race after this debate were Trump and Kasich, both of whom backed out of Thirteen.

The Dems

Thankfully, the Dems scheduled only six debates. Dream on. That got bucked up to nine. Delusionals Chafee and Webb made it through the first. O'Malley until the fifth. Then it was all Hillary and Bernie.

Readers will be relieved that each face-off will not be as detailed as the Republican debates, because for the most part, moderators didn't need whips and chairs (and in Megyn Kelly's case, pepper spray and a Taser).

Debate One:
Las Vegas.
Oct. 13, 2015.

The first debate had Clinton, Sanders, Martin O'Malley, Jim Webb and Lincoln Chafee.

To the surprise of many, the debate was not a sleep aid as predicted. It will be remembered for Bernie Sanders, when moderator Anderson Cooper kept after Clinton for her private server, saying that it "may not be great politics. But I think the secretary is right, and that is that the American people are sick and tired of hearing about your damn emails."

Let's not overlook how she handled Chafee's calling into question her credibility and ethics over the email issue. When asked if she wanted to respond, Clinton flatly said, "No." In many ways, that one exchange was emblematic of Chafee's entire run. He wasn't significant enough to even deserve a response.

Poor Chafee. Later in the debate, the guy was in front of a national audience admitting he voted for repealing Glass-Steagall, a 1933 law that separated commercial and investment banking. Many analysts point to the repeal as the catalyst for the economic crisis of 2008. That's an even worse version of the nightmare we've all had where you show up to school only to realize you're completely naked. But instead of all your classmates pointing and laughing at your little ambassador, they're accusing you of nearly ruining the United States of America. Chafee offered that it "was my very first vote" and basically had no idea what he was voting for. Not unlike having the entire school see your gigglestick, there is no coming back from that. Chafee was done.

Webb complained a lot about not getting equal time. He even implored Sanders to say his name so that he could respond. When it was Webb's turn, he spent a lot of it giving long wonky answers. When asked which enemy he was proudest to have made, Webb got very literal saying, "I'd have to say the enemy soldier that threw the grenade that

SOURCE: DONKEYHOTEY, DONKEYHOTEY.WORDPRESS.COM

wounded me. But he's not around right now to talk to." So, Jim Webb killed a guy.

Sanders did his usual Larry David impression and got applause for that. The economy is rigged. Black lives matter. Free public-college education. Rebuild the crumbling infrastructure. Raise the minimum wage to $15 an hour. Equal pay for equal work. Pure Bernie, who was described as "fervent, grumpy, unfiltered and righteously angry."

For her part, Clinton was poised, unrattled and spelled out her policy agenda without sounding too scripted, which knowing Hillary, must have taken a lot of rehearsing. And she did thank Bernie for the "damn emails" remark.

After O'Malley criticized her, Clinton came back with "I was very pleased when Governor O'Malley endorsed me in 2008."

And poor Donald, his oversized ego must have been bruised when the Dems failed to pay much attention to him. The only real attack came from O'Malley who called him "that carnival barker in the Republican Party."

Debate Two:
Drake University, Des Moines.
Nov. 14, 2015.

Chafee and Webb were gone, giving Sanders and O'Malley more time to go after Clinton.

According to her rivals, she was bad on gun control, terrible on handling the Middle East, wrong to vote for invading Iraq and bad, bad, bad on overhauling Wall Street. "Not enough" was Bernie's growl on her plan.

Hillary was forced to school Sanders and O'Malley on the history of foreign policy and financial reform, which put the audience to sleep at a slightly slower rate than the free-form poetry that Ben Carson calls his debating. And in case anyone was wondering why she only wanted the minimum wage raised to $12, not $15, here, ladies and gentlemen, were international studies backing her position. Clinton knew lots of studies.

Bear in mind, there was a relative air of civility, something so lacking on the Republican side. Though Sanders did go aggressive when criticizing Clinton's ties to big money. "Let's not be naïve about it. Why over her political career has Wall Street been the major campaign contributor to Hillary Clinton? Now maybe they're dumb, and they don't know what they're going to get, but I don't think so."

Interesting concept by Sanders, but he was vastly overestimating Wall Street. These are the same braniacs that gobbled up collateralized debt obligations (CDOs) like they were McDonald's breakfast sausages, leading to the 2007 subprime mortgage crisis. What is a CDO, you ask? Actually, it's a lot like a McDonald's breakfast sausage. To make a CDO, you take a bunch of bits and pieces from different investments, then throw them into the financial meat grinder. Like a McDonald's sausage, what you're left with does vaguely resemble meat, but you have no idea what the hell is in it. In the case of the housing crisis, it turned out to be thousands upon hundreds of thousands of mortgages that people were going to default on. It's possible Wall Street took the same approach with Clinton that it did with practically everything else. "We'll throw a lot of money at her, then hope something good happens."

Hold on there, Bernie, Clinton responded. Most of the money she had raised was from women making small donations. Then she said something totally off the wall to explain why Wall Street was bestowing contributions on her. "I represented New York on 9/11 when we were attacked. Where were we attacked? We were attacked in downtown Manhattan where Wall Street is. I did spend a whole lot of time and effort helping them rebuild." As if the stock-market types cared about that. They would have been happy to move to Jersey or someplace off the terrorist radar.

Sanders worked to his fervent base when he talked about income inequality and got laughs when he said he would raise taxes on the rich, but not to the 90-percent level under Eisenhower. At the mention of a 90-percent tax rate, a host of right-wing bloggers began furiously typing like angry chimpanzees. "Communist" and "welfare state" were commonly used words. But were they right? Is a 90-percent tax rate immediately equal to communism and the end of the free world as we know it? No.

Let's keep three things in mind. First, Sanders said he would *not* raise taxes to that level. Second, Eisenhower's tax rate was only on the wealthiest of the wealthy making more than $200,000 annually or couples making $400,000. That might not sound like a gargantuan income by today's standards, but this was in the 1950s. When you adjust for inflation and the fact that you could buy four gallons of gas for just $1 like your grandpa won't shut up about, that's actually closer to a $9-million income today. America was in World War II during the time of the 90-percent tax rate, and it was being used for the war effort. Third to Sanders' point, sometimes high taxes are necessary, especially when they are being used to keep a mass-murderer from taking over the world.

The winner? OK, Clinton because except for that toe-stub about 9/11, she did not make any major mistakes.

Loser? O'Malley because he didn't shine enough to move up in the polls, though his name was Googled a lot. And Bernie? He did fine with his supporters. The guy is as consistent as the rising sun.

Debate Three:
San Anselm College, Goffstown, N.H.
Dec. 19, 2015.

Before the salvos began, Hillary and Bernie made nice. There had been a data breach with the Sanders campaign receiving Clinton campaign info. He apologized and asserted that this was not the type of race he was running. She accepted the apology and said let's move on. O'Malley must have missed that exchange because he then complained about back-and-forth bickering.

Hillary used that age-old tactic of deflecting incomings by bringing up something else as a shield. Trump with his hate-mongering rhetoric was "becoming ISIS' best recruiter." Clinton might have had a point there. For years, radical terrorists had made America out to be immoral and a place of decadence that spits in the face of their religion. But Trump is actually those things. He could be the poster boy for ISIS if that hadn't literally happened already.

Clinton stayed above the fray, largely refusing to allow herself to be sucked into her opponents' attacks, instead going after whom she judged as the guy she was going to face in the election — The Donald. Gun control? This was after the San Bernardino shootings. It was important, but stopping Trump's radicalization of Muslims, more so.

Well, what about Clinton's hawkishness? Sanders hit her with "Secretary Clinton is too much into regime change and a little bit too aggressive without knowing what the unintended consequences might be."

But what about you, Bernie? ". . . you voted for regime change with respect to Libya. You joined the Senate in voting to get rid of Qaddafi, and you asked that there be a Security Council validation of that with a resolution."

That was Libya. When it came to Syria, neither Sanders nor O'Malley backed the U.S. ushering in a regime change there.

Clinton came back with "I think it's fair to say Assad has killed, by last count, about 250,000 Syrians" and called for arming moderates. So take that, you foreign-policy rubes.

It was not a love fest. Not a mud-wrestling free-for-all.

Debate Four:
Gaillard Center, Charleston, S.C.
Jan. 17, 2016.

This was the last debate before the Iowa Democratic caucuses on Feb. 1. Clinton and Sanders were running pretty close in the polls, 45 percent to 42 percent. Alas, for O'Malley, he was coming in at an underwhelming 3 percent. In other words, maybe 5,000 voters. It makes you wonder why he bothered to show up for this debate. Granted Charleston is a lovely city with January temperatures in the 70s. Maybe he wanted to tour Fort Sumter.

A Clinton ad had pretty much said Sanders was unelectable. He countered in the debate with "When this campaign began, she was 50 points ahead of me. We were all of 3 percentage points. Guess what? In Iowa and New Hampshire, the race is very, very close." To push the knife in a little further, he pointed out that in polls that pitted the former secretary of state against the former builder and him against "my good friend, Donald Trump," Bernie did better.

That hurt. Those numbers meant it was time to go all out against this improbable opponent. It was time for Hillary to adopt her Batman persona. The volume was ratcheted up, and she sounded more like the Hillary of 2008 dive-bombing Obama. As long as she was reaching the shouting level, why not decry Sanders' gun-vote record, which made him buddy of the NRA, notwithstanding the group honoring him with a D-? Remember, he voted against the Brady Bill and other legislation that would make manufacturers responsible for shootings. He did change his mind on that one shortly before heading to South Carolina. And, ready for this, he voted to allow guns on Amtrak and in national parks. On Sanders' part, he got to use the word "disingenuous" when describing Hillary's statements about his record. He had been for instant background checks and closing gun-show loopholes. Was it his fault a lot of Vermonters love their hunting guns?

Hillary assailed the Sanders' Medicare for All, single-payer healthcare plan as playing into the hands of Republicans who want to flush the Affordable Care Act into the sewer. "That is nonsense," Sanders said. "What a 'Medicare for All' program does is finally provide healthcare for every man, woman and child as a right." And in case Clinton was unaware of it, he let her know that 29 million people still didn't have health insurance.

She wants to attack him about gun-control and Obamacare? Sanders would hit her again on the tons and tons of Wall Street loot flooding into her PACs. Think she won't do a quid pro quo?

It was hard to remember there was a third person on

the stage, O'Malley. Poor guy didn't get much speaking time, though not for lack of trying. There was no way this would be his year. Hillary and then Bernie edged him from the get-go. And the .6 percent he managed to tally in Iowa only affirmed that. He dropped out the day of the vote. And then there were two.

Debate Five:
University of New Hampshire, Durham.
Feb. 4, 2016.

Yikes, Hillary was ticked off, and she made it known.

You know, Bernie, talking about her speaking fees were "attacks by insinuation and innuendo," impugning her integrity and a "very artful smear." After all, she had also addressed the American Camping Association. Banks weren't trying to curry her favor. Oh no, they wanted to hear her take on foreign affairs and pantsuits.

"There is this attack that he is putting out, which really comes down to, anybody who took donations or speaking fees from any interest group has to be bought," she said. "And I just absolutely reject that, Senator. And I really don't think these attacks by insinuation and innuendo are worthy of you. Enough is enough. If you've got something to say, say it directly."

Sanders was not to be pushed off his refrain of Hillary Super PACs being funded by banks. "There is a reason why these people are putting huge amounts of money into our political system," Sanders said. "It is undermining American democracy, and it is allowing Congress to represent wealthy campaign contributors and not the working families of this country." And Bernie's campaign money?

It came from 3.5 million individuals contributing an average $27.

This was one of the most interesting questions at the heart of the debates. Can you receive special-interest money without having your integrity compromised? First, let's examine the basic premise in any transaction. The buyer forks over cash, and in return, gets goods or services. For example, when a buyer pays $2.79 to Taco Bell for a Gordita Supreme, he gets a moment of mouth pleasure to try and fill the sadness hole that exists deep in his soul. Clinton, on the other hand, received anywhere from $100,000 to $325,000 for her 91 speaking engagements between April 2013 and March 2015. So, what were those buyers hoping to get in return? Preferential treatment? Inside information? Confirmation of the Illuminati pyramid tattooed across her chest like a prison convict?

The University of Nevada, Las Vegas defended paying Clinton $225,000, pointing out that its fundraiser brought in $350,000 because of her. Tickets to the event went for as high as $3,000 apiece. Wait, weren't all of Clinton's speaking engagements for soulless Wall Street fat cats? No. Only a small percentage were for organizations like Morgan Stanley, Deutsche Bank, Goldman Sachs and UBS Wealth Management. The majority of the speeches were given at other types of organizations, including The Gap, eBay, Beth El Synagogue, A&E Television, the International Deli-Dairy-Bakery Association and the American Camping Association. Which begs the question, where the hell did the American Camping Association get $260,000 to play Clinton? Perhaps, we finally have an answer as to where all that Girl Scout cookie money goes—"You get back on the corner and push those Thin Mints, Mary-Lou! Hillary needs a new Versace pantsuit!"

With such a wide variety of buyers, it's impossible to know what all of them hoped to get out of the exchange. It's likely that many, like UNLV, wanted to capitalize on Hillary's presence. Some of the financial institutions like Goldman Sachs may have wanted to whisper suggestions in a future president's ear like the stereotypical shoulder-devil (or Dick Cheney). And the Gap was obviously trying for a line of Hillary-endorsed pantsuits. So, back to the original question, does that mean Hillary is fundamentally compromised? No.

Just because she spoke before the International Deli-Dairy-Bakery Association does not mean she is now obligated to its nefarious apple-strudel agenda. And as for Hillary taking money from Goldman Sachs, it's probably like when you take money from your grandparents. "Nan-na, I got your $50 check, so I showed up to holiday brunch, but I am not taking 14 cats home with me." At the end of the day, what many of these appearances mean is that Hillary is not a pure-at-heart idealist like Sanders. She's willing to show up and collect what some have estimated to be as much as $2,500 per minute. But it's unlikely Hillary will be taking any cats home with her.

An angry Clinton attacking Sanders might not have been the best strategy running up to the New Hampshire primary, seeing that he was eviscerating her in the polls there. As it turned out, he ran away 60 percent to 38. Still, we're only talking 15 delegates for Bern, nine Hil. Add in the Iowa delegates won, the scorecard showed Sanders only leading by five.

The debate had an "I'm more progressive than you"

theme. The higher level of Clinton vitriol didn't throw Sanders off his message. "Millions of Americans are giving up on the political process, and they're giving up on the political process because they understand that the economy is rigged," he said.

In the aftermath analysis, some called the debate for Hillary because of her foreign-affairs creds. Others gave the nod to Bernie.

No one is more on message than this guy. No matter the context, no matter the topic—even if the topic is "can you believe Hans Solo's son killed him?"—Sanders was uncannily good at changing the conversation back to inequality, the political power of banks and the evils of corporate money in politics.

Debate Six.
University of Wisconsin-Milwaukee.
Feb. 11, 2016.

With Super Tuesday coming in two weeks, this debate was a humongous for them both.

Hillary hit at her opponent's economic plans, saying he should "level" with the American people about what they would cost and if he had a chance of getting Congress to go along with him. In all likelihood, Sanders only had a snowball's chance in Hades of getting those plans through. But who knew? Maybe he would have had a good shot since hell, in the wake of a Trump presidency, has apparently frozen over. Meanwhile, on his part, Sanders wanted Clinton to "Level with the American people about what we can do to make sure they get quality affordable healthcare." He wanted the voters to hear how he really stood on healthcare reform. There was a whole lot of leveling demands going on.

One of the debate highlights was the lively exchange on Henry Kissinger, much reviled by many liberals for prolonging the war in Vietnam, illegally bombing Cambodia and Laos, being a big-time encourager of wiretapping journalists. When there was talk that Kissinger might be asked to take over the scandal-ridden governing body of world soccer, an English journalist wrote, "To his detractors, the notion of Henry Kissinger being summoned by Sepp Blatter to help cleanse the rotten house of Fifa is akin to making the Empress Messalina a United Nations special envoy for chastity." (Fun historical footnote: The empress apparently had a sex competition against a prostitute, with the competition lasting 24 hours and the empress winning with a score of 25 partners.)

To put this in perspective, Bernie was a conscientious objector and anti-Vietnam war protester. Surprised he doesn't like Hank? "[Clinton] talked about getting the approval or the support or the mentoring of Henry Kissinger. Now, I find it rather amazing, because I happen to believe that Henry Kissinger was one of the most destructive secretaries of state in the modern history of this country."

If that wasn't enough, he added, "I am proud to say that Henry Kissinger is not my friend. I will not take advice from Henry Kissinger." Bernie would be more likely to take advice from revolutionary pacifists like Mahatma Gandhi, Leo Tolstoy or Ben and Jerry (creators of Cherry Garcia and Americone Dream).

Hillary had her own rap. Trying to capitalize on Obama's popularity, she went after Sanders' complaints about the president. "The kind of criticism that we've heard from Senator Sanders about our president, I expect from Republicans. I do not expect from someone running for the Democratic nomination."

Debate Seven.
The Whiting in Flint (Mich.) Center.
March 6, 2016.

Super Tuesday hadn't been super for Sanders. He won in four states, she seven. The important thing is not how many, but which. Sanders buried her in Vermont. She smooshed him in Texas. When the counting was done, Clinton gained 518 pledged delegates to Sanders' 347, putting her about 200 pledged delegates ahead of him.

Take notice of the debate venue. Flint, Mich., a city 57-percent black with 42 percent of its population living below the poverty line and everyone unable to drink the lead-polluted water. There were going to be questions about race, job stimulation and yes, how the Republicans running the state screwed up the city's water supply to save some money.

Asked about her "racial blind spots," Clinton skirted the question by going back to an earlier one, giving her the chance to talk about babysitting the children of mi-grant workers and hearing Martin Luther King Jr. Whatev-er works. When pressed, she talked about meeting moth-ers whose children had been killed by the police, and she promised "to tear down the barriers of systemic racism that are in the criminal-justice system, in the employment system, in the education and healthcare system."

Bernie took a while to answer directly. Instead, he told about a black congressman who couldn't get a cab in D.C. 20 years ago because of his race. When he did get to the question, he basically did a "me, too" to what Hillary had said.

This exchange highlighted one of the inherent failings in the Sanders campaign and perhaps even Sanders as a candidate. You see Bernie is very much like a fluffy white terrier dog—not only is he adorable in his feisty gruffness, but he's also color blind. Bernie was never able to galvanize the black vote, largely because he views everything in terms of class. When pressed about his color blind spot, Sanders answered, "When you're white, you don't know what it's like to be living in a ghetto, you don't know what it's like to be poor." This sent the Black Lives Matter movement into a tizzy. Bernie, you know all black people don't live in the ghetto, right? And middle-class blacks still need to worry about being harassed by police or shot, too.

He also had his failings with blacks that did live in the ghetto. "For African-Americans, he never connected the dots from a practical perspective," Tara Dowdell, a political strategist and former "Apprentice" contestant, said. "How would this measurably improve your life? And his color-blind approach to economics ignores the fact that this is the United States of America, where policy and economics and race are tied." It's not surprising that Bernie was not ready to tackle this issue. Despite being in politics for decades, almost all of it was in Vermont. He probably didn't meet the three black people who live in the Green Mountain State.

Jobs? Hillary made the obligatory reference to how well her hubby did in the '90s to create them, Bernie how trade deals had sucked them away.

Moderator Anderson Cooper led into the Flint water crisis with a damning indictment of how the crisis was handled. "The state of Michigan, in an effort to save money, switched Flint's water source to a cheaper, but riskier alternative, the Flint River. Safeguards were ignored. That river water corroded residential pipes, and for nearly two years, lead leaked into the water used in people's homes." So guys, what will you do?

Bernie did a Bernie shout-out about millionaires and billionaires, but managed to squeeze in that the entire nation's infrastructure needed rebuilding.

Clinton called out the Michigan governor to tap into the state's rainy-day fund for emergencies. She got a good one off with "It is raining lead in Flint, and the state is derelict in not coming forward with the money that is required." She didn't do as well when asked if she would fire the head of the EPA for not fixing Flint's water problems. Two hundred words later, the best she could come up with was she would "determine who knew what, when." Bernie? It took him only 16 words— "President Sanders would fire anybody who knew about what was happening and did not act appropriately." He broke the applause meter on that one.

They were both angry and enervated at times. Other times, maybe a bit fatigued. Can you blame them?

Debate 8.
Miami Dade College.
Mar. 9, 2016.

You're in Miami. So, what do you talk about? Immigration and Cuba.

Hillary was smarting from her "oops, what happened in Michigan?" primary loss and was aiming head blows at Bernie. What about supporting Fidel Castro and President

Daniel Ortega of Nicaragua? And she brought up, more than once, that he voted against a 2007 bill that would have opened up a path to citizenship for millions of immigrants in the country illegally.

Wait one second there, lady, he wouldn't support it because the guest-worker provisions in the bill were "akin to slavery."

The former First Lady was more comfortable talking about immigration, the needs of immigrant families and knocking down barriers to housing and jobs, no doubt hoping this would help her in Florida and North Carolina. Bernie, on the other hand, was looking to the primary battlegrounds in Ohio, Illinois and Missouri, emphasizing his standard progressive points.

The questions ranged all over the place from the chance Clinton would be indicted because of the email mess to whether Bernie had supported vigilantes on the border—that's Mexico's, not Canada's.

So who won? Depends on to whom you talked. Clinton came across as forceful and maneuvered through some minefields. Sanders continued to make a strong case for his progressive agenda. The undisputed winner? Bernie's brown suit. Social media went nuts over it. Male candidates wear blue suits, maybe charcoal. But brown? Who would have thought that rumpled and disheveled Bernie Sanders would make a fashion statement?

Debate Nine.
Brooklyn Navy Yard.
April 14, 2016.

As long as they were in Clinton's home state—sort of home state after Illinois, Arkansas and D.C., which isn't a state, but at least should get a congressional seat—a rock-skipping distance from Wall Street, it was a good time for Bernie, so close to delegate extinction, to hit his opponent hard with a litany of "poor judgments." The usual. Taking speaking money from Goldman Sachs. Her vote for the Iraq invasion. Supporting free-trade deals. Oh, and by the way, "Do we really feel confident about a candidate who says she will bring change in America when she is so dependent on big-money interests?" Mr. Sanders asked. "I don't think so."

While Bernie was described as "ferocious," Hillary was again "steely." Being New York, the crowd acted as if they were cheering and booing the Knicks (though the latter was more prevalent of late), catcalling and interrupting.

The crowd loved it when Bernie attacked Madame Secretary for Wall Street ties, and she responded with "I called them out on their mortgage behavior. I also was very willing to speak out against some of the special privileges they had under the tax code." Ahh, don't give an opening like that. It was too easy for Sanders to come back with "Secretary Clinton called them out—oh my goodness, they must have been really crushed by this. And was that before or after you received huge sums of money by giving speaking engagements?"

Another issue you bring up in New York City—Israel. There was a lot of seesawing over whether that country overreacts with too much force to what it perceives as Palestinian provocation. Sanders argued they do. He also said "If we are ever going to bring peace to that region, we are going to have to treat the Palestinian people with respect and dignity." Not words often heard from a candidate.

This wasn't a touchy-touchy, feely-feely debate like

early ones. Voices were raised, sarcasm spread and disparagements cast galore.

Thank the gods of politics and mercy, the primary debate season was over.

Chapter Five:
Run-up to Philly
and Cleveland

The 2016 campaign became (along with Pearl Harbor, the Bay of Pigs invasion, and Jerry Falwell proclaiming "Teletubbies" Tinky Winky gay) a "what the fuck just happened?" moment in American history. It wasn't scripted to play out the way it did. It made no sense. How could someone so ill-equipped, so ill-tempered, so unfit as Donald Trump win the nomination? A lineup of Republican candidates with the collective charisma of a bag of pit vipers? An event of mass insanity among the American people, where they forget they were electing a president and not texting in their vote for "American Idol"?

The debates and primaries tell that shameful story.

As always, the primary season started with the Iowa caucus, a state with a population of three million (only a half-a-million more than Brooklyn) and six Electoral College votes. The number of people there swells considerably every four years as the press, candidates, candidates' families, candidates' entourages, field-office staff and "political tourists" who want to be close to the action, descend much to the delight of local restaurant owners and hotels.

Some Des Moines hotels gouge up to $900 for a room and have 88 to 90 percent occupancy. Casey's General Stores pulled in $36,000 during the summer, gassing up staff cars. All the doughnuts and snacks they sold didn't make their way onto campaign expense sheets, meaning the windfall was considerably higher. You had Ben Carson buying 3,500 ears of corn for $2,184 to be munched on at his "family festivals." O'Malley paying $11,200 for his Iowa headquarters in Des Moines. Chris Christie's people had a check for $512.48 at a fancy steakhouse. At least, it was nice to see one candidate going about business as usual and not pandering to the state.

But it's not about the money. Really. It's the glory of every four years having the spotlight on Iowa, a state known for corn and Johnny Carson. Or as Joseph Jones of a Des Moines development group explained, "For us, it's not about economic impact. We know we're not the first to caucus because we're special. We're special because we're the first."

In that statement lies the problem that so many have with the Electoral College and the election process as a whole. Iowa receives an abundance of extra time and attention from the candidates simply because of its place in an arbitrary election cycle. Not because it most closely represents the voice of the American people. The Electoral College causes candidates to pander to certain states because they represent "swing votes." Meanwhile, a gargantuan like California, which makes up so much of the West Coast, receives fewer visits from some candidates than Iowa despite the Hawkeye State not even having a 10th of the population.

The last couple of cycles, Iowans haven't been spot on

when it came to picking the eventual Republican candidate. Eight years ago, they went for Mike Huckabee, and in 2012, the dazzling Rick Santorum.

In 2016, it was Darth Ted who took the Republican side with 27.7 percent and runner-up Trump 24.3. Mike Huckabee's barely noticeable 1.8 percent convinced him it was time to pack up his evangelical tent on the day of the vote. It took Rand Paul two more days, Feb. 3, to accept the inevitable and pull his name, short on funds and short on votes (4.5 percent). Rick Santorum and his abysmal 1 percent did the same.

The Republican field was cut in half, down to eight, with Rick Perry, Scott Walker, Bobby Jindal, Lindsey Graham and Lonesome George Pataki not having made it to the first of the year.

Over on the Dem side, Sanders and Clinton duked it out to a near tie, with Clinton ending up slightly ahead. How could this have happened? This was supposed to be her year for the taking. Then along came this wild-haired, wild-idea socialist from Vermont.

Bernie backers lined up at precincts. They caused traffic jams. They turned out new voters, voters changing their affiliation from independent, new citizens. As John Nichols of The Nation wrote, these Bernie backers "upset expectations by democratizing democracy. They have renewed the tradition of mass rallies, filling halls usually reserved for rock stars and sports teams. They have upset the tired punditry that says young people can't get excited about politics anymore. They have upset the cynicism that claims the presidential campaigns of our times will be funded mainly by millionaires and billionaires. They have upset the historic 'certainty' that a democratic socialist could not be a viable contender for the nomination of a major American political party." In short, they were Bernie Believers.

But why is Bernie a Bae (Bae is a millennial term meaning "before anyone else") for these younger voters? What was it about Sanders specifically that energized the 20-something demographic in a way we've never seen before? It certainly wasn't his sense of personal style. Nor his haircut. And he didn't try to pander to young voters with pop culture references or slang. Dozens of writers, reporters and publications weighed in. One professor thought it was because of the generation's sense of entitlement. They liked the idea of having things given to them in a way socialism would. Even Mark Cuban, billionaire owner of basketball's Dallas Mavericks, threw in his two cents, though maybe tons of money would be more appropriate. "How can it be a surprise that Millennials are excited about Bernie Sanders? Millennials EXPECT capitalism to reflect a socialist element." Strangely, only Vice.com thought to ask the millennials. They reported from a Halloween rave party/Sanders fundraiser where the young partygoers came dressed as the candidates. So, "Why do you love Bernie?"

"There's a reason other candidates are not hitting the pitch," said 24-year-old Matthew Collura, who co-managed the Millennials for Bernie site. "The pitch is honesty, and as much as I like O'Malley's policies, he's very trained, and I think the classical training that politicians are undergoing is going to end up harming them."

Twenty-five-year-old Moumita Ahmed added, "Top concerns that students have had for years are student debt and the climate crisis, but Bernie was the first candidate to make those his priorities in a forceful way never done before, by laying out his record, which shows he's been a consistent fighter for the environment and for students."

Oh . . . SMH (that's "shake my head, dear Baby Boomers) . . . it's because he's a legit dude who speaks plainly, means what he says and specifically addresses the problems that young people are facing. Everyone seems to forget that for millennials, "the struggle is real." In a world that feels scripted and fake, a world that often tells them one thing (work hard, go to college and you will get a good job) and delivers another (unemployment and mountains of student debt), they just wanted someone they could believe in. They wanted someone who "keeps it 100."

That's likely why Sanders was breaking records similar to Usain Bolt with a 50-mph backwind. In February, he hauled in $43.5 million. Come March, it was $44 million. For the first quarter of 2016, he was up to $109 million from two million donors. No Super PAC mega-money. Only Super Sanders mega-money.

But wait, Martin O'Malley hung in to Iowa. How did he do? Try a "why bother to count it" 0.6 percent. He joined Jim Webb and Lincoln Chafee who had had fallen on their swords in October.

The next stop on the primary circuit was New Hampshire on Feb. 9. The Live Free or Die state showed determination over the years to remain the first primary, pushing the date earlier and earlier. This proved to be no heartstopper for The Donald or Bernie. With New Hampshire being such a close neighbor to Vermont, a Sanders victory could be expected. Not, however, the 20-point trouncing of Clinton, who was no "comeback kid" as her husband had been in the Granite State.

Bernie wasn't one to let an opportunity slip away. Immediately after his victory, he announced he was holding a nationwide fundraiser, "right here, right now, across America," asking people to contribute "whether it's 10 bucks, or 20 bucks, or 50 bucks." His supporters listened and sent $8 million dollars to his website in one day.

Trump shed his Iowa loser label, taking the primary with 100,406 votes (35.3 percent) over the next closest. That would be John Kasich. Yep, he came in with almost 45,000, beating Ted Cruz (33,189), low-energy Jeb (31,310), Little Marco (30,032), Chris Christie (21,069) and Carly Fiorina, who managed to cajole 11,706 to cast their ballots for her. You could be pretty sure they weren't Hewlett Packard people.

The next day, it was bye-bye for her and Christie. Jim Who? Gilmore (.05 percent—an embarrassing 133 votes) stuck it out for another two days. And then there were six.

The Democrats wedged in a Nevada caucus, which Clinton won 52.6 percent to 47.3.

South Carolina was the next, far bigger prize with the Republican winner potentially walking away with between 38 and 50 delegates in a not exactly proportional or winner-take-all contest. The Democratic primary is proportional with some super-delegates thrown in to muddy up the outcome a bit.

The Republican winner has a history of getting the nomination. All had since Reagan in 1980, with the exception of Gingrich in 2012. The state Republican Party even boasts "We take our primaries very seriously. We pick presidents!" With a miss here and there, but that would make the slogan too long.

South Carolina was Clinton country, and she needed

to win big to overcome her trouncing in New Hampshire and future contests that might go either way.

First came the S.C. Republican primary, with the Dems following a week later.

Cruz was pushing for evangelical votes. Rubio was hoping endorsements from big-name South Carolinians would help his cause. Jeb brought out the two former Bush presidents to buoy his drowning efforts. And Trump . . . well, as long as there were several opponents in the running, he only needed 30 percent of the vote to capture the eventual prize.

Which he did with 33 percent, followed by Rubio and Cruz, both with 22 percent. And where was Jeb! The good news was he placed fourth. The bad news was he eked out fewer than 58,000 votes or a pathetic 8 percent and pulled out when the tallies were in. How could this humiliating result have happened? Jeb started with a $100-million war chest and name recognition out the wazoo. The answer is he had been humbled and blindsided by a mendacious political newbie who used pyrotechnics and theatrics to overwhelm his opponents who ran by-the-book, traditional campaigns. In other words, Jeb was out-entertained.

John Kasich did about as poorly, but refused to quit. Ben Carson only got 7 percent, but being a religious type, must have thought there would be a Super Tuesday miracle.

It was Clinton all the way in South Carolina. In 2008, Obama had beaten her badly among black voters. In 2016, she wasn't going to let that happen again. To say it was a resounding victory wasn't saying enough. She topped Sanders six to one among black voters and won 74 percent over all. But Super Tuesday was looming on March 1 with 13 states and one territory going to the polls.

Conventional wisdom had Cruz winning in Texas. Rubio maybe in Minnesota and the Great Duplicitous Donald taking most of the rest. Clinton was figured to do well, but it wasn't clear if it would be well enough to knock Bernie out of the race so she could graciously accept his calling it quits.

(For those who like trivia, Super Tuesday is also called SEC Tuesday because so many of the states have schools in the collegiate Southeastern Conference.)

When the results were in, it was obvious Bernie and faithful followers would not fade quietly into the night. Hillary won big, but Bernie had a glimmer of a maybe with his win in Vermont and Oklahoma. Clinton seized big delegate states like Georgia, Tennessee and Texas, and again showed her popularity among black voters.

Trump triumphed in seven out of 11 states—Virginia, Arkansas, Alabama, Tennessee, Vermont, Massachusetts and Georgia. If he had managed Texas, it would have meant it was time for homeboy Cruz to throw himself on a funeral pyre. But Darth Ted won Texas, Oklahoma and Alaska, proving how influential Sarah Palin was up there having endorsed Trump. Little Marco? They did like him in Minnesota.

It looked as if the race was pretty much over. Still, as long as there were frequent-flyer miles to be had and money left in the bank, why not soldier on? At first that included Ben Carson, who said he was "not quite ready to quit." By March 4, he was quite ready, saying, "I do not see a political path forward in light of last evening's Super Tuesday primary results," But his supporters were not to worry, he would remain committed to "Saving America for Future Generations."

And there was always the "who would have thought?" factor, which indeed, showed up on Super Saturday. For the Democrats, it was that pesky Sanders—again. Poor Hillary. Sure, she scored big in the delegate column with a sizable win in Louisiana, but that guy would not go away. He won Nebraska, Kansas and later Maine.

The pest Trump wanted to lightsaber out of existence continued to be Darth Ted. Out of four contests, Cruz managed Kansas and Maine. In 2012, Kansas went for Rick Santorum, and Romney beat Rand Paul by a smidgeon. It was Louisiana and Kentucky for the frontrunner, who was starting to run even further in front. And Marco? Let's put it this way, he had to take Florida on March 15, and then he was *sure* he would be the nominee. Had to take Florida. Had to. Had to.

Come March 8 and there were still some Beltway insiders who thought Cruz could stop the confounding Trump. Maybe Cruz would win Michigan. Did he have a chance in Mississippi? The wait wasn't long for the answers. Michigan polls closed at 9 p.m. Immediately, Trump was given the W. It took a whole 30 minutes for the Magnolia State to smell extra sweet for the Boastful Billionaire. Cruz won Idaho, and Rubio got one delegate out of Hawaii. Let's not forget Kasich. He walked away with 17 Michigan delegates and . . . no, that was it.

A stunner on the 8th was how Democrats voted in Michigan. Some polls had Hillary up by 20. The voters must have missed those since the state went for Bernie. This revved up his supporters, as if they needed further juicing, and he had the money to continue to the convention floor. Even if he trailed in delegates, there was always the hope of swaying super delegates. These are unpledged party officials and other favored ones who arrive at the DNC and can vote for any candidate they choose. This system was instituted after the big shots felt that they should have more say in who gets the nomination and not only rely on the dumb rank-and-filers. Since the party powerfuls favored Hillary, Bernie had a better shot of appearing as a cover model for Men's Fitness magazine than garnering super-delegate support. After all, the super-delegate kink was in reaction to a too-liberal George McGovern and a peanut farmer from Georgia who distained Washington winning too many primaries.

The next big voting day was Super Tuesday II on March 15. (Whoever names these is about as creative as the Hollywood movie studios. At least, can we call it, "Super Tuesday 2: Attack of the Candidates"?) This was when Marco Rubio would shine —even though his delegate count had sunk deep into the Everglades— and show he deserved to be the party standard-bearer by taking every single, without exception, Sunshine State vote. That wasn't quite what played out. It was more like he was the racehorse Frosted, coming in five-and-a-half lengths behind American Pharoah in the Belmont. Trump obliterated Marco with a tally of 1,077,221 to 636,653, which meant Trump got all the state's 99 delegates.

Little Marco pulled out and petulantly said he wouldn't run for his Senate seat. Take that, fickle Florida voters. If only he had kept to his word. Maybe when he realized he would be out of work, he decided the Senate was a nice place, after all.

In other Attack of the Candidates results, Trump was awarded 54 Illinois delegates to Cruz' nine, Kasich's six and none for Rubio. Trump was victorious in Missouri,

North Carolina and the ever-important American Samoa and North Mariana Islands (Guam). John Kasich was the decided victor in Ohio. At least, *he* could hold his home state, Marco.

Other states had random primaries and caucuses. Cruz pulled nine Wyoming delegates to Trump's one. Utah threw its 40 convention votes to Cruz. Both Trump and Clinton were victors in New York—Trump 89 delegates, Kasich 6, Hillary 139, Bernie 108.

In the April 16 Acela primaries (cute, so named for states on the Amtrak Northeast Corridor—Connecticut, Delaware, Maryland, Pennsylvania and Rhode Island), Trump swept with Cruz and Kasich picking up some crumbs he missed.

The rest of the Republican primaries and caucuses were pretty much a Trump victory tour. As for Sanders, there were some states that went for him, but because the delegates were divided proportionately, he couldn't catch up to Clinton—especially when she walked away with the most delegates from New York, Pennsylvania and California.

But Bernie would not quit. He would take his people to the convention floor. In a sense, he was doing Madam Secretary a favor. If he surrendered, his army of Sanderistas would have felt betrayed. As it was, no matter how quixotic, no matter that the windmill was no longer in poking distance, Bernie would continue the good fight and hold some sway over his followers.

Kasich, on the other hand, gave up his spoiler run on May 4. He said, ". . . as I suspend my campaign today, I have renewed faith, deeper faith, that the Lord will show me the way forward, and fulfill the purpose of my life." Who would have guessed that part of that purpose was thumbing his nose at the Presumptive Trump and not showing up at the convention held in his own state?

The final delegate count looked like this:

Republicans: 1,237 delegates needed for the nomination

Donald J. Trump	1,543
Ted Cruz	559
Marco Rubio	165
John Kasich	161
Uncommitted	23
Ben Carson	7
Jeb Bush	4
Carly Fiorina	1
Mike Huckabee	1
Rand Paul	1
Chris Christie	0
Jim Gilmore	0
Rick Santorum	0
30 delegates remaining	

Democrats: 2,382 delegates needed for the nomination

Hillary Clinton	2,814
Bernie Sanders	1,893
Uncommitted	56
Martin O'Malley	0
56 delegates remaining	

So there you had it, the presumptive nominees were Trump and Clinton. After the primaries, they commenced their victory appearances and rallies on their way to convention coronations.

Hillary hit an unexpected bump on July 5, two hours before she and Obama were to mount the steps of Air Force One for their first joint campaign outing. FBI Director James Comey took to the microphones to announce the results of the bureau's investigation into Hillary's emails.

Let's give some background here. The FBI investigates. It is an agency of the Department of Justice, which does the prosecuting based on the bureau's findings and recommendations. A good thing since there are few FBI agents trained in the law. But Comey went against procedure. "Comey's a dirty cop," said former U.S. Attorney Joseph diGenova. "And if there's one thing a prosecutor hates worse than a criminal, it's a dirty cop . . . He threw this case. He did it for political reasons. He lied publicly about the quality of the case. He lied publicly about the law. He lied publicly about the ability to get documents when he could have used the grand jury and he didn't." Additionally, the bureau should not comment on ongoing investigations nor reveal recommendations. Republicans and Democrats agreed on that. This is to keep the FBI from seeming politicized, which Comey came across unquestionably as being.

Maybe he thought that his "hero" status for defying instructions and not signing a wiretap authorization while his boss, Bush II Attorney General John Ashcroft, was in the hospital unable to do so, made him exempt from following the rules. Of course, he later signed the document after a few tweaks, but that's picky, picky, picky. And it didn't stop Comey from preening before Congress as a man of high principles.

In any case, against the urging of the DOJ, Comey announced that the FBI had not found enough evidence to bring criminal charges against Clinton for emails and private-server usage. He couldn't leave it there. Like a scolding male schoolmarm, he was forced to reluctantly admit his student had passed the test, but took her to task for penmanship and Cheetos smudges on the paper, which demonstrated "extreme carelessness."

Clinton spokesman Brian Fallo responded with "As the secretary has long said, it was a mistake to use her personal email, and she would not do it again. We are glad that this matter is now resolved."

True to Trump form, his response was "The system is rigged. . . . Very, very unfair!" He wanted to "Lock her up." Again, this is probably beating a dead horse, or whatever deceased critter lives on Trump's head, but this is hypocrisy at an extreme.

Trump calling for someone to be locked up for skirting the law is Lance Armstrong calling for an end to performance-enhancing drugs in the NFL. Trump has cut corners and made shady deals every step of the way. To date, there have been more than 3,500 lawsuits filed against him for alleged wrongdoings. To put that into context, if they made a "Law and Order: Donald Trump" edition, where each episode revolved around a Trump lawsuit, that show would run for 67 years straight. Yes, the system is unfair, but not for Donald Trump.

Unfair or not, it was on to the conventions.

Chapter Six:
A Tale of Two Conventions

Veepstakes

John Nance Garner once said the vice presidency wasn't "worth a bucket of warm piss." And he would know, having served two terms under FDR. And then there was Harry Truman assessing vice presidents as "about as useful as a cow's fifth teat."

Given the near contempt with which the position has been held, why is it coveted? It's a path to bigger things (and the Naval Observatory is a pretty cool place to live), that's why. Four VPs took over after their boss was assassinated. Three presidents died in office. Can you imagine how flummoxed John Tyler must have been when he was appointed president after only 10 days as VP? He moved on up after William Henry Harrison thought it was a good idea to give a one-hour-and-45 minute inaugural speech (the longest ever) in a raging snowstorm with no coat or hat. He contracted pneumonia and died soon thereafter. It might be argued that Gerald Ford took over after Richard Nixon expired in office.

Then you have the VPs who went on to win the presidency on their own. George H.W. Bush and Martin Van Buren went directly from second to top dog. Nixon had to wait eight years before he got to move into the White House. And having been vice president opens door. Ambassadorships, book deals, Senate seats, professorships—the title gets noticed on a resume.

Picking these lucky souls who until recently had nothing much to do while in office ("I do not propose to be buried until I am really dead," Daniel Webster said on turning down an offer to run with William Henry Harrison) went from direct vote to smoky backroom party wheeling and dealing to finally in 1940, FDR saying in essence, you know what, I'm running for a third term. I get to pick.

Deciding who will be on the ticket has always been very scientific and well thought out. For instance, George H.W. picked blond and spelling-deficient Dan Quayle because he thought the Indiana senator would appeal to female voters. Kind of a non-threatening, early Justin Bieber. Quayle was the guy who said, "If we do not succeed, then we run the risk of failure." "Verbosity leads to unclear, inarticulate things." "I want to be Robin to Bush's Batman." Barry Goldwater gave the nod to William Miller because the New York congressman "drove LBJ nuts." Richard Nixon added Spiro Agnew under the belief that coming from Maryland, Agnew would balance the ticket geographically, appealing to Northerners and Southerners alike. Apparently, it didn't bother Nixon that his choice once called a photographer "a Fat Jap" and had a tendency to use racial slurs while campaigning.

The one word that should be carved into the forehead of all presidential candidates—or at least, their campaign managers—is "vet." Make the effort to check the past of all potentials for embarrassing, even damaging, problems. George McGovern probably wished he had looked a little harder at Thomas Eagleton. McGovern might have discovered—before the information hit the press buzz saw—that his pick had received electroshock treatment for clinical depression. To be fair to McGovern, Eagleton was not the first, second or whatever choice. Everyone had turned down the South Dakota senator, including Teddy Kennedy. Eagleton was asked to run on the first day of the convention. More was discovered on Eagleton's mental condition—his own doctors indicating he might be a danger to the country. If only those same doctors had a chance to evaluate Donald Trump.

Since then, there has been a more concerted effort—Sarah Palin an exception. C'mon guys, you might have taken more than five days and maybe talked to people in Alaska—to come up with a list of possibles, check them out, leak their names to see if the press or opponents uncover anything and finally announce the "winner" before the convention.

OK, is it any surprise that wasn't quite the scenario in 2016? Hillary Clinton followed the script. Names were floated. Although some Clinton and Sanders supporters would have cheered the selection of liberal Massachusetts Sen. Elizabeth Warren, she was probably never a contender. This despite her spirited social-media attacks against Tweetin' Trump. "You wanna see goofy? Look at him in that hat," referring to his "Make America Great Again" baseball cap. In a turn so ironic it would make Alanis Morissette spontaneously combust, those hats were stitched together in a Los Angeles factory by Latinos. "Just wait until he sees who's making his hats," said Yolanda Melendrez, a Mexican immigrant.

Then there was Sherrod Brown of Ohio. He might have helped Clinton take that state. On the negative side, his Senate seat would be filled by Republican Gov. John Kasich should Brown become vice president.

New Jersey Sen. Cory Booker was often mentioned. A Rhodes Scholar, here was someone who could excite a lot of bases. Not to mention, he's black, which might have appealed to Obama supporters. Booker could deliver powerful speeches, something with which Hillary struggled.

The name of Tom Vilsack, Obama's secretary of agriculture, was bandied about a bit. But being called a "boring Tim Kaine" was not a ringing endorsement.

Which brings us to Tim Kaine. This is a fellow who as Richmond mayor got kudos from black and white leaders. Can you imagine a white guy formally apologizing for a city's role in slave trading? A Roman Catholic who is personally against abortion, he maintained as a public official, he shouldn't force his beliefs down the throat of others. He was viewed as a nice guy. He didn't relish the role of attack dog. However, David Eichenbaum, Kaine's media consultant, said, "He is really able to fillet you before you realize it, and before you know it, you're on the grill. And all done with a smile."

Kaine took off time from Harvard Law to volunteer in Honduras, a country in turmoil. He came to distrust U.S. foreign policies there. One priest warned him to be careful "of who you are talking to—most particularly the Americans." Kaine continued his activism in the Richmond City Council and mayor's office, the Virginia governorship and finally U.S. Senate. The New York Times said that "in hyperpartisan Washington, he is often seen as a centrist" and an "old-fashioned liberal . . . driven by Jesuit ideals."

He was considered the safe choice, although he had called himself boring, which makes you wonder about how yawn-producing Vilsack was. In any event, he got the nod just before the convention and had Bill's blessing.

Kaine may come across as an altar boy, but Trump felt he had ammunition to call the former governor "corrupt" for accepting "hundreds of thousands of dollars" in gifts while in office. (Donald, you know there are synonyms for "corrupt"? How about dishonest, unscrupulous, dishonorable, unprincipled, unethical, amoral, untrustworthy, underhanded, double-dealing, criminal, illegal, unlawful or Trump-like?) Fact-checking found that it was $162,083 in *disclosed* gifts, making them legal under Virginia law. Then there was scandal of the Honduras pin. Members of the eagle-eyed North Carolina GOP spotted it on Kaine's lapel during his DNC speech. He "wears a Honduras flag pin on his jacket but no American flag," the state party blustered. "Shameful." Well, that turned out to be rancid egg in the face. It was actually a Blue Star Service pin for his son, a deployed Marine.

Which brings us to the Traveling Trump Show.

Floating out names? Waiting for reaction? C'mon, that wasn't Trump's reality-show style. If he could have brought Simon Cowell in as a consultant, he surely would have. Trump essentially held auditions, hauling out potential running mates at rallies. Would he pick the person who could yell the loudest? Some observers thought Chris Christie had the inside track. Trump wanted a "fighter," and the pugnacious, heavyweight Jersey governor fit that bill. And besides, Christie, even after his Lap-Band surgery to lose weight, was one of the few people around who could make Trump look less like Minnesota Fats.

But Christie had a major problem. Jared Kushner, Ivanka's husband, let it be known that the former prosecutor would be named running mate over his dead body. The animus is understandable when you realize Christie, as U.S. Attorney of New Jersey, was instrumental in sending Papa Kushner to federal prison.

What were the odds that both the fathers-in-law of candidate daughters would have spent quality time behind bars? That's right, Ed Mezvinsky, a former congressman from Iowa and later Chelsea Clinton father-in-law, was convicted for running a Ponzi scheme. His crimes were far more despicable than Charles Kushner's and without the colorful details.

The elder Kushner got pounded with numerous counts of illegal campaign contributions to Democrats, tax evasion and witness tampering. It's the witness tampering that could have come right out of "All My Children." Charles was in a wrangle with his sister over control of their really big company. He found out that she and her husband might be providing evidence to the feds on the tax evasion. So what would any good brother do? He hired a prostitute to seduce the brother-in-law in a motel room outfitted with surveillance cameras. He then sent the video to his sister and husband, hoping to keep them quiet. In response, they did what any good relatives would do. They turned the video over to authorities.

Charles eventually pleaded guilty to 18 counts of various bad doings and was sentenced to two years. Two years that Christie tried extending to five since Kushner didn't show proper remorse—or maybe because Kushner was a huge donor to Democrats. That would be more than enough for Jared to hate Christie. The fact that the U.S. Attorney trotted out the hooker angle and humiliated the family only served to fan Jared's hatred. Hey, in Christie's defense, he didn't know the kid would marry the heiress. Maybe Christie would have handled the case differently if he had.

Mezvinsky, on the other hand, conned friends and relatives out of $10 million. That included taking his 86-year-old, former mother-in-law for $309,000. He tried to get a pardon from Bill Clinton before the formal indictment. That was a no-go. Then Mezvinsky offered various creative defenses, including the medication he took for trips to Africa made him do it. He ended up spending five years in jail after pleading guilty to 31 of 69 felony charges in 2002. His wife, one-term House Representative Marjorie Margolies-Mezvinsky, dumped him five years later.

Then on the short list was Newt Gingrich. Yes, that Newt Gingrich, the guy who showed up in his first wife's hospital room as she was recovering from uterine-cancer surgery with a yellow legal pad to go over their divorce. He told a friend that "You know and I know that she's not young enough or pretty enough to be the wife of a president." Jackie had been his high-school history teacher, older by seven years. On to Wife Number Two, a 28-year-old congressional staffer. By this time, Newt Man had made it to Congress with the help of Jackie's campaigning. Let's not forget that Gingrich didn't pay child and spousal support to the point that his former wife and kids had to rely on help from their church to survive. Meanwhile, he was reported to be spending $400 a month on dry cleaning and other necessities.

The new wife, Marianne, lasted 19 years, though you might call into question "lasted" since he had taken up an affair for six years with another House staffer (guess it was easier than picking up babes in a bar, especially when you resemble the offspring of a bull toad and the Stay Puft Marshmallow Man) while he was still married to Marianne. This was going on at the same time he was attacking President Bill Clinton for his involvement with White House intern Monica Lewinsky. Newtie (that's what his mother called him) and Marianne were headed for divorce court when she declined an open marriage. He is reported to have said to Wife Number Two, "You want me all to yourself. Callista doesn't care what I do."

Let's move past sordid to substance. The honorable Newt took out the Contract on America. Sorry, Freudian typo. Contract with America. As Speaker of the House, he destroyed the long, long practice of compromise. Bill goes to bipartisan committee. Come to an agreement. Send it out for a full vote. No one is a 100-percent happy, but that's what compromise is all about.

That was not Gingrich's take on governing. His way or no way. Screw the country. As Politico put it, "More than anyone else in the modern history of Congress, it's Gingrich who observers credit for bringing the hyperpartisan, obstructionist approach to Washington that we associate with the capital to this day."

A petulant Gingrich closed down the government twice because the proposed budget was not to his liking. The second shutdown had 800,000 government workers furloughed, and there was talk that 3.3 million people would have to wait for their veterans' benefit checks. Unbelievably, Gingrich said the shutdown was Clinton's fault. He charged that negotiations went south because the Speaker of the House wasn't afforded proper respect when flying to Yitzhak Rabin's funeral on Air Force One. Can you imagine? He had to enter the plane by the back stairs. The press had loads of fun with this explanation. The New York Daily News ran a cartoon on its front page of a diapered, pudgy Newtie throwing a fit. Headline: Cry Baby.

President Clinton absolutely hammered the shutdown at the next State of the Union address, going so far as introducing a man who rescued three people in the aftermath of the Oklahoma City bombing. But as someone who worked for the Social Security Administration, he went without pay during the stoppage.

The American voters expressed their unhappiness by punishing Republicans in the next election. And Gingrich didn't fare very well, either. He had been hit with 84 ethics violations complaints that revolved around a business course, "Renewing American Civilization," Gingrich taught at Kennesaw State College in Georgia. He got into trouble over raising money for The Kennesaw State College Foundation, a tax-deductible nonprofit. It was determined that the class was really a Republican recruitment tool, a "coordinated effort to have the 501(c)(3) organization help in achieving a partisan, political goal." Not a good thing for Gingrich, who was forced to pay a fine of $300,000, money he had to borrow from Bob Dole. Then there was the $15 million he piled up in fundraising efforts that somehow were not mentioned to the Federal Election Commission.

For all of this, Newt Gingrich became the first Speaker of the House to be reprimanded and fined on a vote of 395 to 28. He stuck his tail between his legs and left office.

With that background, you could see why Trump might want him as a running mate. So many marital war and military deferment stories to share. The name of Alabama Sen. Jeff Sessions was pingponged about for a while, at one point, he was even considered a frontrunner. Sessions would go down in history books as being only the second person up for federal judgeship in 50 years not to get the post. His defeat might have had something to do with his calling the NAACP and ACLU "un-American" and "communist-inspired" organizations that "forced civil rights down the throats of people."

Undaunted by his defeat, Sessions became Alabama's attorney general. Any shock that he was accused of promoting voter suppression? When he got to the U.S. Senate, he took a seat on the judiciary committee. He strongly opposed the nomination of Sonia Sotomayor to the Supreme Court because her Puerto Rican background would keep her from making fair rulings. Trump would use the same argument against Judge Gonzalo Curiel, who was presiding over a Trump University case. Although Curiel was born and bred in Indiana, Trump accused him of having an "inherent conflict of interest." And that would be because The Donald wanted to build that wall along the U.S.-Mexican border and the judge's parents were from Mexico.

Also in the mix was Rudy Giuliani. We have Oprah Winfrey to blame for dubbing him "America's Mayor" after 9/11. Gingrich went to his sick wife's hospital room in an attempt to get her to sign off on divorce details. Still, as far as the Distastefulness Derby goes, Rudy comes in second. The former mayor of New York announced at a press conference he was divorcing his wife—before he told her.

Giuliani was also a serial party switcher, depending on which affiliation best suited his ambitions. First, he was a Democrat. When he was up for a job in the Ford administration, suddenly the Dem was an independent. But why stop there? Reagan moves into the Oval Office, and one month later, Giuliani's voter registration card reads Republican. It must have worked for soon the Brooklyn-born rising star had risen to the third-highest post in the Justice Department. He made headlines when he argued that people fleeing Haiti were doing so for economic reasons and not to escape the repressive regime of Jean-Claude Duvalier. According to Giuliani, "political repression, at least in general, does not exist" under Baby Doc, even though 30,000 people were murdered or executed for political reasons during his more than 13 corrupt years in power.

But the really big headlines came when Rudy took over as U.S. Attorney for the Southern District of New York. He went after the Mafia's five families and conducted perp walks—you know, where people are escorted out by cops in front of a cadre of reporters, who just happened to be in the neighborhood. It didn't matter if charges were later dropped and the humiliating damage done. Giuliani got his name plastered in the papers.

That publicity led him to Gracie Mansion after he was elected mayor in 1993, following a close defeat to David Dinkins four years earlier. In office, he took a tough-on-crime approach. When crime rates fell, it was all because of Giuliani's policy, though it was pointed out the decline started during Dinkins' tenure.

After the 9/11 attacks, Giuliani seemed to be everywhere—radio, TV, making speeches. The one place he wasn't so much as he claimed was at Ground Zero. He was there, he said "as often, if not more, than most workers. . . . I was there working with them. I was exposed to exactly the same things they were exposed to. So in that sense, I'm one of them." No Rudy, just because you got to throw out a first pitch doesn't mean you are a New York Yankee. There is no record of how often he was in Lower Manhattan immediately after the attack. It was found that over the following three months, he showed up for a total of 29 hours. The workers racked that up in two days.

Accolades were showered on him, including being named Time magazine's Man of the Year and having an honorary knighthood bestowed on him by Queen Elizabeth II. The praise might have been tempered had some of the information about Giuliani's missteps before and after the attack surfaced earlier.

Perhaps most egregious was his declaring "The air quality is safe and acceptable" around the World Trade Center when in fact, it was more toxic than Godzilla's morning breath. He kept the Federal Emergency Management Agency, Army Corps of Engineers and the Occupational Safety and Health Administration out of the cleanup process. According to Christie Todd Whitman, head of the federal Environmental Protection Agency, the good mayor blocked her attempts to require workers at the site to wear respirators, which would have cut down on ensuing lung-disease cases.

He made poor judgment calls pre-attack. For one, putting the city's Office of Emergency Management (OEM) headquarters in the World Trade Center, especially considering bin Laden's 1993 truck bombing of the North Tower. Giuliani overruled locating the OEM in Brooklyn, which meant on 9/11, the agency was too busy evacuating to coordinate police and fire response.

That left Mike Pence, a bit of a head-scratcher. Conventional wisdom (read that advice from Trump's family) was that Pence would give the campaign conservative creds. And there was no question that Pence was conservative.

Here was a guy who spent 12 years in the House of Representatives never giving up the fight to defund Planned Parenthood. He then shouted hurrahs after the Supreme Court Citizens United decision to treat corporations as real live, breathing voters. He said it was a step closer to the Founding Fathers' vision of free speech." Right, what Thomas Jefferson really meant was "We hold these truths to be self-evident, that all men and giant business entities are created equal, that they are endowed by their Creator (be it by God or filing with their state's secretary of state) certain unalienable Rights, that among these are Life, Liberty, and the pursuit of obscene amounts of money."

Forget about raising the federal minimum wage from $5.15 to $7.25 an hour because it would hurt the working poor. Yeah, small businesses wouldn't be afforded simultaneous "relief," so maybe they would close then the working poor would be out jobs that kept them below the poverty level—figure it out, if you can. He was also against family-friendly legislation like paid maternity leave for federal employees.

All in all, Pence has shown worse judgment than a man trapped on an escalator during a power outage (think about it). More than 30 years after the surgeon general's warning on the dangers of smoking, Pence begged to differ. "Time for a quick reality check. Despite the hysteria from the political class and the media, smoking doesn't kill."

And let's not get all hot and bothered about global warming. Burning fuels is no way responsible for global temperatures spiking because CO_2 "is a naturally occurring phenomenon in nature . . ." This showed a certain affinity to Trump, who was prone to calling global warming a hoax perpetrated by the Chinese. When that statement was widely ridiculed, Trump backtracked saying it was meant as a joke. Give the guy credit. At least, he didn't blame the Martians.

But here is why people were wondering why Pence was under consideration in the first place. His popularity as governor of Indiana had been nose-diving. So much so, there was talk that he would lose his re-election bid to the Dem he defeated. Pence's approval rating was at 43 percent, down 17 points from 2015. He could take comfort that he was far more popular than Kansas Gov. Sam Brownback, who could only muster a 26-percent good-job rating.

What sent Pence over the cliff in the Hoosier State? How about the cockamamie idea of having a government news service that would cherry-pick which stories were sent to reporters? Sort of an Indiana Pravda. It could be like communist Russia, come to Indiana! That idea got dropped quickly when it was mocked across the country.

Then there was spurning $80 million from Washington that would have funded pre-kindergarten in Indiana. As one pol put it, "He wanted to be seen as the guy who wouldn't take money from D.C."

A lot of women did not take kindly to Pence's law that would not allow abortions even when it was discovered the baby had a genetic or physical defect. As a born-again evangelical, Pence never made a secret of his hatred of abortions. A federal judge felt otherwise and knocked down the law.

As egregious as some people found these actions, the one that really screwed his pooch was the Religious Freedom Restoration Act, which opponents argued would let business owners discriminate against the gay and transgender communities. The pushback was intense. Companies dropped Indiana travel plans and conventions to a tune of $60 million. The NBA weighed in against it. Little wonder the Indiana Chamber of Commerce said the bill made the state look less than welcoming and hospitable. President Obama made fun of it at the 2015 White House Correspondents' dinner, saying he and Biden have "gotten so close, in some places in Indiana, they won't serve us pizza anymore."

It didn't take Pence long to sign a "on second thought" amendment that said the act shouldn't be used to discriminate against gays.

Despite all this, Trump tweeted out that Pence was his guy, with the formal announcement coming the next day. There were reports that The Donald had second thoughts. But it was a done deal.

A Tale of Two Conventions

The Worst of Times—The RNC

Those of you who are picky-pickiers will protest that Charles Dickens started out with the "best of times." He wasn't living in this 2016 brawl for the presidency of the United States.

Donald Trump promised "show biz." He teased extravagance and showmanship, befitting of a Hollywood star like himself. And he made good, if your consider reruns on basic cable to be extravagant. Trump's A-lister turned out to be '80s actor Scott Baio of "Charles in Charge."

What became very evident from Day One was that someone who was a self-proclaimed master of putting on a show, Trump and company were not prepared to handle a convention. There was no pace. Anyone who has mounted even an amateur production knows you build to a crescendo. And who was in charge of the speaker's list? You don't announce that Heisman Winner Tim Tebow would take the podium without asking him. (He didn't.) On Day One, you were shaking your head over some of the choices, and not only Charles.

How about Willie Robertson, a son on the pseudo-reality show, "Duck Dynasty," who once said the Bible called LGBT members "drunks and thieves." His ringing endorsement of Trump was "I have three things in common with Mr. Trump. We're both successful businessmen. We've both had hit TV shows. And we both have intelligent wives who are much better looking than we are." He left out that they both inherited their companies from their bigoted fathers. Fred Trump had the reported KKK affiliations, while Willie's father, referencing the LGBT community, said, "It is nonsense. We have to run this bunch out of Washington, D.C. We have to rid the earth of them."

And what pol wouldn't be eager for Antonio Sabato Jr.'s endorsement? The former underwear model and soap-opera guy declared, "We had a Muslim president for seven-and-a-half years. I don't believe he is [a Christian]. I believe that he's on the other side . . . the Middle East. He's with the bad guys." There are more things wrong with this statement than a plot line of "General Hospital." Obama is not a Muslim, the Middle East are not the bad buys, and Obama's birthplace has been proved time and time again. Like his acting career, Sabato should have let the birther conspiracy die a quick and unceremonious death. Frothing Rudy Giuliani's gloom-and-doom speech was something to behold. The guy looked like he had missed his rabies shot as he screamed, "You know who you are, and we are coming to get you" to any potential terrorists in the audience.

Then there was the Trump's phone call to Fox while two survivors of the Benghazi attack were onstage accounting harrowing details and accusing Clinton of failing to do her job. So what happened? Fox left the convention hall to cover Trump's lambasting of Ohio governor and former rival John Kasich's refusal to attend the RNC in Cleveland. When Bill O'Reilly asked Trump if he thought Kasich was a sore loser, Trump said, "Well, I don't want to say that, but you know what? It was a very contentious primary. He lost very, very badly, and maybe if I were in his position, I wouldn't show up either."

Melania Trump's speech was supposed to be the highlight of the night. Before she opened her mouth, she was overshadowed by her husband making a grand entrance. The soon-to-be nominee usually waits until the last night to make a triumphal appearance. But Trump needed his ego-induced camera fix whenever he could get it. He came in backlit by a blinding, glowing light. Queen's "We Are the Champions" blasted through the hall. Apparently, no one told him this was a political convention and not the WWE Summer Slam. Let's just be thankful he wasn't wearing the customary pro-wrestling Speedos. Queen, of course, was quick to protest their song being used since they didn't authorize it nor did they endorse The Really Rich One.

When it was finally Melania's turn, she spoke softly, consulted the teleprompter often, but didn't deliver on her main objective. Humanize her husband. Fine, maybe that was an impossible task. She did say, "Donald is intensely loyal. To family, friends, employees, country." She forgot to mention that Donald has repeatedly cheated on his wives, tried to deny healthcare to family members with a sick infant, spoken openly about exacting revenge on employees and notoriously has no friends. Melania also went into her immigrant background when talking about a man who wanted to put up a big wall to keep immigrants out. But really, trying to equate your tough times as a model working in Paris and Milan with the hard times of American workers raised a few eyebrows.

First reaction was she did a competent job. Second reaction was "Did Michelle Obama help write her speech?" An eagle-eared blogger thought some of Melania's lines sounded familiar. And through the wonders of the internet, found the plagiarized material in Michelle's 2008 DNC speech. To compound the stupidity, Melania had laid claim to complete authorship. "I wrote it with [as] little help as possible," she told NBC's Matt Lauer shortly before making a fool of herself—as if those puffy things on the sleeves of her dress weren't enough..

Because the first night was mismanaged so much, it ran long. That left poor Iowa Sen. Joni Ernst, the GOP's Great Gal Hope, speaking to the backs of people hurrying up the aisles with network TV cameras off and the band stopping mid-song.

Day Two was filled with reactions to Mrs. Trump's Mi-

chelle lift. What was the big deal? Trump people asked.
Chris Christie tried to defend her saying it couldn't be
counted as plagiarism, "not when 93 percent of the speech
is completely different." Why is 7 percent a big deal anyway? It's not like the FDA would have a problem if Trump
Vodka contained 93 percent vodka and 7 percent goat
urine, right?

Paul Manafort, Trump's soon-to-be ex-campaign manager, somehow managed to blame this on Hillary. "This is
once again an example of when a woman threatens Hillary Clinton, how she seeks out to demean her and take
her down." At least, he didn't accuse Clinton of tampering
with the teleprompter.

The Twitter response was immediate.

> Thank God #Melania didn't go with her original open-
> ing tonight: "Hi, my name is Michelle Obama . . ."
> "Life is like a box of chocolates"—Melania Trump
> "Melania really sounded like a first lady! A specific,
> current one."
> "What a man, what a man, what a mighty good man."
> #FamousMelaniaTrumpQuotes

Leave it to Stephen Colbert to trump them all. He
had actress Laura Benanti do a spot-on imitation of Melania. "My fellow Americans," she said, "this is truly the best
of times, it is the worst of times. I did not plagiarize my
speech last night, I would never do such a thing. I would
not, could not with a goat. I would not, could not on a
boat. That is because I learned honesty during my humble
upbringing, in West Philadelphia born and raised. Thank
you. On the playground is where I spent most of my days."

The last part was a lift from "The Fresh Prince of Bel-Air," in case you aren't up on TV trivia. Benanti even nailed the teleprompter squints.

Despite the distraction, the show must go on. There were formalities to get out of the way. Nominate Pence as vice president. Check. Trump as president. Check check.

The celebrities for the night were top golfer Natalie Gulbis—top if you consider being ranked 121st on the WPGA tour as such—and Dana White, president of the Ultimate Fighting Championship (UFC). You know. Ronda Rousey, Conor McGregor, kicking, punching, tossing and other mayhem in a cage.

One of the main eventers for the evening was Chris Christie. He, after reminding everyone that he had been a federal prosecutor, offered an indictment of Hillary Clinton. After each "charge," he asked the crowd "guilty or innocent." Shouts of "Lock her up," echoed through the convention hall like whatever sound lemmings make right before they plunge over the side of a cliff. Incidentally, he did not ask for the jury's verdict on whether he had a part in the Bridgegate scandal. Nor did he make reference to another prosecutor, James Comey, exonerating Clinton of criminal wrongdoing.

Tiffany Trump, the daughter that's not attractive enough for Donald to want to date, took to the podium. She spoke of her father's supporting her by writing "sweet notes" of encouragement on her report card. "Donald Trump has never done anything halfway, least of all as a parent," she said. What she neglected to mention was her mother, Marla Maples, had said she raised Tiffany as a single parent. Only once a year did the girl visit her father's Florida estate, Mar-a-Lago, for two weeks. Tiffany told an interviewer, "He's not the dad who's going to take me to the beach and go swimming, but he's such a motivational person." So you can only wonder how much father-daughter quality time there was in those two weeks.

Tiffany's performance was bright and chipper, yet somehow sad, like Cinderella waxing poetic about her father to a congregation of field mice. You also had to wonder if this was an attempt to win her father's attention—although he wasn't in Cleveland that night, maybe he was watching back in Trump Tower.

Donald Trump Jr., of course, had more exposure to his father. Junior described Senior as hardworking, someone who "didn't hide out behind some desk in an executive suite. He spent his career with regular Americans. He hung out with the guys on construction sites . . . pouring concrete and hanging sheet rock . . . He listened to them, and he valued their opinions as much and often more than the guys from Harvard and Wharton, locked away in offices, away from the real work." Junior left out that Pops had a history of not paying those guys on construction sites.

Donny's attempt at humanizing his father was mentioning grandpa tries to teach granddaughter how to swing a golf club and that dad had his older kids work under regular guys like "Vinnie Stellio, who taught us how to drive heavy equipment, operate tractors and chainsaws, who worked his way through the ranks to become a trusted adviser of my father. It's why we're the only children of billionaires as comfortable in a D10 Caterpillar as we are in our own cars." Perhaps being a Caterpillar stockholder, Trump's children received the special models with Bose sound systems, climate-control air conditioning and seat massagers.

Therein followed the obligatory Hillary bashing and the fiction that she wants to banish the Second Amendment. Junior also made it clear he really, really doesn't like teacher tenure. And he really, really likes school choice. "Our schools used to be an elevator to the middle class. Now they're stalled on the ground floor," he said. "They're like Soviet-era department stores that are run for the benefit of the clerks and not the customers." This from a guy who attended exclusive private schools. He's stepped foot in fewer public schools than Holden Caulfield.

Be that as it may, there was chatter after the speech about Junior going into politics. More and more came out about his retweeting white supremacists, doing radio shows with white supremacists and joking about gas chambers. Referencing Hillary Clinton, Junior had said, "They've let her slide on every indiscrepancy, on every lie, on every DNC game trying to get Bernie Sanders out of this thing. If Republicans were doing that, they'd be warming up the gas chamber right now." On the upside, he appears to think the gas chamber is a bad thing, so that's comforting.

A speaker later, it was Ben Carson's turn. He delivered another one of his "say what?" discourses as he went off prompter. Somehow he made a leap from Hillary Clinton admiring community organizer Saul Alinsky to Hillary admiring Lucifer. A perfectly logical leap—at least in Carson's mind —since Alinsky once wrote about Lucifer being the first radical.

An Atlantic magazine contributor may have summed it up best. "Two more days left in the convention, but it's going to be hard for anyone to match moon-bat tone of Ben Carson's Lucifer/Alinsky speech."

Day 3, Pence spoke. Donald made still-another appearance. Third Trump kid spoke. Some women got time at the mic. But the guy who stole the show was Ted Cruz. The lovable Canadian-turned-Texan thumbed his nose at the whole party-unity push. He stood defiant in his refusal to endorse Trump. "I am not in the habit of supporting people who attack my wife and attack my father." But that wasn't enough. He ended by saying, "Don't stay home in November. Stand and speak and vote your conscience."

This so riled the crowd, his wife had to be led out by security. And Trump, once again, got the spotlight turned on him when he walked over to his family-seating area and flashed a thumb's up. Give the man credit for restraint. It might have been more in character if the finger had been the middle one.

And then it was the day, Day Four, that Trump had been salivating over like a large-breasted blonde. He would stand before millions and accept the nomination. His people managed to line up speakers with a tad more star power for the occasion. NFL quarterback Fran Tarkenton, now promoting an anti-AARP group (hey, didn't you know the AARP is a bunch of communists who supported Obamacare?), Jerry Falwell Jr. (Sr. is now cursing the Teletubbies from the afterlife) and Peter Thiel, PayPal co-founder who ran against the Silicon Valley tide of endorsing Clinton.

It was left to daughter Ivanka, daddy's favorite, to introduce her father. (If you were playing a drinking game for every time she said, "my father"—28—you would have been sloshed and in the ER by the end of her speech. To be fair, she probably needs to remind Trump that he is her father whenever possible.) She got high marks for poise and making a case for Père Donald. She said he would read about a person "facing some injustice or hardship" and set up a meeting at Trump Tower so he could help him or her out.

She also made a case for her clothing line. The $138 pink dress she wore sold out the next day.

So, how did the main attraction do? He shouted like loudspeakers hadn't been invented, he pointed, he delicately put his thumb and index finger together, thumbs went up, standard Trump stuff. He also managed to stay on teleprompter for the 75 minutes he was at the podium.

In that time, Trump made it clear that the country was not going to hell in a handbasket. It was already there, and HE was the only one who could fix it. He could get rid of crime as soon as he took over the White House. ISIS, you be warned because Trump would exterminate you like a nest of roaches in a Trump-owned condo.

Along the way, he used misinterpreted, cherry-picked and sometimes out-and-out false numbers to back up claims that the country was crime ridden, under siege from immigrants, had falling income, with more than 50 percent of black youth unemployed, suffering "disastrous" trade deals that were killing American manufacturing and so on.

He got hits on Hillary, which led to applause, booing her and cries of "Lock her up." He took one well-aimed shot with "My opponent asks her supporters to recite a three-word loyalty pledge. It reads: 'I'm With Her.' I choose to recite a different pledge. My pledge reads 'I'm with you, the American people.' I am your voice."

Those watching the speech might have missed Bernie Sanders' tweets in reaction to Trump saying the progressive's supporters "will join our movement, because we will fix his biggest issue, trade deals." To which Bernie tweeted,

"Those who voted for me will not support Trump who has made bigotry and divisiveness the cornerstone of his campaign."

When the Man of the Hour blamed the mess in the Middle East on Obama and Clinton, Sanders swiped back with "Trump is wrong. The real cause of instability in the Middle East was the Bush-Cheney invasion of Iraq. By the way, where is President Bush?" Probably on a ranch somewhere trying to make a Nativity scene out of taxidermied animals.

The consensus was the speech was a success. However, the convention not so much. There were unacceptable pauses on-air that TV anchors struggled to fill. Speakers were slotted at strange times. "The underwear model had a better speaking slot than Jodi Ernst," said Stuart Stevens, the strategist who ran Romney's 2012 convention. Parts of Tuesday were so soporific that a producer joked it might be better to cut away from the convention to announce director Garry Marshall's death.

Not that Trump saw it that way. He tweeted that it was "one of the best produced, including the incredible stage & set, in the history of conventions." And the ratings were through the roof, he exulted. Except they weren't. His acceptance speech was watched by fewer people than John McCain's. When the overall the ratings didn't prove to be as big as Trump promised, he blamed the GOP. "I didn't produce our show," Trump told The New York Times. "I just showed up for the final speech."

The Best of Times — The DNC

Humorist Will Rogers is often quoted as saying "I am not a member of any organized political party. I am a Democrat." He would have been astonished by Democratic National Convention, organized, polished, moving and strong.

There was some worry that Day One might devolve into a 1968 convention melee with Bernie supporters going ballistic—and to be sure, there was a fair amount of booing. Emails had been leaked showing DNC staffers, including chairman Debbie Wasserman Schultz, plotted ways to undermine Sanders. DNC chief financial officer Brad Sanders wrote, "Can we get someone to ask his belief. Does he believe in a God. He had skated on saying he has a Jewish heritage. I think I read he is an atheist. This could make several points difference with my peeps." After Sanders voiced concern that the DNC was undermining his campaign, Wasserman Schultz chided him via a DNC email saying, "Spoken like someone who has never been a member of the Democratic Party and has no understanding of what we do."

This is not a sentence that should appear in print often, but Donald Trump was right. There was some rigging going on to a small extent.

This did not sit well with Berniebros. The revolutionaries were beyond outraged. They protested outside the Philadelphia Wells Fargo Center where it's usually drunken Flyers fans doing the shouting. And Sandernistas took it inside. Even Bernie had a hard time quieting them. He made it clear, however, that the mission now was to defeat Donald Trump. "Hillary Clinton must become the next president of the United States. The choice is not even close."

If you want someone in your corner, recruit Michelle Obama. She absolutely delivered for Clinton. She began her pattern of disdaining Trump by not mentioning him by name. That somehow made her pounding him more effective. She talked about advice she gave her daughters when it came to dealing with tormentors. "When someone is cruel or acts like a bully, you don't stoop to their level. No, our motto is, when they go low, we go high."

She made the speech wonderfully personal, talking about the first day her young girls went to school. "I watched those 7- and 10-year-olds get into those black SUVs with those big [Secret Service] men with guns," she said. All she could think of was "What have we done?" It was Hillary Clinton, she asserted, who would protect all the children of America. And more than that, she pointed out "Hillary Clinton lets my daughters take it for granted a woman can be president of the United States."

One of the best lines of the night went to comedian Sarah Silverman, a Sanders supporter. When she got a cue from the side to stretch her time onstage, she ad-libbed, "You Bernie-or-bust voters are being ridiculous."

And nothing like closing out the evening with Paul Simon singing "Bridge Over Troubled Water." The RNC, on the other hand, had country singer Chris Janson, famous for such hits as "Buy me a Boat," "White Trash" and "Power of Positive Drinkin." Although when you examine Janson's lyrics, he may have been the perfect choice for a Trump campaign. In "Buy me a Boat," he croons

> "I keep hearing that money is the root of all evil
> And you can't fit a camel through the eye of a
>   needle . . .
> 'Cause it could buy me a boat, it could buy me a
>   truck to pull it"

Perhaps he was talking about Trump's $100-million yacht, the Trump Princess.

Day Two was a big one for Hillary. The vote was in, and no surprise (especially after reading the leaked DNC emails), she was the nominee. Bernie Sanders showed his disappointment was not overriding. The enemy was Donald Trump. Vermont was moved to last in the roll call so that Sanders could ask for a unanimous vote for his one-time opponent. It's like that old saying, "The enemy of a megalomaniacal douchebag is my friend."

Day Two was a day for Bill. He started his keynote with "I met a girl." On to him proposing three times and only getting a "yes" on the third and that after he bought a tiny house she had admired. Bill was supposed to make Hillary more likeable. As was Melania with Trump. Bringing in anecdotes is always a good thing, so the nod goes to Bill—and no plagiarism accusations followed his speech. He showed the Big Dog—though that vegan diet had made him not as big—still could get a crowd going. He could advocate forcefully for his wife, the candidate. "She's the best darn change maker I ever met in my entire life. This woman has never been satisfied with the status quo on anything. She always wants to move the ball forward. That's just who she is."

Meryl Streep spoke, opening with a scream that became a viral sensation. She followed with a rousing speech, highlighting the need for "grit and grace" in female leaders. No one has ever said Streep doesn't give her all to any role she plays. If Hillary could have made some kind of "Freaky Friday" body-swap with Streep, inherited Streep's stage presence and diction, she probably would have won the election.

On a somber note was the appearance of Mothers of

the Movement—women whose children had been killed, children whose names had been in headlines for days, months and longer—Eric Garner, Trayvon Martin, Dontré Hamilton, Michael Brown, Sandra Bland and others. The anguish of these mothers was hard to watch.

Day Three was a combination of "America Is Already Great" optimism and "Trump Is the Suck Master" evisceration. Maybe those Trump words weren't used, still viewers got the drift. The speakers ran from the expected, Barack Obama, Joe Biden to the somewhat unexpected, Mike Bloomberg. Trump brags about his many billions, though who knows how many he has. No disputing the former N.Y. mayor's $40 billion.

Mayor Mike made it very clear he had no use for the "dangerous demagogue." And boy, Bloomberg didn't build his fortune on a million-dollar check from his daddy. "I'm a New Yorker, and I know a con when I see one," he said. "The richest thing about Donald Trump is his hypocrisy." As long as he was at it, he exhorted the country to elect a "sane, competent" person.

Joe Biden was not to be outdone, calling Trump's cynicism "unbounded. His lack of empathy and compassion can be summed up in the phrase I suspect he's proud of and he made famous: 'You're fired!' I mean think about that. . . . How can there be pleasure in saying 'you're fired'? He has no clue about what makes America great. Actually, he has no clue. Period."

Leave it to Obama, however, to take the oratory to a new level. He was under some pressure to do so since Michelle had set the bar so high. POTUS reportedly stayed up until 3 in the morning of his speech rewriting it. What he gave was met with euphoric applause.

"Fair to say, this is not your typical election. It's not just a choice between parties or policies, the usual debates between left and right. This is a more fundamental choice—about who we are as a people and whether we stay true to this great American experiment in self-government."

He pushed the belief that Americans "are stronger together—black, white, Latino, Asian, Native American, young, old, gay, straight, men, women, folks with disabilities, all pledging allegiance, under the same proud flag, to this big, bold country that we love. That's what I see. That's the America I know!"

Obama got the crowd to wildly chant Hillary, Hillary, Hillary. And after mentioning Trump by name, asked the crowd not to boo, but to vote.

While Obama can always whip a crowd into a frenzy, his speech posed one of the more important questions asked at the DNC. What does a choice to elect Donald Trump say about the United States as a people? Are we a country based more on bluster than substance? Are we hopelessly distracted by shiny objects like a flock of magpies with attention deficit disorder? Or are we just that frustrated, like the early 20th-century men who received monkey-testicle implants to treat erectile dysfunction, that we will try literally anything?

It would be hard to top the speechmaking of the previous three nights. Still, there is nothing like basketball great Kareem Abdul-Jabbar introducing himself as Michael Jordan to the confused conventioneers. "I said that because I know that Donald Trump couldn't tell the difference." Slam dunk.

Abdul-Jabbar was not the only Muslim to address the

convention that night. The other was Khizr Kahn, a Pakistani who had come to the U.S. from the United Arab Emirates, His son was a U.S. Army captain in Iraq and died trying to stop a vehicle with suicide bombers and explosives in it.

"Our son, Humayun, had dreams also," Khizr Khan. "Dreams of being a military lawyer. But he put those dreams aside the day he sacrificed his life to save his fellow soldiers."

Khan went on to condemn Donald Trump's anti-Muslim stance before asking the Republican nominee if had ever been to Arlington Cemetery. "To look at the graves of brave patriots who died defending the United States of America? You will see all faiths, genders and ethnicities. You have sacrificed nothing," he said. "If it was up to Donald Trump, [Humayun] never would have even been in America. He vows to build walls and ban us from this country. Donald Trump, you're asking Americans to trust you with their future. Let me ask you, have you even read the United States Constitution? I will gladly lend you my copy." At that, he pulled a miniature version from his coat pocket.

This ignited one of the most captivating sub-battles of the 2016 campaign: Trump mind (and his Twitter account) vs. the Kahns. Trump went on attack against the Gold Star military family. And he made the attack more egregious by saying, "If you look at his wife, she was standing there, she had nothing to say, she probably—maybe she wasn't allowed to have anything to say, you tell me."

The following day, Mrs. Kahn explained her silence. "I was very nervous, because I cannot see my son's picture, and I cannot even come in the room where his pictures are, and that's why when I saw the picture on my back, I couldn't take it." Mr. Khan, was not so diplomatic, adding, "Trump is totally void of any decency because he is unaware of how to talk to a Gold Star family and how to speak to a Gold Star mother."

Looking to get the last word in, Trump appeared in an interview with ABC News' George Stephanopolous. When asked what he would say to the grieving father, Mr. Trump replied, "I'd say, 'We've had a lot of problems with radical Islamic terrorism.'" Wow? What will Trump say to his son, Barron, after the kid's hamster dies? — "We've had a lot of problems with rodent lifespans"? Trump also added, ""I think I've made a lot of sacrifices. I work very, very hard."

This exposes one of the biggest character flaws of Donald Trump. He literally did not understand the concept of self-sacrifice. He has never been selfless. Everything he's built, all the work he's put in, has been for him. His name, his fortune, his fame. He has always put his own personal gain ahead of his family, his children and certainly, his wives. There is a better chance of a blue whale passing through the eye of a beading needle than Donald Trump becoming benevolent. Just don't tell Trump that because he may try to have a blue whale captured and liquefied so it can make the squeeze. But back to the convention.

The nominee's acceptance speech ended it. Hillary Clinton is not known for being a powerful speaker. Some of the criticisms appear sexist—she shouts, she's shrill. But in truth she just is not a powerful speaker. All candidates have their flaws. But in this, her most important speech to date, she did very well, getting high marks even from some conservatives.

A theme throughout the speech was unity. "Powerful

forces are threatening to pull us apart. Bonds of trust and respect are fraying," she said. "And just as with our founders, there are no guarantees. It truly is up to us."

She gave a nod to people occasionally mistaking her for a mechanical death-android with "My job titles only tell you what I've done. They don't tell you why. The truth is through all these years of public service, the 'service' part has always come easier to me than the 'public' part." And a nod to her obsessiveness. "I sweat the details of policy," she said. "Because it's not just a detail if it's your kid—if it's your family. It's a big deal. And it should be a big deal to your president."

She was not above taking swipes at her opponent. "He spoke for 70-odd minutes, and I do mean odd," she said in reference to Trump's acceptance speech. "He had zero solutions."

Point of fact, Hillary was incorrect in saying Trump offered zero solution. From the start, he has suggested building a border wall was a solution. Maybe Hillary meant viable solutions. Building a wall will not make America great again. It's just going to be like Hulk Hogan—a big stupid thing that doesn't do anything productive.

Hillary also dissed him for claiming to know more about ISIS than the generals and for calling the U.S. military a disaster. Her plan would strike ISIS from the air "and support local forces taking them out on the ground. We will surge our intelligence so that we detect and prevent attacks before they happen. We will disrupt their efforts online to reach and radicalize young people in our country. It won't be easy or quick, but make no mistake—we will prevail."

As a sop to Sandernistas, Hillary promised to work

with Bernie to get free public-college education. She also thanked Sanders for putting economic and social justice issues "front and center, where they belong."

She concluded by saying, "That is the story of America. And we begin a new chapter tonight. Yes, the world is watching what we do. Yes, America's destiny is ours to choose. So let's be stronger together. Looking to the future with courage and confidence. Building a better tomorrow for our beloved children and our beloved country. When we do, America will be greater than ever. Thank you and may God bless the United States of America!"

And just like that, in a cascade of balloons and pyrotechnics reflecting off of Hillary's almost blindingly white pantsuit, the DNC was over.

Chapter Seven:
On to the Issues —
Sort of

S ort of? Well, trying to figure out where Donald Trump stood from one moment to the next millisecond was the equivalent of watching two hummingbirds having sex. The positions changed constantly, and you weren't real sure what was happening.

Shut down the borders to all Muslims one day. Later no, he didn't say that even though it was spelled out in a press release. He said he said, "You have to be very careful. We have to be very, very strong and vigilant at the borders."

He's opposed to the government mandating the purchase of health insurance. But wait, in a televised interview, he liked the mandate because he didn't want people dying in the streets.

Always against going into Libya except when he wasn't. Syria? Let them and ISIS fight it out. On second thought, invade Syria with "boots on the ground."

Let Trump be Trump, his first campaign manager, Corey Lewandowski, said before he was fired, starting a whiplash change in Trump's staff. There were reports that Lewandowski got canned because he was clueless about running an operation. There were also reports that his affair with the 27-year-old press secretary, Hope Hicks, she of the "no comment," ended with a shouting match on the street. Lewandowski, by the way, married his best friend's wife after BF was killed on 9/11. Lewandowski probably should have steered clear of the former model, who is a Trump pet. She lives in a rent-free Trump apartment and according to The Washington Post, sent her boss's dictated tweets to someone else to post. One wonders if Trump toddled over to her apartment at 3 a.m., baggy eyed and bathrobed, yelling, "Hope, we need to let the world know that Miss Universe is a disgusting loser!" It didn't help Lewandowski's tenure that Jared hated him. (An unnamed Trump campaign official, [cough] maybe Lewandowski [cough], described Kushner as "a snaky little motherfucker, a horrible human being.")

Lewandowski was followed by Paul Manafort, who was supposed to instill order and calm Republican jitters. He then became a "low-energy" (Trump's word, not ours) liability when reports came out of his possible illegal lobbying for the former president of Ukraine, a big-time Putin pal. In came Steve Bannon, CEO of Breitbart (it shouldn't be dignified with "News" since much of what appears is white-supremacist fiction) and Kellyanne Conway, who at one point apparently wasn't getting a paycheck. No matter, her polling company was raking it in since she was appointed campaign manager.

Let Trump be Trump, which why seriously talking about his issues is less productive than searching for the hidden meaning in a Justin Bieber song. Still, here goes. WARNING: Hillary's are not as entertaining—or scary—as Señor Trump's.

Immigration

Build a wall. Build it tall. And keep out those Mexican rapists and criminals. According to the master builder, he would erect it for $8 billion, which changed to $10 billion, then $12 billion—because he is the best at building. And that fantastic wall will be 1,000 miles by maybe 50 feet tall. And not to worry, the Mexicans would pay for it. The only problem was people who know what they are talking about, like actual engineers, put the price tag of materials alone at more than $17 billion. And the logistics would be a "ridiculous," one expert said. Just think of the housing for the 1,000 workers that would be needed to complete the job in a Trump first term. That's not to mention building roads to transport materials or maintenance of the wall, which could cost as much as $1 billion per year. And Mexican President Peña Nieto said, "At the start of the conversation with Donald Trump, I made it clear that Mexico will not pay for the wall." Perhaps that's why in a "60 Minutes" interview, Trump backed off from his assertion he would use concrete and steel, changing to saying some of it could be fencing. He could cut costs even further by only posting signs in certain areas that read, "Stay out! Seriously! We mean it!"

So we keep all those terrible people from invading us from the south. But those "radical Islamic terrorists" from the east are even more threatening. Don't let them in. There might be terrorists hidden among the 4.7 million Syrian refugees fleeing five years of war and deprivation. Or as Donald Jr. tweeted, "If I had a bowl of skittles and I told you just three would kill you. Would you take a handful? That's our Syrian refugee problem."

Funny thing, a year earlier, Papa Trump told his friend and fellow sympathizer, Bill O'Reilly, that he hated the concept of taking in refugees, "but on a humanitarian basis, you have to."

Three months later, he was calling for a complete ban on Muslims entering the U.S. for any reason. Of course when he was visiting Scotland to open a golf course, he hedged. Muslims from nice places like Great Britain, they could come in. But not from bad places. And maybe rich Muslims like Dubai's Hussain Sajwani, who Trump had called "a good friend" and "great man," could come over to negotiate deals that would make lots of money for the candidate.

What about those already in the country? A "deportation task force" would be created to focus on "identifying and quickly removing the 2 million plus most dangerous criminal illegal aliens in America." This was something of a pullback from an earlier position. Trump had said all 11 million undocumenteds would be deported. Even with the scaleback, let's consider what rounding up 2 million people would actually look like. It would take massive squads of police and military to track down the possible illegals. Then, with prisons already overflowing, special camps would need to be built to hold the deportees until they could be processed and shipped back. If you are disturbed because this sounds eerily familiar, that is good. It means that you have at least an elementary grasp of world history and some semblance of a soul. The other option Trump could try would be privatizing deportation, the way Uber has done with taxis. Sure, why not? Instead of Uber, Trump could have an app developed called "Beaner." For every illegal a private citizen apprehends, the catcher would get tax credits and free stays at a luxury Trump hotel. "Wait," you say, "that sounds immeasurably divisive and racist." True. But so were half the things Trump said while campaigning, so at least it's consistent.

Hillary? She called for immigration reform that would lead to full and equal citizenship. She would end family detention, close private immigrant-detention centers and help more eligible people become naturalized.

A leaked speech had her calling for "open borders," which Trump pounced on in the third debate. She was talking about energy, she claimed, electricity flowing from country to country. A Duke public-policy professor felt it was a "broader call for greater hemispheric cooperation on a variety of issues, including trade." He noted that the leak was only an excerpt. ". . . without seeing the rest of her speech, I would also guess that the 'open borders' she mentions relate to the movement of goods and capital, but not people."

Though Hillary never said so, you might believe that the only wall she wanted to build was around Donald Trump.

The Economy

Trump would tear up NAFTA, despite it tripling trade between Canada, Mexico and the U.S. from $290 billion in 1993 to more than $1.1 trillion in 2016. Yes, some American jobs were lost because of the agreement, and yes, some were created.

Then he would impose tariffs of up to 35 percent on imported goods. Because Trump lives in a penthouse on top of Trump Land, the notion of retaliation never made it up the high-speed elevator to him.

Trump being a good Republican, of course, wanted to cut taxes big time. The biggest winners would be the wealthy. Trump would have you believe that by capping deductions for the wealthy and closing special-interest loopholes, "The tax relief will be concentrated on the working and middle class taxpayer. They will receive the biggest benefit—it won't even be close," he said with a straight face.

However, others, who can add and subtract, disagreed. His plan would represent around a paltry 2-percent savings for the poor and middle class, with many single parents actually seeing their rates increase. And big bucks would go to those top 1-percenters in the form of a 12-percent savings. Trump would benefit additionally by reducing the rate on something called "pass-through" entities, of which he owns a ton. But please don't think that anything nefarious was afoot. "It wasn't something we took into consideration when we made this plan," Trump economic policy adviser Stephen Moore said.

Furthermore, Citizens for Tax Justice crunched the numbers and found Trump's tax proposal would slash federal revenues by $4.8 trillion over the next 10 years, which would add trillions to the national debt.

Hillary, on the other hand, would raise taxes on the wealthy with what she called the "fair share surcharge." If you make $5 million or more, the top rate would be 43.6 percent. For the benefit of Fox business journalist Maria Bartiromo and others who missed this day in school or slept through the class, that does *not* mean you would be paying that percentage on all your income. Bartiromo insisted that Ben and Jerry of yummy ice-cream fame would be paying 92 percent of everything they made if Bernie

Sanders had his way. (They liked Bernie so much, they created a flavor in his honor—Bernie's Yearning, mint ice cream with a layer of chocolate at the top, which represents the economic gains that have gone to the wealthiest 1 percent since the recession. "Beneath it, the rest of us.") The U.S. has something called a graduated income tax. That means Warren Buffet shells out the same $1,800 on the first $15,000 he earns as someone who makes a total of $15,000. Higher brackets are assessed incrementally. Note: Trump isn't used as a reference point since, proudly, he hasn't paid federal taxes since the 1990s.

When it came to trade pacts, Clinton had her own case of "hummingbird sex." She tried to back off from her support while secretary of state of the Trans-Pacific Partnership (TPP). Candidate Clinton wasn't so sure it was the "gold standard" she once called it.

She wouldn't assess tariffs that would make foreign products more expensive and theoretically, but not probably, get Americans to buy homegrown items. She touted a plan that would increase American production by dangling tax incentives in front of companies that build in the U.S.

When it came to creating jobs, Trump was the guy who could do it. Count on 25 million new ones over 10 years. And how would he achieve that? By building a better business environment, by reducing taxes, eliminating pesky regulations. The Trump campaign complained that the FDA "even dictates the nutritional content of dog food." Sure, who cares if your dog's food is actually made out of petroleum jelly and ground-up tires? Not Trump. He's never owned a dog.

Clinton wanted more job training, $275 billion on infrastructure spending and investment in new energy that would boost the number of jobs in those areas. The infrastructure money would come, she said, from corporate tax reform.

But hold it right there, cowgirl, Donald would spend $550 billion and he'd pay for it by creating a fund that people would invest in and by getting low-interest deals. And if that didn't work, he would put on a show in the barn.

Healthcare

Trump would rip up Obamacare and replace it with "something terrific." (Hope he gets a big shredder installed in the Oval Office for all the ripping he's going to do.) That something would be making the cost of health insurance a tax deduction, opening up the borders, oops, the state borders so that a Floridian could shop around and buy into a Colorado plan. And permitting the importation of cheaper prescription drugs from other countries.

OK. But after he has done his shredding, what happens to people covered under the Affordable Care Act? Will insurance companies revert to denying coverage because of pre-existing conditions? Sons and daughters up to age 26, would they no longer be on their parents' plans? The problem with this and other Trump proposals is that he will not be the boss giving orders to apprentices who can be fired. He will have to deal with the unruly Congress, many of whose members take marching orders from lobbyists. Buying prescriptions overseas might sound great. How do you think the pharma industry is going to like it? These guys spend close to $3.4 billion on lobbying.

Hillary, she would work on tweaking it, not throwing the legislation into the shredder. Getting more people

enrolled with more generous subsidies. Premiums would
be limited to no more than 8.5 percent of incomes as opposed to the current 9.66 percent.

But wait, there's more. Open Medicare to 55-year-olds
and add a public-option plan. That's a government-run
health insurance agency that competes with the private
sector.

The Supreme Court

Of course, this became a big issue what with Antonin
Scalia's seat still unfilled, two justices older than 80 and
a third 78. As one millennial, Jeremy Karpf, wrote, "Who
those justices are will affect whether Roe v. Wade protects
a woman's right to choose, Citizens United v. FEC continues to allow dark money to influence political campaigns
and Obergefell v. Hodges allows same-sex couples to marry. Ultimately, the president alone will not singlehandedly
seat the new justices. Congress must confirm any nominee, but the person we elect president will determine who
is nominated."

In the third presidential debate, this was one issue that
provoked a substantive discourse. Trump wanted a justice
who would help overturn Roe v. Wade. Clinton wanted
Citizens United overturned. Trump wanted a court that
would forcefully uphold the Second Amendment, and
once again, falsely accused Clinton of trying to do away
with it and "take your guns away." Apparently, Trump is
blissfully unaware of how difficult it is to repeal a constitutional amendment. In fact, only one has been—Prohibi-
tion. A good thing because many Americans needed cases
of hooch to get through this election cycle.

Terrorism aka ISIS

This is a complicated issue with no easy answers from either side. One might think with Hillary's years of dealing with Gordian knots, she might have an edge. On the other hand, she can't shout as loud or angrily scrunch her face as much as Trump. Shoot, one look at him, and ISIS types might decide to surrender forthwith.

The list of issues went on flailing around in the shouts of Trump's Make America Great Again and Hillary's assurance the country would be Stronger Together, a slogan she choose after passing on 84 others. This vital bit of information was revealed in a hacked email that WikiLeaks thought was important to leak.

Chapter Eight:
He didn't just
say that . . .

There is an old saying, "Actions speak louder than words." It's as if Donald Trump is fighting his own, very public, battle to prove that statement false. He is the mouth-author of some of the most ridiculous things ever heard. Bask in a few of the most outrageous, most perplexing, most "Is this real life, or am I having some kind of fever dream?" quotes from The Donald.

"If Ivanka weren't my daughter, perhaps, I would be dating her." (The comment was made on a 2006 episode of "The View" when Ivanka was 24.)

The only way this could have been creepier is if Trump had been gently stroking a Cabbage Patch doll's crotch when he said it. Suggesting sleeping with your daughter (Trump bragged about sleeping with a lot of women he dated) isn't too far behind cannibalism and being a member of an Osmonds tribute band on the taboo list.

"Cause I like kids, I mean, I won't do anything to take care of them. I'll supply funds and she'll take care of the kids." (Fortune, 2016)

Donald Trump has the parental instincts of a father grizzly bear. That is to say he might eat his own young if he wasn't trying to fuck them. Hyperbole aside, this quote illustrates just how little Trump actually cares about his own children when they can't be useful to him.

"Black guys counting my money; I hate it! The only kind of people I want counting my money are little short guys that wear yarmulkes every day." (USA Today, 1991)

Well, at least Donald didn't actually use the N-word. So, on the racist scale that puts him slightly ahead of David Duke, Paula Deen and baseball jerk John Rocker. Of course, that's like being the tallest worker at the Willy Wonka Chocolate factory. Is it coincidence that both Trump and the Oompa Loompas are orange?

"You know, it really doesn't matter what the media write as long as you've got a young, beautiful piece of ass." (Esquire, 2013)

No Donald, finding a 20-something woman who's desperate enough to sleep with you does not erase the reports of the terrible things you've done.

"When Mexico sends its people, they're not sending the best. They're not sending you, they're sending people that have lots of problems and they're bringing those problems with us. They're bringing drugs. They're bring crime. They're rapists . . . And some, I assume, are good people."

Trump goes on a tirade against Mexican immigrants, says they're rapists and then tacks on that some "are good people" at the end. It's meeting someone and saying, "Wow, your face looks like a bullfrog's after getting a battery-acid enema. Your hair looks like someone skinned a giant, diseased hamster . . . And your teeth, they look nice."

"All of the women on 'The Apprentice' flirted with me—consciously or unconsciously. That's to be expected."

Trump is that delusional guy you knew in college who thought every woman was trying to sleep with him. You were like, "Man, she just asked to borrow a pencil." "Bro! That's secret girl-code for she wants the D!"

"The beauty of me is that I'm very rich."

Well, it's not his body, face, hair or personality. So if we're not counting the ability to lie without reservation as something beautiful, then sure, let's go with rich.

"The point is, you can never be too greedy."

Apparently Donald has never read the story of King Midas, heard about the 2008 collapse of the housing market or watched "The Price is Right"—"You had 90 cents! Why, why would you spin again?!?!?!"

"My Twitter has become so powerful that I can actually make my enemies tell the truth."

Captain America had his shield. Wonder Woman her lasso. And Trump has a Twitter account that apparently works as a truth serum, as well as an insult-delivery system.

"Look at those hands, are they small hands? And, [Republican rival Marco Rubio] referred to my hands: 'If they're small, something else must be small.' I guarantee you there's no problem. I guarantee."

Yes, that needed to be mentioned again. Trump started

talking about his penis during a presidential debate. The only way that could have gotten cruder is if he dropped his pants and showed everyone. And don't think he wouldn't have done it if Viagra had paid him millions to become their spokesman.

"Number one, I have great respect for women. I was the one that really broke the glass ceiling on behalf of women, more than anybody in the construction industry."

Trump saying he has great respect for women is like saying Pablo Esocbar had great respect for U.S. customs officials. It's like saying John Wayne Gacy had great respect for teenage boys. It's like saying the bear had great respect for Leonardo DiCaprio in "The Revenant."

"Sorry losers and haters, but my I.Q. is one of the highest—and you all know it! Please don't feel so stupid or insecure, it's not your fault.

You know who feels the need to brag about their IQ? People who are terribly insecure and have done nothing of note that actually validates their intelligence.

"It's like in golf. A lot of people—I don't want this to sound trivial—but a lot of people are switching to these really long putters, very unattractive. It's weird. You see these great players with these really long putters, because they can't sink three-footers anymore. And, I hate it. I am a traditionalist. I have so many fabulous friends who happen to be gay, but I am a traditionalist."

So . . . Donald Trump doesn't like gay marriage or long putters. And yes, equating the lifestyle of a huge group of people to a game designed to entertain rich assholes is very trivializing.

"He's [John McCain] not a war hero. He was a war hero because he was captured. I like people who weren't captured."

Donald Trump saying John McCain isn't a war hero is a pewee football coach saying, "Dan Marino wasn't a great quarterback because I like people who win Super Bowls." This is Trump, a guy who dodged Vietnam like it was a gym-class dodge ball. The hypocrisy is so thick and slimy, Ted Cruz could use it as hair gel.

"I think apologizing's a great thing, but you have to be wrong. I will absolutely apologize, sometime in the hopefully distant future, if I'm ever wrong."

There's a word for a person who cannot admit they're wrong. Narcissist. Or douchebag works, too. This quote confirms what people have suspected — that Trump thinks he is infallible. He probably would think he was the second coming of Christ, too, except that Jesus got captured and tortured like that "loser" John McCain.

"The concept of global warming was created by and for the Chinese in order to make U.S. manufacturing non-competitive."

Yes, and all the scientific data is probably a Chinese conspiracy, too. Think about it, where were all the thermometers made the scientists used to collect the otherwise irrefutable data? China.

"I watched when the World Trade Center came tumbling down. And I watched in Jersey City, N.J., where thousands and thousands of people were cheering as that building was coming down. Thousands of people were cheering."

This never happened. He just made it up. Donald

Trump lies more effortlessly than Michael Phelps swims when it suits his purpose. And he does it so frequently that trying to debunk his falsehoods is like trying to wipe up the ocean with a sponge mop.

"I would bring back waterboarding, and I'd bring back a hell of a lot worse than waterboarding."

The U.S. president-elect is advocating the use of torture "a lot worse" than waterboarding. Let that sink in. Taking into account that a waterboarding victim described it as "being drowned, albeit slowly" and said that now, "if I do anything that makes me short of breath, I find myself clawing at the air with a horrible sensation of smothering and claustrophobia," what worse things does Trump want to use? The gas chamber? Genital mutilation? Force them to watch unending reruns of "The Jerry Springer Show"?

"Hillary wants to abolish — essentially abolish the Second Amendment. By the way, if she gets to pick, if she gets to pick her judges, nothing you can do, folks. Although the Second Amendment people, maybe there is, I don't know."

What . . . the . . . fuck. Trump just vaguely suggested the assassination of Hillary Clinton. This is not something to be ever joked about. Ever. Especially with Trump supporters who we know, by virtue of believing his campaign promises, have no grasp of the difference between fiction and reality.

Chapter Nine:
Hillary Missteps, Misspokes and Pillorying Hillary

O nce upon a time, Hillary Clinton was First Lady of the United States of America with an 80-percent approval rating. When she left the secretary of state office, she was at 65 percent. So what happened? How did she become untrustworthy, unlikable, a liar, "such a nasty woman" and crooked?

Some of it can be attributed to that "vast right wing conspiracy" Hillary was always talking about. You're only paranoid if they aren't out to get you, and Hillary managed to enrage plenty Republicans. Rubbing people the wrong way is kind of Hillary's super-power. It started back when she was First Lady. Then the opposition blitzkrieg began when it became obvious she, an uppity woman, was running for president. "Everybody thought Hillary Clinton was unbeatable, right?" Republican Majority Leader Kevin McCarthy boasted. "But we put together a Benghazi special committee . . . What are her numbers today? Her numbers are dropping." And everyone wonders why Hillary bothers with tin-foil hats and secret emails.

Unfortunately for her, Hillary helped attackers by bringing along more baggage than Kim Kardashian on a weeklong getaway. She chose to set up the private email server. And when it was brought to light, she was dismissive, saying, "Everything I did was permitted. There was no law, there was no regulation, there was nothing that did not give me the full authority to decide how I was going to communicate. And people across the government knew that I used one device. Maybe it was because I'm not the most technically capable person and wanted to make it easy as possible. And now I think it's kind of fun. People get a real-time, behind-the-scenes look at what I was emailing about."

That is a terrible answer. Truly awful. For starters, not being "technically capable" isn't a valid excuse when your boss stumbles across porno on your work computer (I don't know how it got there, Boss. I'm not technically capable). Forget about when you're secretary of state and national security is involved. Second, at no point did she admit fault or say how she was going to make amends. Instead, she said, "Everything I did was permitted," which was categorically false. It wasn't illegal, but she needed to obtain approval before using a private server. She should have said something like "I made a bad error in judgment. I'm sorry. I will better educate myself on the technological aspects so something like this never happens again, and I will work to be more transparent to the American people." Then the entire thing could have been over before it started. Finally, NOTHING about this was fun. Except maybe the email about someone robbing a Domino's Pizza in a

Hillary Clinton mask. That was kind of fun . . . except for the poor employee who was shot in the leg. So no, NOTH-ING about it was fun.

If you know you're going to be running for president, don't speak three times before Goldman Sachs, even for $675,000. What's so wrong with Goldman? "The first thing you need to know about Goldman Sachs is that it's everywhere," journalist Matt Taibbi explains. "The world's most powerful investment bank is a great vampire squid wrapped around the face of humanity, relentlessly jamming its blood funnel into anything that smells like money." It is a reviled financial company, largely held responsible for the Great Recession. The Atlantic even ran an article titled, "Is Goldman Sachs the Root of All Evil?" If that question even needs to be asked, a political candidate should avoid Goldman like a vegan avoids Big Macs. No, they couldn't be that bad. Yes, they could. For reference, here are some of the worst things overhead in the Goldman Sachs elevator:

"If I could choose between world peace and a reasonable fortune, my first Lambo would be orange."

"Listening to Obama talk about the economy is like listening to a chick talk about football."

"If you can only be good at one thing, be good at lying . . . because if you're good at lying, you're good at everything."

And according to an anonymous attendee, Hillary's speeches were "pretty glowing about us" and that "it's so far from what she sounds like as a candidate now. . . . She sounded more like a Goldman Sachs managing director." When you pile that on top of Hillary's other questionable financial dealings, it is shadier than a solar eclipse.

It didn't help that when Hillary and Bill left the White House, she said they were "dead broke." Most Americans would like to be as broke. They bought a $1.7 million house in tony Chappaqua, N.Y., in the year before changing their 20500 zip code, and a $2.85-million crash pad in D.C. in December 2000. Many Americans would question the destitute claim. In Hillary's world, she probably was dead broke, but that only goes to show how far out of touch she'd become with normal life. Granted, it's hard to relate to Joe Sixpack when you've been living in the White House and flying around on private jets for the better part of a decade.

When Steve Bannon's Government Accountability Institute (GAI) went after the Clinton Foundation, the basis had been laid for believing the "pay for play" allegations of Clinton using her position as secretary to state to establish a quid pro quo for wealthy donors. Legitimate news organizations jumped on the story and spent 16 months investigating it. And like the Benghazi hearings, wrongdoing was not found. Still, the GAI report made Carly Fiorina's accusation that the foundation spent 90 percent on administration, with only 10 percent going to charities, sound plausible. That is until you remembered Carly Fiorina is only slightly more trustworthy than Bernie Madoff. Records showed the exact opposite was true—10 percent administration and 90 percent charities.

The Clinton Foundation backs public-health, economic-development, women's-rights, AIDS and climate-change programs. Compare that to the Trump Foundation, which bought two giant portraits of Donald and paid to defend a lawsuit to take down a too-high flagpole.

Another blot on her reputation—the Vince Foster

conspiracy. Yes, it's true that Hillary chewed him out, Sergeant Hartman style, days before his death. Probably not the best thing to do to someone who suffers from anxiety and depression, but the death was definitely a suicide. Foster even left a note saying, "I was not meant for the job or the spotlight of public life in Washington. Here ruining people is considered sport." Somehow that has not stopped people from speculating that she had him killed, and of course, Trump fanned the flames on Foster's funeral pyre.

"He knew everything that was going on, and then all of a sudden he committed suicide," Trump said. "I don't bring [Foster's death] up because I don't know enough to really discuss it. I will say there are people who continue to bring it up because they think it was absolutely a murder. I don't do that because I don't think it's fair." Donald, what the hell? That's like saying, "There is a lawsuit against Donald Trump for raping a 13-year-old girl. I don't bring it up because I don't really know enough to discuss it. But people say he absolutely has a fetish for Dora the Explorer." By the way, if you think that example was too off-base, there actually was a suit filed against him and fellow billionaire Jeffrey Epstein. The plaintiff claimed Trump assaulted her at a series of sex parties that Epstein threw in 1994. Both Epstein and Trump denied the allegations, although Epstein did plead guilty to soliciting a minor in 2008.

The problem is Hillary is more secretive than Bruce Wayne when someone brings up the Batcave. If you appear to be hiding something, voters are going to think you *are* hiding things. In her defense, she has been under an electron microscope for decades and is understandably taciturn. Hillary admitted, at one point, of keeping the press corps at arm's length, which would only amp up their attention. Still, if you have pneumonia, be forthright about it. That way you don't give more grist to Rudy Giuliani's "she's got serious health problems" mill.

Another piece of advice. Don't go into coal country and say "I'm the only candidate which has a policy about how to bring economic opportunity using clean renewable energy as the key into coal country. Because we're going to put a lot of coal miners and coal companies out of business, right?" She might as well have told them she was going to personally douse their houses in kerosene and light a match.

All they heard was she was going to put them out of their jobs, not what she followed with about generations of those working in the mines "losing their health, often losing their lives to turn on our lights and power our factories. Now we've got to move away from coal and all the other fossil fuels, but I don't want to move away from the people who did the best they could to produce the energy that we relied on."

Despite Bernie barking in her ear, Hillary completely missed what turned out to be the central aspect of the campaign. The working middle-class was hurting bad, or at least, thought they were, and instead of positioning herself as their champion, she talked about closing plants.

Hillary also probably wanted a take-back over her "deplorables" comment. "You could put half of Trump's supporters into what I call the 'basket of deplorables.'" It was probably only 10 percent who fit that description. For example, some Trump supporters at his rallies were truly deplorable as evidenced by one cold-cocking a 69-year-old woman with an oxygen tank in her backpack. Or the mob yelling "light the motherfucker on fire" and "kick his ass" as a Black Lives Matters protester was dragged away. One young black woman was seen on tape being shoved by a Trump backer as the candidate was exhorting the crowd to "get them out, get them out." The shover later said he wasn't a racist. Sure, and Mussolini wasn't a fascist, he just favored a hands-on approach.

There was backlash, but not as much as Mitt Romney saying 47 percent of Americans are dependent on government and see themselves as victims and feel entitled to food, housing, healthcare. And if that wasn't bad enough, he added, "I'll never convince them that they should take personal responsibility and care for their lives." Come the end of September, Trump's campaign manager conceded that the Trump supporter who yelled Jew-S-A, was, indeed, deplorable for doing so.

However, despite all the scandals, missteps, and screw ups, Hillary's biggest mistake may have been following Michelle Obama's advice. During the convention, Michelle said her motto was going high when bullies went low.

That is what Hillary tried to do, take the high road. When Trump attacked with a low blow, she held her ground, but didn't retaliate. She tried to appear calm and benevolent instead of "shrill" and "nasty." This was a mistake, especially considering who she was facing. She didn't need to go as low as Trump, if that were possible. But we can boil the campaign down to one moment in the second debate.

"People have been destroyed for doing one-fifth of what you did," Trump said after making several false claims about Hillary's emails. "You ought to be ashamed of yourself."

She made sure to state that the claims were false, and then asked voters to fact-check Trump on her website. She followed with, "It's just awfully good that someone with the temperament of Donald Trump is not in charge of the law in this country."

"Because you'd be in jail," Trump fired back.

And she said nothing. She smiled, glanced away with an "Oh Donald!" look on her face. But in that moment, her silence was deafening. In that moment, she needed to get off the high road and be Drill Sgt. Hugh Rodham's daughter. She needed to eviscerate him.

"Do you really want to talk about going to jail?" she could have said, "Do you want to tell the American people how you committed fraud with Trump University and swindled working-class people out of their life savings? Do you want to talk about the thousands of lawsuits because you haven't paid your workers? The alleged mob connections? People have been put away for a long time for the things you've done, only their daddies weren't millionaires."

It would have been ugly. It would have been messy. And in that one moment, Hillary Clinton could have saved her presidential bid.

Chapter Ten:
The Trajectory
of the Race

Columnists, newscasters and reporters had their thesauruses working overtime. Every time shocking revelations came out or a new F-bomb dropped about Donald Trump, they needed new words and phrases to describe the Republican nominee.

"Demagogue." "Fraudster," "Head case." "Fake philanthropist." "Liar," "Flip-flopper." "Ignoramus." "Tax evader." "The divider." "The authoritarian." "The misogynist." "Enemy of democracy." And all those were from just one extraordinary New York Daily News editorial denouncing Donald J. Trump.

The Cleveland convention gave him a bump in the polls, up about 3 to 6 percent, depending on the poll. Nothing unexpected. Convention bounces are almost standard operating procedure. This was evidenced by Clinton pinging up seven points.

There were about three months to Election Day. It's the time that sane candidates attempt to enlarge their tent, expand their base. They address issues that matter to their followers. Make themselves more appealing to independents and undecideds. Go after disgruntled Democrats.

271

Maybe even be a smidgeon conciliatory. Sane was not a word used to describe Trump in that Daily News editorial. The insanity of Trump came immediately after his dark-and-disturbing convention speech. A lot of people voted for Ted Cruz in the primaries. Big deal to Donald. Darth Ted lost. He was yesterday's burnt burrito. So what would Trump gain by bringing up his tweet that showed his glamorous, much-younger wife and Ted's, who nobody was going to book to follow Gisele Bundchen on a fashion runway? Don't give a press conference in which you trash Cruz and Kasich while praising the National Enquirer and Corey Lewandowski, you know the campaign manager you fired in June. If you're going to be bizarre, might as well say with your running mate standing next you, "If I don't win, we're going to have to blame Mike."

And that was only the beginning. Carrying on the convention disorder and poor planning, Trump had to cancel a rally in Ohio because his staff couldn't manage to line up proper security. As the Democrats were highlighting Michele Obama and Joe Biden, The Donald thought that since leaked DNC emails brought down chair Debbie Wasserman Schultz, maybe more could destroy Hillary. "Russia, if you're listening," he called out. "I hope you're able to find the 30,000 emails that are missing [from Hillary's private server]. I think you will probably be rewarded mightily by our press." Hey, that was tantamount to urging illegal hacking by a hostile foreign nation.

Then came his attack on the Gold Star mother and father at the DNC. What did he hope to accomplish? Now he had the leader of the Veterans of Foreign Wars lashing out. "VFW will not tolerate anyone berating a Gold Star family member for exercising his or her right of speech or expression." Joining the backlash were 11 other Gold Star families who wrote, "Your recent comments regarding the Khan family were repugnant and personally offensive to us."

"Repugnant" wasn't only used by them to characterize the Big Guy. (By the way, when it was reported that for his height and weight, Trump was obese, he grew an inch. He went from 6'2" to 6'3". Michael Jordan sprouted from 6'3" to 6'6" in college. He was in his teens. He wasn't 70, when people are generally losing inches.) Obama used the word "repugnant." David Letterman used it. Ditto Senate Majority Leader Mitch McConnell.

Trump throughout the campaign appeared genetically incapable of cutting his losses. When asked what kind of sacrifices he has made, he answered "I think I've made a lot of sacrifices. I work very, very hard. I've created thousands and thousands of jobs, tens of thousands of jobs, built great structures. I've had tremendous success. I think I've done a lot." Good going equating building hotels and casinos with losing a son protecting fellow soldiers. You could almost hear retching across the country. Alienate vets even more by when a follower gives you a Purple Heart medal, saying you had always wanted one, but getting it this way "a lot easier," meaning a lot easier than being wounded or killed serving in the armed forces.

Moving on. Speaking of getting wounded, why don't you shoot yourself in the foot, kneecap or other parts of your body by refusing to endorse the most powerful person in the Republican Party? Yes, we are talking about Paul Ryan, Speaker of the House. Trump was in a Donald snit because Paul waited until June to endorse him. Ryan had the effrontery to say he wasn't "quite there yet." Until he was there yet.

Someone apparently forgot to tell Trump that should he be moving to the White House, he would need Ryan's support to get anything done. No matter. In Trump World, Ryan was a loser because ran with that loser Romney. Trump would find some way to oust him from the speakership. As it was, Donald warmly embraced Ryan's Tea Party primary rival, Paul Nehlen, because the guy had chastised the speaker's "constant knee-jerk reactions to anything controversial Donald Trump might say." That's right, Paul, don't say the Khans' sacrifice "should always be honored." What an attack on The Donald. Trump backtracked right before the primary. Someone must have told him Nehlen was going to lose 80-percent big time.

What about inciting violence even beyond your rallies where you tell people you want to punch protesters in the face and you will pay the legal fees of anyone who does? Not smart. However, Trump really crossed the line with his insupportable "If [Clinton] gets to pick her judges, nothing you can do, folks. Although the Second Amendment people — maybe there is, I don't know." Don't think the Secret Service was thrilled. Martin Luther King Jr.'s daughter, Bernice, definitely not. To her, Trump's words were "distasteful, disturbing, dangerous."

At the end of July, Trump was in Colorado Springs for a rally. The billionaire Koch boys were having their own "rally" across I-25 in the posh Broadmoor Resort. Rooms run from $300 to $600, but surely the Kochs swung a deal for their fellow big-bucks conservatives who meet periodically to plot the takeover of the world.

Some of the donors tried to arrange a meeting between the Trump and the climate-change-denying brothers. They would be only five miles apart. The brothers declined. Back in April, Charley Koch had said it was possible that Clinton would make a better president than the Republicans in the race, though he later dialed back from that.

How did Trump handle this slight? How do you think? He claimed he turned down an invitation, you know, the one that had never been sent. He had other troubles. One of his posse used an elevator bypass key without knowing how to turn it back on. Trump and entourage were stuck until firefighters lowered a ladder. To show his appreciation, Trump lambasted the local fire marshal for turning away attendees because capacity in the rally hall had been exceeded. "This is why our country doesn't work," Trump bellowed soon after the department's firefighters rescued him. That fire marshal "didn't know what he was doing" and "was probably a Democrat." Forget that the Trump people had been warned about capacity limits, but handed out more tickets anyway.

By mid-August, with falling poll numbers, Trump started his ever-deafening drumbeat of the election is rigged, the election is rigged. He had as much evidence of that as Chicken Little had about the sky falling. Actually, less, since at least the chicken was beaned by an acorn. And while he was at it, he lambasted the media. "If the disgusting and corrupt media covered me honestly and didn't put false meaning into the words I say, I would be beating Hillary by 20 percent."

Remember, this was the guy in the primaries who got almost $2 billion in free television coverage. Harvard found he got favorable coverage 74 percent of the time from USA Today, 73 percent from Fox News and if you can believe it, 63 percent from the later-to-be excoriated, New

York Times. Bad polling numbers meant Whining Trump has to find someone to blame.

That led to the big staff shake-up, which led to Breitbart's Steve Bannon coming out of his sewer lair. He got his campaign chief executive (whatever that meant) title, and Kellyanne Conway was elevated to campaign manager.

Some backstory on Bannon and Conway is in order about now.

Bannon, a former naval officer, made a ton of money at Goldman Sachs and received an interest in "Seinfeld." By 2013, reruns had earned $3.1 billion. Oh, those royalty checks keep adding up. He dabbled here and there in show business, first working with Sean Penn on something called "The Indian Runner," which was based on a Bruce Springsteen song. Penn called the Republican primaries a defecation on America. And Springsteen? Well yeah, he said, "The republic is under siege by a moron," the moron being Donald Trump.

For those who are lucky enough to be unfamiliar with Breitbart, it has been called "a haven for people who think Fox News is too polite and restrained" and Trump Pravda. Here are a few of this self-proclaimed news site's headlines.

"Gabby Gifford—The Gun Control Movement's Human Shield"

"Planned Parenthood's Body Count Under Cecile Richards Is Up To Half A Holocaust"

"Birth Control Makes Women Unattractive And Crazy"

Bannon is an equal-opportunity hater. Hates the Dems. Hates the Republicans. He once told a Daily Beast reporter that he was a Leninist. "Lenin wanted to destroy the state, and that's my goal, too. I want to bring everything

crashing down, and destroy all of today's establishment."
(He later had amnesia about the conversation, while not
directly denying that was his sentiment. Probably not a big
deal to Trump, who would have thought the Lenin under
discussion was a dead Beatle.)

From what Bannon's ex-wife said, you can add Jews
to the list. Bannon didn't want his daughters to attend a
school because it had too many Jewish students. "He said
that he doesn't like Jews and that he doesn't like the way
they raise their kids to be 'whiny brats' and that he didn't
want the girls to go to school with Jews."

As long as you're insulting people, how about backing conservative women like Sarah Palin, Ann Coulter and
Michelle Bachman to lead the country because they would
be "pro-family, they would have husbands, they would love
their children. They wouldn't be a bunch of dykes that
came from the Seven Sisters schools up in New England."
Uhh, should someone tell Steve that Ann Coulter has never been married and doesn't have kids?

Add blacks to the hate list. A former Breitbart insider
said Bannon used racist slurs that made editorial meetings
sound "like a white supremacist rally." No word concern-
ing Bannon's position on puppies and kittens.

He and Trump seemed a perfect fit, especially considering the Breitbart honcho's purported penchant for
referring to women as "cunts." What a marriage made in
heaven, or perhaps, more appropriately, the gutter. An
aside: You would think with all his Goldman Sachs-Sein-
feld-Breitbart millions, Bannon could afford a dermatolo-
gist. Pictures of him show a blotchy face and a nose akin to
W.C. Fields, whose drinking was legendary. Bannon's rud-
dy snout might come from the Irish Curse: red nose and

short hose. Though, the world can only hope he doesn't feel the necessity to refute the short penis part.

Moving on to the less-noxious addition to the Trump menagerie, the jutting-jawed Mrs. Conway, often called a gender-gap expert.

Kellyanne had been moving in political circles for a long time. After doing a law-school, lawyering stint, she transitioned into the wonderful world of polling. The way she described it sounded like *so* much fun. "I'm a female consultant in the Republican Party, which means when I walk into a meeting at the RNC or somewhere, I always feel like I'm walking into a bachelor party in the locker room of the Elks club."

In 1995, she set up her Polling Company and got corporations like American Express, Hasbro and Vaseline to sign on for finding out what women would buy. Then there was her list of political clients—Newtie, Mike Pence and always a crowd pleaser, Dan Quayle.

Should you think that Trump was Kellyanne's most problem client, nope. Remember Todd Akin? That was the ignoramus who said rape victims couldn't become pregnant because of some miraculous force field that kept the rapist's sperm from reaching the egg.

Then there was Kellyanne's argument that there would be less rape in the military if women were physically stronger. "If we were physiologically—not mentally, emotionally, professionally—equal to men, if we were physiologically as strong as men, rape would not exist," she said. "You would be able to defend yourself and fight him off." This blithe statement overlooks the fact that men are raped, too. As for sexual assaults in the military, Trump maintained it was bound to happen "when they put men and women together." So, the assaulter wasn't to blame, it was the fault of the DOD brass.

With the new staff in place, Trump took what Conway called a "decisive presidential move." He went a-calling on Mexican President Enrique Peña Nieto. This was right before Trump was to make a speech on immigration in Phoenix. Trump and the president had a cozy one-on-one, then held a joint press conference.

That's when the weirdness of Trump going to Mexico in the first place got weirder. Beaming from whatever alternate universe he was occupying, the nominee said that he and el presidente had discussed the Great Wall of Trump, but not who would pick up its tab. Back on earth, after the press conference (Trump spoke last), Peña Nieto made it very clear that he had made it very clear not one Mexican peso would go for the wall. Maybe Trump hadn't been paying attention, his apparent attention-deficit disorder might have kicked in. His mind certainly seemed to be wandering when the president talked about the 6 million American jobs created by NAFTA.

On to Phoenix. There were those who predicted Trump would tone down his anti-immigrant rhetoric in the hope of winning over Hispanic voters. If that was the aim, someone forgot to tell Trump or maybe his mind was wandering again. He painted that picture of a dark American landscape that needed a "deportation task force" that would round up the dangerous criminals in the country illegally. Amnesty? Forget it, not on his watch. And those 11 million he frequently threatened to deport? He didn't put them in the roundup. Still, the speech smacked of pure Steve Bannon.

Over on the Clinton side, there were no upheavals, no

rapid firings and hirings. Many of her staff members had been with her in one capacity or another for years. These were experienced people. Compare Clinton campaign manager Robby Mook to Steve Bannon. Mook's credentials included helping Jeanne Shaheen win a New Hampshire Senate seat and Terry McAuliffe the Virginia governorship. He also worked on Clinton's unsuccessful 2008 presidential push as state director in Nevada, Indiana and Ohio. Campaign chairman John Podesta? It's rumored he was on Thomas Jefferson's staff. Kellyanne worked as a senior adviser on Gingrich's 2008 team and was president of a Ted Cruz Super-PAC. Steve Bannon's campaign resume is pretty much blank. Though who knows, maybe he ran for fifth-grade class president.

September

We toddled into September with Trump trailing in most of the polls and many people wondering why he wasn't further behind. It came down to the "We Don't Trust Her" people. Clinton's unfavorable ratings were in the mid-50s. Donald's were at 60 percent in a bunch of other polls.

Which is to be expected with the way he so artfully turned off black, Hispanics and Muslims. What kind of an appeal to African Americans was asking "What do you have to lose?" by voting for him? That was a question he asked at a rally in the almost all-white Lansing, Mich. Oh gee, I'm not in Detroit? Or what about characterizing black neighborhoods as "war zones" with families barely able to make it on food stamps. (Should a staff member tell him food stamps were replaced by EBT cards?)

"You're living in your poverty, your schools are no good, you have no jobs, 58 percent of your youth is unemployed—what the hell do you have to lose?" Apparently, many blacks felt they had a lot to lose, at one point giving Hillary a 91-percent to 1-percent lead over Trump.

Finally, Trump, who had been pushing the birther movement big time since 2011—getting lots of coveted media attention—finally conceded "President Barack Obama was born in the United States." Would he let it lay there? It's Donald Trump. He had to offer another conspiracy theory. Hillary Clinton had started the whole kerfuffle back in 2008. Trump's birtherism did not sit well with black communities. Rep. G.K. Butterfield, D-N.C., and chairman of the Congressional Black Caucus, summed up the distaste by calling Trump a "disgusting fraud." Hillary weighed in by saying Trump had championed "the birther movement to de-legitimize our first black president" and that his presidential campaign was "founded on this outrageous lie."

Why the Trump change of heart? For expediency sake, did you need to ask? Conway was pushing to tone him down, to make him look less racist and hate mongering.

Speaking of conspiracies, what about Hillary's health? Right-wing conspiracists would probably like to tie her to the assassination of JFK had she not been a 16-year-old high-school student in Park Ridge. At least with her health, there was something on which to base the "she's desperately ill" propaganda. It started in December 2012. Back from a trip to Europe, the secretary of state became dehydrated battling a stomach virus. She fainted and hit her head. A mild concussion was diagnosed. She had to postpone testifying before the Benghazi committee (talk about conspiracies). The briefly U.N. ambassador under George W., John Bolton, accused Clinton of suffering from a "diplomatic illness." "You know," he explained, "every foreign-service officer in every foreign ministry in the world knows the phrase . . . When you don't want to go to a meeting or conference, or an event, you have a 'diplomatic illness.' "

Later, a blot clot was found behind Clinton's ear, and she was put on blood thinners. Don't think it stopped there. Suddenly Karl Rove, the George W. adviser of dirty-tricks fame, was saying Clinton had suffered a "traumatic brain injury," and the proof was the glasses she started to wear. Technically he was right. A concussion is the mildest form of traumatic brain injury. One result of conking your head can be sensitivity to light. Sunglasses, light, light, sunglasses, moving on.

Come 2016 and apparently Rudy Giuliani and TV blathering head Sean Hannity had graduated from medical school. Giuliani had seen her coughing, coughing so much she had to drink some water and suck on a lozenge. The American public should not be fooled into thinking it was allergies. And what about the time she had to be helped up stairs while boarding an airplane? So what if she tripped and the Secret Service was keeping her from falling? It was more proof that Hillary was a sick, sick lady.

Sean Hannity pointed to a picture of a Hillary Secret Service agent carrying a diazepam pen that treats seizures. When more sane heads examined the photo, turned out the guy had a small flashlight in his hand.

Dr. Sean also wondered about her facial tics and that she paused between words. A doctor on his show, who had never met Clinton, much less examined her, came up with "I'm wondering about a word called 'aphasia,' where you're searching for words, you suddenly lose those words and that can be the sign, again, of some kind of traumatic brain injury or the aftereffects of a 'concussion.'" Trump spokesperson Katrina "Tea Party" Pierson backed up that diagnosis, though she called it "dysphasia." That earned her a rebuke from the National Aphasia Association.

"Aphasia does not affect intelligence. . . . Aphasia is not a term applied to an individual who is selectively pacing her speech in order to deliver an appropriate and thoughtful message, or a person in her 60's who might occasionally pause on a word. A diagnosis of aphasia by a campaign spokesperson in a political campaign is inappropriate and offensive to the approximately 2 million Americans and their families who struggle with communication following a stroke or other brain trauma."

This was far from the only time that Mrs. Pierson (she was married to Mr. Pierson for only three months, maybe Ms. Pierson would be more appropriate) got caught up in an ignorance web. According to her, Barack Obama invaded Afghanistan and was to blame for the death of Capt. Humayun Khan, whose father spoke at the DNC. Never mind Captain Khan died in Iraq in 2004 and the U.S. invasion was in 2001 when Obama was in the Illinois Senate, not known for running U.S. foreign policy. She was the one who said Donald Trump couldn't have groped a woman because first-class seats didn't have moveable armrests. Something that was quickly shown to be a lie.

It certainly bolstered the conspiracy theorist on Clinton's health when she had to be helped away from a 9/11 memorial. Her doctor later said she was suffering from pneumonia. Clinton soon emerged from Chelsea's apartment looking pretty chipper. Except, doncha know, the person was actually a body double, or at least that's what the internet intelligentsia said. What about Trump's health? you might ask. Not to worry, back in December, his doctor, one Harold Bornstein, had said unequivocally that his patient would be "the healthiest individual ever elected to the presidency." On top of that absurdity (do you really think Jefferson took a prostate exam that didn't exist or Lincoln had his blood pressure checked with a cuff that wasn't invented until 1881?), the note was infused with hinkiness, starting with a salutation of "To Whom It My Concern" to saying all Trump's tests were positive. In doctor talk, positive results can be negative. Bornstein also noted that his patient—why was Trump seeing an endocrinologist, anyway?—had lost 15 pounds in the previous year. Whoa, that means The Donald was way into obesity. There was speculation the good doc had not written the note, but rather Trump had.

What were some of the fun reveals in September? One came from Politico. How about a shitload of Trump campaign expenditures being paid to Trump, if you consider $8.2 million a shitload. Instead of holding events at more reasonable venues, Mar-a-Lago was rented to the tune of $432,000. Another $142,000 went to Trump Restaurants. Trump campaign headquarters was, naturally, in Trump Tower to the tune of $1 million. Thirteen hundred had gone to his bottled-water company and $5,000 to the Virginia winery owned by son Eric.

Other big news was the Green Party candidates, Jill Stein and Ajamu Baraka, were cited for trespass and vandalism during a North Dakota oil-pipeline protest. The vandalism stemmed from Stein spray-painting "I approve this message" on a bulldozer.

Her Libertarian counterpart, Gary Johnson, was making headlines of a different nature. When asked about Aleppo, the Syrian city being bombed by Syrian and Russian aircraft, he asked "What's Aleppo" When asked for a foreign leader he admired, all he could come up with was the former Mexican president, of which there were many more than one. After his brain thawed, he remembered the fellow he held in esteem was Vicente Fox. And what about Johnson's attitude toward global warming. Why worry? The sun would someday encompass the earth, anyway. Granted maybe not for a billion years. Is it any wonder his polling numbers dropped to a meager 5 percent?

This was all minor stuff compared to the month's main event—the first presidential debate. Some Clinton supporters worried Trump would skewer her as he did his primary opponents. Others pointed out it wouldn't be as easy for him to barbecue Hillary because with only two debaters, moderators could press for follow-ups, maybe even fact-check. It would be harder to pivot off topic. And Trump would have to be careful about mocking Clinton. That wouldn't boost his numbers with women. It's funny how women get turned off by a Mr. Macho bragging about the size of his penis. They don't appreciate a man calling women "dogs," rating their looks on a scale from one to 10 and speculating about how big his 1-year-old daughter's breasts would be.

Before the big day arrived on Sept. 26, there would be what was billed as the "Commander-in-Chief Forum," dramatically staged on the U.S.S. Intrepid floating museum in New York Harbor. With a town-hall setup, moderator

Matt Lauer would ask questions about national security, foreign and veteran affairs, with Trump on stage first, followed by Clinton. The audience would have its turn with each candidate. That's what it was supposed to be. As it turned out, it quickly became clear that the "Today Show" host was better suited pressing Martha Stewart on how to cook a fabulous chicken fricassee than presiding over a political give-and-take.

Lauer soft-balled Trump and let him get away with the debunked lie that the Republican convert had always, always he says, been against the invasion of Iraq. Lauer spent about 15 minutes of Clinton's 30 hammering on her emails before moving on. As it turned out, it was the morning-show host who was hammered. As political commentator Norman Ornstein tweeted out, "Lauer interrupted Clinton's answers repeatedly to move on. Not once for Trump. Tough to be a woman running for president."

One executive at NBC, the network that carried the forum, called Lauer's performance a "disaster." Look on the bright side. It quickly gave birth to the hashtag "Lauering the Bar."

In Trump's rigging mode, he had complained about the debate scheduling. Somehow, the Clinton people had deviously arranged to program against NFL games, thereby reducing audiences and his chances to dazzle so many more people.

"I'll tell you what I don't like," Trump carped. "It's against two NFL games. I got a letter from the NFL saying, 'This is ridiculous.' "

Oh, Mr. Trump, that was so easy to refute. First, the schedule was arranged in September 2015—before you got the nomination—by the non-partisan Commission on Presidential Debates. And no, you were hallucinating again. The NFL sent no such letter.

The debate did go on at Long Island's Hofstra University without Gennifer Flowers, the long-ago Bill dalliance, in the audience front row. Trump started out obviously minding his handlers. His usual bellicosity was absent. Early on, he even asked if he should call Hillary Secretary Clinton. "Yes, is that OK? Good. I want you to be very happy. It's very important to me." Hope the audience had barf bags. And maybe surgical masks since Trump kept sniffling throughout the night.

He calmly reiterated his plan to lower the tax rate to 15 percent. He spouted the usual Republican line that this would be a job creator and "it would be a beautiful thing to watch." He ran with the renegotiating trade deals.

Clinton came back at Trump for espousing "trickledown economics," which she modified to "Trumped-up trickle down."

A side note. Back in 1949, Harry Truman had this to say about the concept. "The reactionaries hold that government policies should be designed for the special benefit of small groups of people who occupy positions of wealth and influence. Their theory seems to be that if these groups are prosperous, they will pass along some of their prosperity to the rest of us. This can be described as 'the trickle down theory.' The vast majority of us reject that theory as totally wrong." Kinda funny the right-wingers who touted the term didn't realize that Truman coined it as a term of disparagement. When you think about it, it does sound like someone is wizzing on you.

Truman may have had temper issues—when a critic panned Margaret Truman's singing, POTUS fired off a letter promising the reviewer he would "need a new nose, a lot of beefsteak for black eyes, and perhaps a supporter below" should they ever meet—but Trump frequently showed less restraint than a toddler who throws "Goodnight Moon" across the room because he doesn't want to go to bed. Sure enough, Clinton started to get under his notoriously thin skin. She brought up Trump's background of privilege and daddy's help, in an obvious attempt to remind working-class voters that the self-proclaimed mogul was not a bootstrapper.

When moderator Lester Holt tried to move Trump to the next question, no way. Trump had to deny he had been given a big gift from his father. It had only been an itsy, bitsy loan. The Washington Post real-time annotator jumped on that because the paper's fact-checker had earlier given four Pinocchios to the truth-deficient candidate.

"Trump's claim that he built a real-estate fortune out of a 'small' $1 million loan is simply not credible. He benefited from numerous loans and loan guarantees, as well as his father's connections, to make the move into Manhattan. His father also set up lucrative trusts to provide steady income. When Donald Trump became overextended in the casino business, his father bailed him out with a shady casino-chip loan—and Trump also borrowed $9 million against his future inheritance. While Trump asserts 'it has not been easy for me,' he glosses over the fact that his father paved the way for his success—and that his father bailed him out when he got into trouble."

Did the fact-checkers get combat pay during this election cycle?

When Holt got Trump back to the job-creation question, an opening the size of the Dragon Hole in the South

China Sea was created for Clinton. Donald did his riff on jobs going to Mexico and China. When Hillary got her mic time, she talked about how bad off the country had been during the Great Recession and that "Donald was one of the people who rooted for the housing crisis. He said, back in 2006, 'Gee, I hope it does collapse, because then I can go in and buy some and make some money.'"

Trump interrupted with "That's called business, by the way." It was probably about then that Kellyanne Conway was wishing she was at her boss' new hotel on Pennsylvania Avenue knocking back $100 Benjamin Franklins. (That would be vodka, rye, potato, raw oysters and caviar.) He would also brag that not paying federal taxes was a sign he was "smart."

Trump's taxes gave Clinton a good head slam. When he called the U.S. a "debtor nation" because money was squandered on her ideas, she came back with "And maybe because you haven't paid any federal income tax for a lot of years."

Trump wasn't completely without comebacks. Judged The Donald's best line of the night: "Hillary's got experience, but it's bad experience."

If you like moments of tension, it was served up when Hillary called Trump's years of birtherism a "racist lie." "He has a long record of engaging in racist behavior," she added for good measure. Trump countered that in the 2008 campaign, she was disrespectful to Obama. "I watch the way you talk now about how lovely everything is . . . it doesn't work that way," he said. "When you try to act holier than thou, it really doesn't work." This criticism sounded a bit hollow given the president was rallying hard for his former opponent.

Now, you didn't think Clinton was going to let Trump slide on his global-warming stance, did you? "Donald thinks that climate change is a hoax perpetrated by the Chinese. I think it's real."

Another interruption. "I did not. I did not. I do not say that."

The interruptions kept on coming as Clinton hit Trump with his contradictions and questionable statements.

"Wrong."

"It's lies."

In all, Mr. Etiquette interrupted 51 times. That's 51 times in 90 minutes. He would have done better if he had been interrupted before saying that maybe the DNC might have been hacked by "somebody sitting on their bed that weighs 400 pounds, OK?" Not Russia, you morons.

Trump hadn't prepared much for the debate. Usually, candidates have someone act the part of the opponent. Bring up expected topics to prepare reactions. Read through binder after binder on issues. Trump, on the other hand, nah, he didn't need that stuff. He would wing it because it had worked so well in the primaries, and the very force of his personality would cow Clinton.

That didn't work out so well. The viewer started to feel that he didn't stay on point because he wasn't sure what the point was. For instance, he rambled going from B-52s "old enough that your father, your grandfather could be flying them" to China and North Korea to the horrible deal with Iran. Hillary, being Hillary, was ultra prepared. So much so that she had practiced confronting Tempered Trump and Terrible Trump.

The three most memorable takes from the debate? One, when Trump said, "I have much better judgment than she has. There's no question about that. I also have a much better temperament than she does." She came back laughing (as was the audience) with "Whoa. OK" and a shoulder shimmy shake.

The second: The split screen. On the left, Trump, on the right, Clinton. One reporter described it as "one listening, or rather, responding with practiced smiles and looks to camera (Clinton) or head-shakes, eye rolls, winces, pained smirks, smug smirks, smirky smirks, and rude, unruly, infuriating interruptions galore (Trump)."

The third? It was as if Trump was the second banana, straight man feeding setup lines to Clinton. Lester Holt asked The Donald what he meant when he said Hillary didn't have the "presidential look." Trump turned that into "And I don't believe she does have the stamina. To be president of this country, you need tremendous stamina."

To which she fired back, "As soon as he travels to 112 countries and negotiates a peace deal, a ceasefire, a release of dissidents, an opening of new opportunities in nations around the world, or even spends 11 hours testifying in front of a congressional committee, he can talk to me about stamina."

Oh Donald, you didn't have any notion what your stamina slam, which could be viewed as sexist, opened up. Hillary went on the offensive. "He had tried to switch from looks to stamina. But this is a man who has called women pigs, slobs and dogs, and someone who has said pregnancy is an inconvenience to employers, who has said women don't deserve equal pay unless they do as good a job as men."

All that was only the one of the one-two punch. Then came:

> Hillary: And one of the worst things he said was about a woman in a beauty contest. He loves beauty contests, supporting them and hanging around them. And he called this woman "Miss Piggy." Then he called her "Miss Housekeeping," because she was Latina. Donald, she has a name.
> Trump: Where did you find this? Where did you find this?
> Clinton: Her name is Alicia Machado.
> Trump: Where did you find this?
> Clinton: And she has become a U.S. citizen, and you can bet . . .
> Trump: Oh, really?
> Clinton: . . . she's going to vote this November.

Great theater. Trump even said that if his opponent won, he would "absolutely" support her, though Holt had to use an elephant-tooth extractor get that out of him.

Polls that had a basis in science gave Clinton a decisive victory over Trump, who managed to scrounge up some dubious onliners that declared him the winner. He blamed his faulty mic for distracting him. It was faulty. However, you're supposed to arrive in time to do a sound check and find out there is something wrong. No explanation for the nonstop sniffling.

The debate was Monday. The next day, instead of letting the Miss Universe surprise die out of the news cycle, the former beauty-pageant honcho had to bring it up again. He called into Fox News just so everyone would know Machado had "gained a massive amount of weight, and it was a real problem."

For some reason, the Trump didn't fire his tweet barrage until early Friday morning. Had someone hidden his Android phone? Keep in mind, hell hath no fury like a Donald scorned. Obviously forgetting Ms. Kellyanne's gender-gap lessons, he let loose with "Wow, Crooked Hillary was duped and used by my worst Miss U. Hillary floated her as an 'angel' without checking her past, which is terrible!" In another tweet, he urged his believers to check out Machado's sex tape, a futile task since none existed.

There must have been some very happy faces over at Clinton headquarters as Clinton tweets sallied forth. "This is . . . unhinged, even for Trump." "What kind of man stays up all night to smear a woman with lies and conspiracy theories?"

Trump was very proud of his tweeting at odd hours. Shows he's up and prepared. Melania, on the other hand, when asked which habit she wished her husband stopped, answered, "tweeting."

Still, the tweeting craziness served to obscure a story from Newsweek that reported in 1998, Trump people met with Cuban government officials and others to explore the possibility of building a hotel on the island nation. This was in clear violation of the complete trade embargo put into place by JFK in 1962. It should be mentioned that a few months after this little illegal foray, Trump was running for president. And guess what he said then. Not a penny, not a peso would go to Cuba while Fidel Castro was still around if Trump were president. Should have been an asterisk, "Unless I can make money there."

October

The month did not start auspiciously for the Trump camp. On the first, The New York Times published a story based on Trump's 1995 New York state tax returns the paper received anonymously. Note the "state." If they had been federal returns, the paper faced prosecution. A couple of weeks earlier, Times executive editor Dean Baquet had said he'd run with hacked or leaked Trump federal returns should they have plopped on his desk. Luckily for him, the records plopped in the office mailbox of one of his reporters, Susanne Craig. "I don't think it's a crime to check your mailbox," Craig said "And that's what we did, and then we did some reporting." And reporting they certainly did.

Bottom line was the champion of the blue-collar and middle-class, angry white guys had declared a $916-million loss that meant he didn't have to pay any federal income taxes for, oh, 18 years. Hit the pause button here. Trump's fervent supporters were having tax payments deducted from their paychecks, and their hero skated.

The Times didn't stop there. A later story spelled out how he did it. To make it simple, Trump was going under from his Atlantic City casinos and Plaza Hotel debacles. He owed a lot of money. If his debts were forgiven, the IRS would consider that income. However, Trump and his lenders set up a swap of debt for partnership equity. His own lawyers cautioned that the maneuver might not get pass an IRS audit.

It wasn't only the Times microscoping Trump finances. David Fahrenthold of The Washington Post started investigating The Donald's boast of being a really magnanimous philanthropist. Really big. Note to yourself: Never get on David Fahrenthold's radar screen. This guy noticed how Trump like to brag about his generosity. Millions, the candidate said.

A blip showed up after Trump held that "I'm pissed at Fox" fundraiser for veterans in January 2016. He claimed to have raised $6 million and would chip in a million from his supposed billions. During the several months after that, the Post reporter tried to uncover which groups had received the money. And came up zilch. When questioned, Trump responded, "Instead of being like, 'Thank you very much, Mr. Trump' or 'Trump did a good job,' everyone's saying, 'Who got it, who got it, who got it?' . . . I have never received such bad publicity for doing such a good job."

That begged the question of who got the money. The answer was the money was not forthcoming until Fahrenthold shamed—Clinton's word—Trump into cutting checks. Why did it take so long to disperse the checks? Why the vets needed vetting, naturally.

Fahrenthold didn't stop there. He began searching for charities that might have received the more than $100 million Trump former manager and forever cheerleader Corey Lewandowski claimed were donated. The reporter did it the old-fashioned way, making a handwritten list of organizations, calling them and noting which were beneficiaries of Trump generosity. Fahrenthold found that despite pledging a lot of his money, little was handed out. Ivanka's ballet school, however, was gifted with more than $16,500.

The WashPo reporter also uncovered highly questionable Trump Foundation dealings that could lead to court action. Add that to list of Trump University and shitload of other lawsuits Trump was facing.

If the Trump people were counting on accused rapist and WikiLeaks co-founder Julian Assange to drop a race-changing October Surprise, it must have been a letdown. Assange had been holed up in Ecuador's London Embassy for four years fearing extradition to Sweden where he would be tried for the alleged rape and sexual molestation of another woman. He was going to make a big announcement from embassy's balcony. When the embassy said no, a taped speech was broadcast from Berlin. It turned out to be more of an infomercial for WikiLeaks than anything else. To spice it up, Assange suggested there was more to the murder of Seth Rich, a DNC staffer, who had been gunned down in July. Maybe Rich leaked material to WikiLeaks, and maybe . . . D.C. police, who actually investigated, labeled it a "botched robbery."

The vice-presidential debate on Oct. 4 must have come with a sigh of relief for the Trump staff. Mike Pence, a former radio talk-show host, comported himself well. Tim Kaine, usually a nice, genial guy, must have gotten poor advice to come across as a Rottweiler that hadn't been fed for several weeks. What was curious was how Kaine concentrated on Trump and didn't go into Pence's record. When the subject of abortion inevitably arose, Kaine attacked Trump's call for women who have abortions to be punished. (To which Pence responded the top of his ticket wasn't a "polished politician like you and Hillary Clinton.") Kaine didn't mention Pence's fight in the house to stop federal money from going to Planned Parenthood. Or the Indiana governor's Religious Freedom Restoration Act.

Even though he defended Trump, Pence seemed more like he was laying the path for his own run in 2020 or 2024.

Pence came away with the win over Kaine. Still, you can bet Mike and wifey Karen didn't break out the Champagne. He is abstemious to the point that he won't attend a function where alcohol is served unless Karen is with him to save him from demon drink.

Three days later, the Trumpies had another reason to smile. WikiLeaks released those emails that purportedly showed that Clinton said one thing in public about trade and another to Wall Street and bankers.

But let's face it. There are leaks, and there are LEAKS. In the case of Trump, it was more like Hoover Dam bursting. On Oct. 7, the same day of the WikiLeaks "revelations," the "Access Hollywood" tape of Trump and Billy Bush from 2005 was released by The Washington Post. Trump was filming a cameo on the soap, "Days of Our Lives." Billy, an "Access Hollywood" host, and Trump were caught on an open mic discussing the future candidate's conduct with women.

In The Gospel According to Trump, if you're famous, women let you do whatever you want. The vile, and that's putting it mildly, Trump talked about putting moves on who was later revealed to be another "Access Hollywood" anchor, Nancy O'Dell. "I did try and fuck her. She was married." This was while Wife Number Three, Melania, was pregnant with Offspring Number Five. (Do the math. Barron was born Mar. 20, 2006. The video recorded Oct. 24, 2005.)

When Trump and Disciple spot the soap actress sent to escort them to the set, they started acting like prepubescent boys sneaking a peek at Playboy in the corner drugstore.

"Sheesh, your girl's hot as shit. In the purple," Billy is

heard to gush . . . "Yes! The Donald has scored." Referring to the woman, Donald enthuses, "Look at you, you are a pussy . . . I better use some Tic Tacs just in case I start kissing her."

Trump immediately dismissed the tape as "locker-room" banter and that Bill Clinton had said worse things on the golf course. He apologized "if anyone was offended." "If anyone"? Turns out there were lots of anyones. One was John Gotti's widow. Remember, the Teflon Don? On hearing the tape, Victoria Gotti tweeted that Trump was a "crude obnoxious megalomaniacal mutt . . . I was married to #1 gangster and would have cut his throat if he ever said such a foul thing to me."

Republican National Committee Chair Reince Priebus: "No woman should ever be described in these terms or talked about in this manner. Ever."

John McCain: ". . . [Trump's] demeaning comments about women and his boasts about sexual assaults, make it impossible to continue to offer even conditional support for his candidacy."

Former Secretary of State Condoleezza Rice: "Enough! Donald Trump should not be President. He should withdraw."

Speaker of the House Paul Ryan: "I am sickened by what I heard today. Women are to be championed and revered, not objectified."

Even the Tic-Tac people had something to say. "Tic Tac respects all women. We find the recent statements and behavior completely inappropriate and unacceptable." Advertising Age wondered what Tic Tac had done to deserve Trump.

With the second presidential debate coming up fast,

Trump finally got around to apologizing in a 90-second video.

"I've never said I'm a perfect person nor pretended to be someone that I'm not. I've said and done things I regret, and the words released today on this more than a decade-old video are one of them."

Wait, wait, there was more where he finally used the "A" word.

"Anyone who knows me, knows these words don't reflect who I am. I said it. I was wrong, and I apologize."

This was the first time he said he was sorry for anything specific. If you're Donald Trump, you never have to say you're sorry. Even though he was advised against it, he couldn't help getting some digs in at Hillary and Bill. "I've said some foolish things, but there's a big difference between the words and actions of other people. Bill Clinton has actually abused women, and Hillary has bullied, attacked, shamed and intimidated his victims."

He probably should have left out the "words and actions" bit. Women emerged to accuse Trump of taking inappropriate sexual actions against them. All liars, according to Trump, who is always the most truthful person in the room. An incredulous Republican strategist reacted with "That [response] took 10 hours?"

It took Melania more than a week to rush to the defense of her husband. She didn't approve his words, but Billy had egged him into "dirty and bad stuff" boy talk. Had she been coached to say this? Did Donald really want to come across as so easily manipulated by such a powerhouse as Billy Bush? Melania, check your pre-nup.

Which brings us to the second presidential debate. It would be a town-hall setup. The moderators asking questions. Undecideds in the audience asking questions. No lecterns. Talking to the people in the hall and the people watching. There would be a chair for each candidate to sit on while the other was speaking. That's the way it was supposed to be.

Instead, Trump hulked around the stage, back and forth behind Clinton with his grumpy-cat, scowly face. It was especially creepy coming in the wake of the sex-talk tape.

Again, he started out even toned, using what Samantha Bee of "Full Frontal" characterized as "the voice you hear when you're being chloroformed." Then he resorted to Full Frontal Trump. Again, he threatened, à la a South American dictator, to jail Clinton if elected for her egregious email conduct. For her part, Clinton apologized and said she took full responsibility. But she didn't leave it there, instead she went wonky, making her seem less than sincere.

If you are going to threaten prosecution and prison time, why not call your opponent "the devil" with "tremendous hatred" and *again* bring up the sexual improprieties of her husband. Trump surely wanted to get his money's worth out of bringing Bill's accusers (thank you, Steve Bannon) to the debate. One of the women, Juanita Broaddrick, said Bill raped her. Then in an affidavit, changed her mind said no rape, then later yes rape. Another claimed she suffered greatly as a young rape victim when Clinton, the lawyer for the defendant, made her take a lie-director test. The problem is the judge's denial of the request for a polygraph was found.

Trump didn't keep his dissing to Hillary. He went after former Miss Universe Alicia Machado again. He was tweeting because he wanted the world to "just take a look at the person that she built up to be this wonderful Girl Scout who was no Girl Scout." Oh, he never told his millions of followers to check out Machado's sex tape. No, he did not, even though millions read the message.

And he dissed his own running mate, Mike Pence. Pence had said that if Russia kept up air strikes in coordination with Syria, the U.S. should be ready to bomb Bashar al-Assad's military targets.

But hold on there, Pence, you hadn't discussed this with the top banana (maybe top tangerine is more accurate), who for good measure, said he disagreed twice.

This wasn't the only time the dark cloud of Russia appeared. Clinton said that the Kremlin had a hand in recent hacks. Mind you, a couple of days before the debate, the director of National Intelligence and the Department of Homeland Security said, yes indeedy, Putin and company were trying to "interfere with the U.S. election process." In case anyone missed the point, Hillary said, "And believe me, they're not doing it to get me elected."

"She doesn't know if it's the Russians doing the hacking," Trump said. "Maybe there is no hacking."

If you want a blooper, try the Democrat's tortuous explanation of why she seemingly said one thing in paid speeches and another to the public. Well, you see, it was Abraham Lincoln's fault. She cited Steven Spielberg's, "Lincoln." "It was a master class watching President Lincoln get the Congress to approve the 13th Amendment," she said. "It was principled, and it was strategic."

"And I was making the point that it is hard sometimes to get the Congress to do what you want to do, and you have to keep working at it. And, yes, President Lincoln was trying to convince some people, he used some arguments, convincing other people, he used other arguments. That was a great—I thought a great display of presidential leadership."

Boy, how Trump the Tiger pounced on that. He accused her of lying about the speeches. "Now she's blaming the lie on the late, great Abraham Lincoln. . . . Honest Abe, Honest Abe never lied."

The "late, great," that's a description that doesn't usually (maybe never) gets put before the name of the 16th president. Kudos to Trump, however, for knowing Lincoln's nickname.

Speaking of tortuous, try blaming Hillary for his not paying taxes. It was her fault for not closing loopholes that let him get away with owing nothing. Never mind she was merely a senator during a Republican presidency. Trump doesn't let annoying details and rational thought get in the way of his narrative.

In addition, Hillary also had a lot of nerve complaining about him not paying taxes when some of her big donors didn't either. "I know Buffett took hundreds of millions of dollars." As it turned out, Trump knew no such thing. The following day, Warren Buffett, who got his entrepreneurial start not with money from daddy, but by selling chewing gum when he was a kid, released his tax returns for 2015. They showed that on an income of $11,563,931, he had taken deductions of $5,477,694, two thirds of which were for charitable contributions. Furthermore, the Oracle of Omaha had been paying federal income tax every year since 1944 when at age 13, he sent the feds seven bucks. (The equivalent of $95 today.)

If Trump had his way, those loopholes will continue,

perhaps even widen because "builders" deserve breaks. Never mind that the actual builders—carpenters, electricians, plumbers, plasterers, pipefitters, welders—are paying their fair share.

The last question came from the audience. "Would either of you name one positive thing that you respect in one another?" Trump liked that Clinton never gives up. Clinton respects his children. "His children are incredibly able and devoted, and I think that says a lot about Donald." Daddy wasn't sure if that was a compliment. Who knows? If you took a not-very-close look at the kidlings, it was clear that the apples didn't fall far from the diseased Trump tree.

Ivanka was sued for ripping off shoe designs. Her clothing line was manufactured in China. She lied about Hillary not having a child-care program more comprehensive than hers. *And*, at the height of hypocrisy, she told a former marketing director, Marissa Velez Kraxberger, she would have to think about giving her maternity leave. After all, Ivanka returned to her executive suite, or maybe it was merely a cramped cubicle, a week after her first child. When Kraxberger heard Ivanka tout a proposed maternity leave plan, she said she "felt like I was going to be ill."

So how many nannies does the hard-working Mommy Ivanka have? What does she pay the nanny or nannies? Do they get maternity leave? For the answers to those questions, move to Colorado, smoke recreational weed, and it might all become clear to you.

Ivanka had a slimy role in the debacle of the Trump Ocean Resort in Baja, Mexico. People laid out deposits on condos that The Donald promised would be in "the most spectacular place in all of Mexico," deposits to the tune of $32.5 million were taken. Buyers were led to believe that Trump was the builder. Ivanka shilled for the project, saying "We are developing a world-class resort befitting of the Trump brand. I'm very excited about it. I actually chose to buy a unit in the first tower." One buyer at a VIP reception recalled a joking Ivana saying that "she was my upstairs neighbor, and she could borrow sugar from me."

Surprise. Trump Ocean Resort was never built. Trump was never the builder. He had only branded his name on the project. Lawsuits followed. And no sugar was borrowed.

The two older boys? Get the Yuck-o-meter going. Junior showed a disturbing "penchant for interacting with the alt-right," as The Daily Beast put it. Let us count the ways.

He posted a picture of a group of Trumpites and the big guy labeled the Deplorables. As disturbing as the screaming Chris Christie was, more deplorable was the inclusion of Pepe the Frog, which the alt-right, who are anti-Semitic, anti-Hispanics, anti-black and really, really pro-Hitler, use as a propaganda symbol. The poor frog will appear with a "14" on one eyelid (for some reason that stands for "we must secure the existence of our people and a future for white children") and ever-popular "88" on the other ("Heil Hitler"). Poor misunderstood Junior. He didn't know anything about the little green frog. Maybe he thought it was Kermit.

Nor did he realize that there would be people who would be offended by his "warming up the gas chamber" statement."

Those taking offense were obviously prone to political correctness, something the kid decried while being interviewed by white-nationalist radio host James Edwards. If you have managed to stay ignorant of Edwards, count yourself lucky. According to him, "interracial sex is white genocide," "slavery is the greatest thing that ever happened" to blacks and the dream of Martin Luther King Jr. "is our nightmare."

When the interview exploded on the internet, Donny backed off. No, no, he was unaware Edwards would be present. "Had I known, I would have obviously never done an interview with him." And yet there was Edwards roaming around the RNC with press credentials, proclaiming this proved he was going mainstream.

Let's revisit the Skittles tweet likening Syrian refugees to the candy. The Skittles company did not find this acceptable. "Skittles are candy. Refugees are people. We don't feel it's an appropriate analogy," Vice President of Corporate Affairs Denise Young responded. "We will respectfully refrain from further commentary as anything we say could be misinterpreted as marketing."

White supremacists were elated by Donny and gleefully endorsed his father.

We shouldn't be too hard on the boy. It was son like father. Daddy retweeted an image of Hillary with cash flowing around her and what looked like a Star of David. How subtle was that?

Eric, Eric, Eric. Taking a page from Daddy's foundation, questionable activities were found at the Eric Trump Foundation, as The Daily Beast reported. And then there was the Great Wall of Scotland, two miles to shore up beach erosion. Eric was in charge of Trump golf courses. Shortly after this course was purchased, Eric and Junior went to Doonbeg to survey the property bought for a bagpipe squawk. Only problem, the area had been unmercifully pounded by rain. Without a howdy-doo to local authorities and law, trucks were dumping enormous stones to counter the erosion.

And why does Trump and Company need the two-mile stone wall? Global warming may be a Chinese hoax everywhere else, not on this stretch of the Scottish coastline.

Amanda Marcotte of Salon called out the "preening" boys for having "grotesque soul rot that happens when mediocre white men have enough wealth and privilege that they're fooled into thinking they are actually something special."

More newspaper endorsements rolled in for Clinton in October. It got to the point that Trump only had one major paper supporting him. That's only if you call The Las Vegas Review-Journal major. The Review-Journal was owned by Israeli hawk Sheldon Adelson. The Trump people had counted on $100 million from the casino owner, but had to settle for five. There was the "bigly" (Trump's pronunciation of big league) paper that came out for Trump in May. Another one had gushed over him earlier—the state-run North Korean DPRK, which called Trump a "wise politician" and "far-sighted candidate."

There were papers backing Clinton that hadn't endorsed a Democrat in almost forever. That would be 148 years for the San Diego Union-Tribune, 126 years the Arizona Republic, 76 years The Dallas Morning News. If newspapers could vote, the election was over.

On Oct. 19, 10 days after the second one came debate number three, the 25th counting all the primary, vice presidential and presidential. That's not right. There was a 26th, The Free & Equal Election Foundation debate at the University of Colorado in Boulder. Even the prospect of Ed Asner moderating couldn't get Gary Johnson and Jill Stein to take the stage with candidates you most likely never heard of.

The Trump-Clinton heavyweight fight had Chris Wallace of Fox News as referee.

What were the big takeaways? Hillary wore a white pantsuit, having previously worn red and blue.

Trump saying that late-term abortions were terrible because "You can take baby and rip the baby out of the womb. In the ninth month. On the final day. And that's not acceptable." (Obstetricians were quick to point out that what he described is called giving birth.)

In a question on immigration, Trump answered he would be getting rid of the drug lords and bad people. "But we have some bad hombres here, and we're going to get them out." His pronunciation of "hombres" unleashed Twitter hilarity since it came out "hambre," Spanish for "hungry." This is the same man who lectured a rally in Reno on how to properly say their state's name. Nuh-VAH-da, he insisted, even though people in the crowd instructed him it is nuh-VAD-uh. Michelle Obama made the same mistake in 2008. She, however, when corrected, repeated "Ne-VAD-a, Ne-VAD-a, Ne-VAD-a! I know how to bounce back from my mistakes."

What would be a debate without mentions of Russia and Vladimir Putin? Julian Assange and gremlins must have had some downtime since WikiLeaks counted the number of times the former Evil Empire and its short leader had come up—178. ISIS was second at 132, tax policy 119 and Trump tax returns 71.

In Donald Senior's expert opinion, Vlady was dismissive of Obama and Clinton. She came back with "Well, that's because he'd rather have a puppet as president of the United States." The best Trump could muster was "You're the puppet." You can only hope the children of America weren't watching this.

Chris Wallace pushed to get relevant answers. He asked Hillary what she would do about the Social Security and Medicare trust funds running out of money. She promised to use the revenue from increased taxes on shoring up Social Security. "My Social Security payroll contribution will go up, as will Donald's, assuming he can't figure out how to get out of it." Poor Donald, unable to control himself, he had to interrupt with "Such a nasty woman." This inadvertently gave birth to the Nasty Woman Economy. Yep, get your red-hot Nasty Woman T-shirts, pillows, hoodies, mugs, bumper stickers and other paraphernalia. Say it loud, and wear it proud.

Yet, that comment was rivaled by another more serious one. And this was where Wallace further showed he was in command, able to get the candidates to answer questions and keep the crowd under control. (Though he couldn't stop the audience from laughing when Trump proclaimed "Nobody has more respect for women than I do. Nobody.")

When he asked Trump if he would accept the results of the election, Donald shuffled around, diverting to favorite themes, the rigged election, Hillary being crooked. "She shouldn't be allowed to run . . . she's guilty of a very, very serious crime." The dishonest and corrupt media. Wallace wouldn't let him get away with it.

"Not saying that you're necessarily going to be the loser or the winner," Wallace pressed, "but that the loser concedes to the winner and that the country comes together in part for the good of the country. Are you saying you're not prepared now to commit to that principle?"

No he wasn't. "What I'm saying is that I will tell you at the time. I'll keep you in suspense. OK?"

That was a truly a holy-shit moment.

Less than a month left, but who was counting?

There was now three weeks left before Election Day. WikiLeaks dumps on Clinton's campaign chairman, John Podesta, kept Washington insiders busy reading them. Many were mundane—complaints about salary, churlish swipes at other staffers, staffers talking up themselves. There was dirt. Nothing game changing, though headline shoppers did find anti-Chelsea material in aisle 4. How about "Aide calls Chelsea Clinton a 'spoiled brat.' "

The aide turned out to be long-time Bill buddy Douglas J. Band. He was angry that Chelsea, who was on the Clinton Foundation board, called for an audit. She was afraid people from Band's consulting firm were "hustling" clients at foundation functions.

"I don't deserve this from her," Band complained in an email, "and deserve a tad more respect or at least a direct dialogue for me to explain these things. She is acting like a spoiled brat kid who has nothing else to do but create issues to justify what she's doing because she, as she has said, hasn't found her way and has a lack of focus in her life." Leave it to The New York Times to follow up. In a story, "Chelsea Clinton's Frustrations and Devotion Shown in Hacked Emails," she came across as someone genuinely concerned for her father's good name and how the foundation was run.

For instance, after visiting earthquake-ravaged Haiti, into which the foundation was shoveling money for rebuilding efforts, she wrote, "To say I was profoundly disturbed by what I saw—and didn't see would be an understatement. The incompetence is mind numbing."

It was Band who coined Clinton Inc., which certainly was not a term that served Hillary well. Another distraction.

With Election Day fast approaching, the candidates did what candidates do. They took to the hustings, where The Donald was again shown to be the great unifier. Seriously. Michelle Obama and Hillary had bad blood in 2008, Michelle taking exception to Clinton's attacks on Barack. The two were definitely not best buds then. The thought of Trump winning overrode past grievances. As if FLOTUS' DNC speech hadn't been beyond powerful, she outdid it in New Hampshire. In a trembling voice, again without using Trump's name, Michelle gave what was probably the most powerful speech of the election. Even once-Obama hater, conservative radio talk-show host Glenn Beck praised it as the "most effective political speech" since Reagan.

The First Lady pulled no punches in attacking Trump's sexual-predatory inclinations as seen on the "Access Hollywood" tape. She decried the sexist overtones that pervaded the campaign.

"Now is the time for all of us to stand up and say enough is enough," she said. "This has got to stop. Right now."

Jena McGregor of The Washington Post wrote that Michelle's "epic" speech should be "required viewing for every leader" because of "the absolute master class she offered in that elusive quality of leadership: 'authenticity.' " It is something that comes from the gut and not the teleprompter.

Obama was on the stump for Clinton. As were Bernie, Elizabeth Warren, Joe Biden, LeBron James, Beyoncé, Pittsburgh Steelers Hall of Famers Mel Blount and Franco Harris, the impressive list went on.

Out for Trump? Trump and Pence and Chris Christie, though his campaign appearances were cut off after two of his cohorts were convicted in the Bridgegate scandal. Trump said he "didn't have to bring J. Lo or Jay Z—the only way she gets anybody. I am here all by myself. Just me—no guitar, no piano, no nothing." And thank the gods of kindness, no singing.

In New Hampshire, Trump did have John Sununu on the stage with him. Not the younger Sununu, who was running for governor, the older one who had been Papa Bush's chief of staff. His introduction, undoubtedly, delighted the candidate. "Do you think Bill was referring to Hillary when he said, 'I did not have sex with that woman?' "

As it turned out the October Surprise, more like the October Cataclysm, didn't come from Julian Assange. FBI Director James Comey once again bulled himself into the election, this time far more egregiously than in July. Rudy Giuliani cackling like the Wicked Witch of the West foreshadowed what was to come by saying the Trump campaign had "a couple of surprise left."

With only 11 days before the election, Comey dropped what Mort Zuckerman, editor-in-chief of U.S. News & World Report, called a "stink bomb."

The FBI was investigating the odious Anthony Weiner, estranged husband of been-with-Clinton-forever adviser Huma Abedin, for allegedly being pervy with a teenage girl online. FBI found, oh no, Mr. Bill, that a laptop used by Weiner and his wife contained emails to Clinton from Abedin. This demanded a re-opening of the Clinton email case that had been churlishly closed in July.

The important thing to note is that agents had not examined the emails when the self-righteous Comey sent a three-paragraph letter to Congress. "The existence of emails that appear to be pertinent" were found. "Appear to be pertinent"? There would be a review "to determine whether they contain classified information, as well as to assess their importance to our investigation." Would be? And just to make this all very clear, "the FBI cannot yet assess whether this material may be significant." And gee, who knows how long this assessment would take. The DOJ had advised the letter flew in the face of procedure. As Kurt Eichenwald of Newsweek saw it, the director "acted with a lack of accountability that has not been seen since J. Edgar Hoover held the post. It is unforgiveable." (Eichenwald and Fahrenthold were certainly deserving of Pulitzers.)

As it turned out, Comey did a "never mind" two days before the polls closed. In the meantime, 40 million people had voted early by Nov. 6, many within "the stink-bomb to oops" time frame.

No understatement to say Comey was vilified—and not only by Democrats. George W.'s attorney general Alberto Gonzales, no ethical poster boy, pounded the FBI head.

"You don't comment on investigations, because commenting on the investigation may jeopardize the investigation. And that's the box he's put himself in." Gonzales had no problem with Comey holding back on the "maybe there would be, maybe there wouldn't be" investigation until Nov. 9. That would give voters "the opportunity to vote on Election Day without information that may in fact be incomplete or untrue."

Sen. Harry Reid scorched Comey in a letter. "Through your partisan actions, you may have broken the law. . . . The clear double standard established by your actions strongly suggests that your highly selective approach . . . along with your timing, was intended for the success or failure of a partisan candidate or political group."

The law to which he referred is the Hatch Act, "an Act to Prevent Pernicious Political Activities." George W. Bush's ethics lawyer (why does that sound like an oxymoron?) filed a Hatch Act complaint, as did the Department of Justice.

As Nixon chief of staff Bob Haldeman, talk about someone who had big-time ethical problems, said, "You can't put the toothpaste back in the tube." Whatever damage Comey did to the Clinton campaign was done. How much damage would remain to be seen on Election Day.

November

Speeches continued. Obama took to using the catchphrase "c'mon, man." That's "c'mon, man" as in "This is a guy who, like, tweets they should cancel 'Saturday Night Live' " because of Alec Baldwin's pitch-perfect take on the candidate. "Really? I mean, that's the thing that bothers you, and you want to be president of the United States? C'mon, man!" Trump, a "champion of working people," c'mon man.

A surprise visitor on the trail was Melania Trump. Judging by her reaction when her husband mentioned on national TV that she, a good speaker, would be making speeches, she was surprised that she would find herself addressing a rally in suburban Philadelphia. Or maybe she was taken aback that anyone commended her oratory skills. But there she was saying as FLOTUS, she would combat cyberbullying. As one tweeter put it, "If Melania Trump wants to combat cyber bullying on social media, she should start by changing the password to her husband's Twitter account." Let's give Melania a break. After 20 years in the U.S., maybe her command of English is still not great, and she didn't understand what she was reading. Besides, she might have been fretting over the AP story that documented she worked in the U.S. undocumented in 1996.

And then it was finally Nov. 8, ending a campaign that felt like it stretched back to when Oliver Cromwell ran for Parliament.

Chapter Eleven: Aftermath — Winners and Losers

On Wednesday, Nov. 9, many Americans awoke like they'd just spent a night of blackout drinking—"What did we do? Did that really just happen?" Unbelievably, Donald Trump had won.

He won the Electoral College, that is. He tallied 290 and Clinton 232 with Michigan votes still to be counted. Sixteen Electoral College delegates hung in the balance, but Michigan wouldn't put her over the top despite winning the popular vote that nudged up past two million and got to nearly 2.9 million.

Put this into perspective. Although Al Gore took the popular vote by 540,000, Bush won the Electoral College. To be more accurate, he won the Supreme Court.

But two million and counting? For future "Jeopardy" contestants, there were three other candidates who took the popular, but lost the Electoral. The easy one is Gore in 2000, then Grover Cleveland in an 1888 EC loss to Benjamin Harrison though having 90,000 more popular votes and Samuel Tilden, ahead by 250,000, going down to Rutherford B. Hayes in 1876. (There is an asterisk on that list that could trip you up in Final Jeopardy. In the 1824 race, four candidates deadlocked the Electoral College. John Quincy Adams won on a vote in the House of Representatives even though Andrew Jackson had garnered the most yeas in the election.)

What made the Trump triumph in the EC count especially nutty was his supporters were of the type from which the Founding Fathers were trying to protect the country with the Electoral College. The FFs were worried about the unwashed, uneducated lower-class urbanites holding too much sway. The EC was designed to give more power to the agrarian elites. In 2016, the urbans were more elite, and you had a mass of rurals and low-income whites willing to vote for someone who promised them a better future by draining the swamp in Washington. Sadly a narcissistic billionaire who only looks out for himself may not be the best person to deliver them from hardship. Deals with devil don't usually end well unless you're Carrot Top or Kesha.

When the shouting and tears abated, number crunching and analysis began. Three days after the election, The Washington Post found that "razor-thin margins" in three states—Pennsylvania, Wisconsin and Michigan—made the difference.

"This election was effectively decided by 107,000 people in these three states. Trump won the popular vote there by that combined amount. That amounts to 0.09 percent of all votes cast in this election." That count was later lowered to 80,000.

It didn't take long before the Trump camp was telling all those people who rallied around him not to take what he said literally. The supporters did have to take it literally when he appointed Steve Bannon as his chief political strategist. Apologists immediately started a chant that the boy was misunderstood. He was not really anti-Semitic, racist, Muslim hating. One even said Bannon couldn't be racist because he went to Harvard. That's less convincing than saying someone couldn't be homophobic because he shops at Banana Republic.

So, who were the winners and who were the losers? Here's a non-inclusive list since almost every citizen of the United States would be in the losing column.

Sandra Lee's Winners

Melania Trump, now free to proudly display cleavage again. Also, the Trump win might give her a four-year extension on her marriage. At 46, she was way past The Donald's preferred window for women. Melania, however, has certain qualities that Trump adores. He once told Howard Stern she doesn't fart or "make doodie." (Take advice from Melania, ladies, the secret to a successful marriage is separate bathrooms, even though many Trump followers can't afford that luxury.) Another reason Melania was a winner? She was staying in the New York penthouse with son Barron rather than moving to Washington. She would be freed from hubby during the week as he attended to pesky needs of the country in D.C. Her not moving to the White House would come at a security cost to the American taxpayer of $1 million *a day*.

Retired super-hawk generals. There were a lot of them that Trump was going to keep off the streets by giving them jobs, raising concerns that a president with zero, zilch military experience, except maybe having seen "Operation

Petticoat," would be relying too much on these gung-ho warriors without the counterbalance of civilian advice.

Chicago Cubs. Wait. That wasn't the election. That was the World Series.

Mike Pence. Still employed, which it didn't look likely had he run for re-election in Indiana.

Misogyny. Wow, think of how many millions became acquainted with the word. Of course, some might have thought its definition was "crotch-fondling slab of rancid meatloaf." (Thank you, Samantha Bee, always so wonderfully precise in your descriptions.)

Nixon Enemies List. Yes, 37 kept track of those "active in their opposition" to his administration. Journalist Daniel Schorr and actor Paul Newman took it as a great honor to have been included. Author Hunter S. Thompson was ticked he wasn't. Nixon wanted to take it further than keeping track. However, IRS Commissioner Donald C. Alexander politely declined to audit the "enemies." Go ahead, ask. Why does the list make the winners column? Compared to Trump's Shit List, Nixon's foray into getting even will look benign.

Putin. His congratulatory telegram (does anyone else send telegrams?) to Trump read: "building a constructive dialogue between Moscow and Washington, which is based on principles of equality, mutual respect and taking into account one another's true positions, is in the interest of our peoples and the world community." That was code for what the editor-in-chief of the state-run TV network and international news agency said. "If Trump recognizes our Crimea, cancels the sanctions, reaches an agreement with us about Syria and releasing Assange, I'll retire. For the world will be perfect."

The Obamas. It was a helluva ride. Life would never be "normal" again, not with those nice Secret Service agents always lurking. Still, Michelle could shop at Target, and Barack wouldn't have to pore through briefing notebooks at 1 in the morning.

Sandra Lee's Losers

Obviously, **Hillary**, the election was hers, and then it wasn't. A few days after the election, she stated the obvious. FBI Director James Comey had a direct hand in her loss. "Our analysis is that Comey's letter raising doubts that were groundless, baseless, proven to be, stopped our momentum." The Comey investigation letter several days before the election battered Clinton, and surprisingly, the "Oops, never mind" one was also damaging. Suburban white women fell off the fence on the side of Trump having been reminded before they went into the voting booth that Clinton was "untrustworthy."

James Comey. We can only hope he is forced out of the directorship and goes into a more suitable profession, maybe garbage collection. Nah, garbage collection is too honorable for him.

Bill Clinton. If he had kept his pants zipped, Trump couldn't have used the Bubba's sexual improprieties as an indictment of Hillary.

Cuban Americans (maybe). Apparently missing the headlines that Fidel Castro died, Trump started muttering about terminating the détente and outreach with Havana. That would put a kibosh on travel to Cuba and trade that would help all those relatives back in the homeland.

Chris Christie. Oh, little Chris, what did you feel like after publicly endorsing Trump to have him say "Get in the plane and go home. It's over there. Go home"? And then a week later, standing behind your former rival as he issued a long-winded (what else?) Super Tuesday victory speech, you were described as having a "glazed look." More like Mother Superior Margaret Mary having taken you behind the woodshed for a good whooping. As a doggy bone, Trump tossed you the transition lead before the election. But what God Trump giveth, he can taketh away. And you were demoted, to put it nicely. You would be out of a job in Trenton come 2018, to the relief of many Garden State residents. Maybe you were destined to be a toll taker at the George Washington Bridge.

Barron Trump. This poor 11-year-old looked unhappy in every picture (except for the balloon drop at the end of the convention). It was not the sullen or surly unhappy that you might expect from a Donald spawn, rather sad unhappy. To what could have only added to his unhappiness, all kinds of "medical" opinions popped up on the Web. No doubt about it, the kid was autistic. A video was put together showing body movements that showed as much, not wanting to be touched by Mike Pence (who would?) and other proof the boy had the condition. It was reminiscent of the nonsense Giuliani and friends put together showing Hillary was suffering from brain damage. Daddy Donald's debate riff on vaccinations causing autism (no proof whatsoever, though there is correlation between the older age of the father and likelihood of a child developing autism) didn't help. Who cares? Give the poor boy breathing room. He will never have much for the rest of his life, no matter how protective his mother is.

Pollsters. You botched this one, big time.

Washington swamp. Nah, don't expect Trump to carry out his promise of draining and cleaning it. Not unless the bankers and billionaires he's adding to his administration get out with Scrubbies and power hoses. **Trump supporters.** He ain't coming through, people. Coal miners, you heard him say you're "going to start to work again, believe me. You're going to be proud again to be miners." No way. Utilities are shutting down coal-fired plants because natural gas is way cheaper. "Look at steel, it's being wiped out." He would champion the industry and bring back the jobs. Reality check. The reason Trump used Chinese steel in his buildings was because it's cheaper. AND unless The Donald was going to become The Good-Guy Arnold in "Terminator 2," President Trump would have to destroy all the robots and automations that took away so many jobs in so many industries.

All you wearers of Make America Great Again hats and T-shirts, not necessarily made in America, you don't matter to him anymore. He will screw you over as he has so many workers and contractors and ex-wives and anyone who didn't serve his sociopathic agenda. You voted for him. You live with him. Unfortunately, so will the rest of us.

Aaron's Winners

Kellyanne Conway. Kellyanne will go down as a campaign manager who did the impossible. She was able to persuade not quite half of the American people that a megalomaniacal billionaire with no political experience was the answer to their problems. It's a "mind freak" that even Criss Angel had to be jealous of. And think of all the career opportunities this has opened for her. Maybe Kim

Jong-un needs an American spokeswoman to make him seem more warm and cuddly? Or perhaps Bill Cosby needs a new career manager to rehab his image? The possibilities are endless if she sets her sights very, very low.

Russian Hackers. It's crazy to think that some 17-year-old kid in Russia had a major hand in the U.S. election. "What should I do today?" he thought to himself. "I could play 'Starcraft' . . . no, I will destroy American democracy." It's unfortunate the game the hackers decided to play was creating mayhem in the U.S. election, but they definitely were successful. With data leaks and fake news stories, they toyed with this election like it was the game of "Words with Friends."

Bernie Sanders. For Bernie, it was never about winning elections. If that was the case, he'd have quit back in those early Vermont days after getting beaten like a Black Lives Matter protester at a Donald Trump rally. For Bernie, it has always been about getting the message out. He accomplished that in this election. His supporters fawned over him like he was a member for One Direction, and he's been on more talk shows post-election than most A-list celebrities. People are starting to listen, and whether the DNC likes it or not, he is going to have a much bigger role in the party.

Donald Trump's Twitter account. The account saw a surge of almost 8 million new followers between July 4 and Nov. 21. Numerous tweets have led to heated debate, news stories and more angry women than the phrase, "Are you wearing *that?*" It has also been unceasingly active, even sending off 3 a.m. tweets, which makes us consider a frightening possibility: Donald Trump's Twitter has become sentient. We always thought it would be Skynet that would take us down, but this may have been the first step toward the intelligent, artificial life (the intelligent part is highly debatable) that eventually enslaves the human race.

Barack Obama. Until this election, many liberal voters were maligning Obama's presidency. With the stark contrast of the 2016 election, those same voters are like teenagers who moved out of their parents' house after years of complaining. Suddenly the refrain became "That house was magical! Laundry did itself, and food just appeared out of nowhere!"

Trump University Students. When they enrolled in Trump University, the students didn't think they would make money by suing Donald Trump. However, that's exactly what happened when Donald Trump settled the fraud case for $25 million. So perhaps they did learn one of Trump's most important business tactics.

Aaron's Losers

Hillary Clinton. The ball was on the 1-yard line. The presidency was Hillary's for the taking. Then the campaign had a collapse so epic it can best be described in terms of the New England Patriots 17-14 loss to the New York Giants in 2008. In fact, the Pats and the Hillary campaign have a lot of common ground. They have a leader that struggles to show normal human emotion, people really hate them, and they constantly get accused of cheating. In the end, the Clinton campaign fumbled the ball as if their hands were coated in Vaseline and the tears of little girls everywhere.

The Electoral College. As long as we're on football metaphors, does anyone feel like they're hearing about the college BCS every time the Electoral College comes up? It's a stupid, outdated system that employs math that virtually no one understands. This election saw a candidate win the popular vote by a number greater than the entire population of Chicago, the third largest city in the country, but lose the election. If the NCAA could pull their heads out of their bureaucratic behinds, the U.S. should be able to do the same.

Feminism. Every time a bell rings, an angel gets its wings. And every time a Donald Trump gets elected, the dreams of 10 million young woman die a little. Trump's treatment of the fairer sex and statements on women were egregious—and validated by the election result. This probably set feminism back more than boob jobs and Britney Spears combined.

Evangelicals. What happened to voting on religious principle, people? Guess what, God didn't look down upon Job during his hardships and say, "Well . . . you were not faithful to my word . . . but I'm cool with that because some billionaire promised you tax cuts and a lot of other bullshit." Evangelicals have made their religious principles the focus in presidential elections, and now they helped elect someone who treats the seven deadly sins like a weekend to-do list. For shame.

Ted Cruz. Through this election, a whole new wave of people have come to know Ted Cruz. And to know him is to hate him. If Ted wishes to keep that number from growing, perhaps he could move to an uninhabited island or Antarctica. His freshman college roommate said it best, "Ted Cruz is a nightmare of a human being."

Debbie Wasserman Schultz. Her emails undermined Bernie Sanders' campaign, leading to her resignation as

DNC chair. Wasserman Schultz screwed up worse than Steve Harvey at the Miss Universe pageant. That is to say she tried to crown the wrong person, and we're sure as shit not going to going to trust her with anything important again.
The American People. In the end, the biggest losers in this election were the American people. Rich. Poor. Republican. Democrat. White. Black. Muslim. Especially Muslim. Hispanic. Especially Hispanic. We all lose in this together. The United States is a vessel that ferries us across too-often turbulent waters. Well, we just pointed that vessel at a fucking iceberg and turned the helm over to a sociopathic captain who has no idea how to steer. Some may benefit in the short term, but in the long term, like Botox injections and tattoo portraits of your high-school sweetheart, no good can come of this.

***

Democracy in disarray? More like democracy thrown into the gutter. OK, not that bad. We can only hope. Trump won't find it that easy to bully through his agenda—once he figures out what that is. He'll discover the office is more than middle-of-the-night, sleep-deprived tweets.

Whatever the outcome, the country will endure. It may have to suffer through another deregulatory recession. Fingers crossed there will be no disastrous military incursions. People dying without healthcare insurance. The country will overcome. Fuck, why did it come to overcoming Donald J. for Jerk Trump?